The Motley Fool

MILLION DOLLAR PORTFOLIO

The Motley Fool

MILLION DOLLAR PORTFOLIO

HOW TO BUILD AND GROW A PANIC-PROOF INVESTMENT PORTFOLIO

DAVID AND TOM GARDNER

COLLINS BUSINESS

An Imprint of HarperCollins Publishers

While the method of investment described in this book is believed to be effective, there is no guarantee that the method will be profitable in specific applications, owing to the risk that is involved in almost any kind of investing. Therefore, neither the publisher nor the author assumes liability for any losses that may be sustained by the use of the method described in this book, and any such liability is hereby expressly disclaimed.

ISBN-13: 978-1-61523-331-1

For our mother

CONTENTS

PREFACE

The concept for this book draws its origins from a meeting Tom had in New York with one of the world's great commercial leaders, Lew Frankfort, the impassioned chief executive of Coach. With a near 30-year tenure at the business, Frankfort is widely—and correctly—credited with transforming a troubled leather goods business into the world's leading handbag company. In its eight years in the public markets, Coach stock has turned a $10,000 investment into $150,000, earning investors 40% returns *per year*.

What Lew told Tom at that meeting in February 2007 changed The Motley Fool forever. Few companies do enough customer research, he said. Instead, they develop new products and services solely on the experiences, insights, and instincts of their internal team. "That won't work indefinitely," he cautioned. "You've got to be more obsessed with researching customers than with generating ideas. To be great for generations, your intuition alone about what customers want today *will not suffice*. Talk to them every day. Listen to them. Make an eternal effort of gathering and analyzing as much information about them as you can."

Tom returned to Fool Global Headquarters in Alexandria, Virginia, and we immediately created our Customer Insights division, headed by Ginni Bratti. She and her team now spend every day meeting with investors in face-to-face focus groups, over the phone, through video interviews, at member events, via surveys, and in our online community at fool.com. Today, we're inundated with customer statistics, comment lists, audio and video files, and memories of breaking bread (and uncorking wine) with our members from Minneapolis to Bermuda, Shanghai to Copenhagen, Stockholm to San Francisco, and beyond. Every day we listen and therefore learn more about what you—our fellow Fools—need to become better investors.

Just months after forming the Customer Insights team, we leaned heavily on customer feedback to design the most successful service in The Motley Fool's 15-year history, *Million Dollar Portfolio*, which is the origin of this book. By listening, we heard that investors like you want to:

1. View our best recommendations across all investment philosophies
2. Study how we build an active portfolio of stocks
3. See us invest alongside you
4. Get a clear picture of our performance against the stock market
5. Talk to other smart investors online

Million Dollar Portfolio (mdp.fool.com) is our answer to these and thousands of other requests from people like you. We now manage, in full view, $1 million of our own hard-earned capital. That money is allocated into the best investment ideas drawn from the research of dozens of analysts across our newsletter services and thousands of investors throughout our community. The portfolio includes value investments, dividend-payers, and growth stocks, as well as small-, mid-, and large-cap stocks from domestic and international markets. We announce all of our investment decisions before purchasing any stock, giving our members the opportunity to transact before we do. And we welcome both positive and negative feedback in the lively, ongoing, unedited interaction among our members online (which no other investment company in the world offers). Together, we are thrashing the market's average return.

This book distills all of that thinking into 11 chapters that will teach you how to build your own million-dollar portfolio using our very best strategies across all stock-investing disciplines. What you will find in these pages are philosophies that in certain scenarios stand in direct opposition to one another. The principles needed to invest effectively in domestic mid-cap growth stocks do not perfectly replicate those needed to win with international small-cap turnaround stocks, of the sort that Motley Fool star investor Bill Mann has uncovered for years. Don't let these contradictions throw you. The more you invest, the more you'll come to realize just how many roads there are to prosperity for disciplined investors.

As students of the great masters—from Ben Franklin and Ben Graham to Warren Buffett and Peter Lynch—we're committed to teaching the timeless principles of successful investing using plain language. We want you to enjoy every page of this book and to leave these pages equipped to lay a permanent foundation for your financial independence. It is through the habit of continual saving, the discipline of regular investment, the deployment of fifth-grade mathematics, the use of a collection of superior investment strategies, and the power of your imagination that you will meet with enduring success.

What you will find in this book is the unveiling of the core strategies that have led our newsletter services to beat the market substantially. The ambitious aim of this work is to assemble these competing investment approaches into a single strategy that will help you take your portfolio to $1 million and beyond.

Here's a quick peek at the performance of some of our investing newsletters:

	RETURNS	S&P 500 (OVER COMPARABLE PERIOD)
Stock Advisor	53%	11%
Hidden Gems	24%	2%
Income Investor	16%	9%
Rule Breakers	11%	−1%

As you read, remember that the greatest investors in history are multifaceted. They're like the brilliant performer Frank Miles, who at our company's annual meeting in 2008 juggled knives, torches, bowling balls, and stun guns—before twirling by on a unicycle. If they were baseball hitters, they'd draw walks, spray the ball to all fields, hit for power, and bunt. If they were composers, they could play all four families of musical instruments in the symphony. You see, the true master investor could never be categorized solely as a growth or value or income or even a domestic investor. Because the truly great investor can do it all. So, too, we believe, can you.

Since the creation of The Motley Fool in 1993, our greatest pleasures have come when we recognize that our work is an adventure into things we cannot yet see. No one knows what's next. We can merely calculate the probabilities. And so, the art and the mysteries of commerce and investing richly reward the adventuring spirit and the prepared mind. One meeting in New York with the CEO of Coach has changed the fate of The Motley Fool. We hope this book will change yours.

—David and Tom Gardner

A NOTE ON THE FINANCIAL COLLAPSE OF 2008

OCTOBER: This is one of the peculiarly dangerous months to speculate in stocks in. The other are July, January, September, April, November, May, March, June, December, August, and February.

—Mark Twain

On September 29, 2008, the S&P 500 cratered 9%—the worst single day for the broad-market index since the crash of 1987. And yet that was merely one in a series of steep declines in 2008 that wiped out more than five years of market gains. In fact, at its low, the S&P 500 touched prices unseen since May 1997. That's 11 years of 0% returns!

Having endured that, you may well be scratching your head as to why you'd ever read an investment book. Who wants to buy stocks when the market is fragile and faltering? The answer might surprise you: *Warren Buffett, the world's greatest investor.* One of our top analysts at The Motley Fool, Anand Chokkavelu, discovered something fascinating about Buffett. He had around $45 billion sitting in cash at the end of 2004. And 2005. And 2006. And 2007. In fact, at one point, Buffett had 20% of the asset base of his company, Berkshire Hathaway, in money market funds. But when the market crumbled, he adapted. In the four weeks ending with October 13, Buffett put $20 billion to work in the world of equities.

You see, for long-term investors, now is precisely the time you should be reading an investment book and determining what to do with your savings. But the last thing you'll want to do is to invest without fully understanding the risks you're taking. The lesson from the Mark Twain quote that leads us in to this chapter is simple: *Do not speculate* (the same as the mantra of Hettie Green, America's first female mogul investor). And so let's stay out of speculation mode by reviewing together exactly what happened with this market crash, and then we'll wend our way through the book, assembling the ideal approach for building your everlastingly rock-solid stock portfolio.

SO, WHAT HAPPENED?

For answers, we turned to Fool analyst Matthew Argersinger. What started out as a "subprime" mortgage problem in late 2007 quickly snowballed into a full-blown financial crisis in 2008, laying waste to multibillion-dollar investment banks like Bear Stearns and Lehman Brothers. AIG, the largest insurer in the world and a former Dow component, was forced to take more than $120 billion in emergency loans from the U.S. government and to give up 80% of its ownership equity to taxpayers just to keep its doors open. Fannie Mae and Freddie Mac—the structurally flawed backbones of America's $12 trillion home mortgage market—imploded under massive losses. Washington Mutual became the largest U.S. bank failure in history.

By the end of the month, the financial sector was literally falling to pieces. Within days, the U.S. government abandoned CPR techniques and reached straight for the defibrillator. When on October 3 the U.S. Congress committed to spend up to $700 billion to purchase distressed assets and buy stakes in America's largest banks, the total investment by U.S. taxpayers crossed the $1 trillion mark. That's the largest bailout of any kind in history! Yeesh. Just let that sink in for a moment. . . . Now that you have, the natural question is:

HOW DID IT ALL HAPPEN?

You can point to three overarching themes: cheap money, leverage, and greed. Let's take 'em one by one.

Cheap Money

In general terms, sharp increases in the availability of money can often lead to unsustainable booms in the prices of securities, real estate, and commodities. In the wake of the economic recession that ensued after the dot-com bust and September 11, the Federal Reserve, under then-Chairman Alan Greenspan, reduced interest rates to 1% and held them there for over a year. With interest rates at historic lows, the cost of all types of loans—mortgages, auto loans, credit cards—shrank dramatically. Cheap money allowed homebuyers to purchase pricier houses than they could otherwise afford while flexing more spending muscle at the shopping mall. At the same time, access to cheap credit allowed public companies, as well as private equity players, to borrow money and buy up other companies at extremely high valuations.

In short, all of this cheap money fed higher asset prices. That eventually contributed to a speculative boom in real estate, to massive debt-fueled consumption on the part of consumers, and to an explosion in leveraged buyouts.

Excess Leverage

But if money and credit were the flames that lit the fires of the credit ka-boom, excess leverage was the gasoline. As asset prices rose and money stayed cheap, both consumers and companies took on enormous amounts of debt. Consumers refinanced their houses and borrowed trillions against their homes' equity to satisfy increased spending habits. At the same time, corporations—particularly banks and financial institutions—levered up their balance sheets with new types of asset-driven securities and de-rivatives. Some of these securities, like those tied to subprime mortgages, offered extremely tantalizing yields. And most of them—thanks to "sophisticated" financial engineering and the blessing of myopic credit agencies—came with triple-A credit ratings. They were simply too good to pass up (and too good to be true). Besides, the prevailing belief at the time was that housing prices rise without interruption, *always*.

Greed

Underpinning all of this excessive leverage and wanton risk-taking was pure, unadulterated greed. By the late stages of the housing bubble, mortgage lenders like Countrywide were giving mortgages to people who had no business buying a home. But that didn't matter because—under the new financial securitiza-tion schemes—new loans were simply packaged into highly rated securities and sold off to investors. Mortgage lenders weren't getting paid to underwrite a good mortgage; they were being re-warded for writing just *any* mortgage. On the other side of the table, Wall Street banks like Bear Stearns and Lehman Brothers were making a killing writing and selling securities and deriva-tive instruments based on those dicey mortgages. And banks, hedge funds, and insurance companies were more than happy to lever up on these high-yielding securities to boost their returns. Meanwhile, executives at each of these firms were pulling in hundreds of millions of dollars in salaries, bonuses, and stock options. Finally, let us not ignore that a subset of consumers speculated in real estate to a ridiculous extreme, expecting that they could endlessly flip their properties onto eager buyers at inflated prices.

It didn't take long before homebuyers, having bought more house (or houses) than they could possibly afford, simply stopped making their monthly mortgage payments and walked away from their properties. Suddenly, those coveted mortgage securities that no bank could seem to get enough of were worth a whole lot less (some bordering on worth-*less*). Credit froze as banks curtailed lending and rushed to de-lever their debt-choked balance sheets. Hedge funds that had borrowed heavily to invest in these now defunct securities rushed to sell other stocks to meet margin calls. Prices for all types of assets plunged. Wall Street and the mortgage industry's house of cards came tumbling down, destroying trillions of dollars in stock market wealth in the process and leading to the largest government rescue in American history.

That's the most succinct way we can explain what happened. Next question…

WHAT IS THE FOOLISH INVESTOR TO DO?

It's never a good feeling to see the values of 401(k) accounts, IRAs, and brokerage accounts get thrashed. In times like this, it's best to take a deep breath, stop obsessing over the day-to-day gyrations in the market, and get some perspective on the current crisis.

Bear markets—commonly labeled as a decline in a market index of 20% or more—emerge every five years or so. The average length of a bear market is 15 months, with an average decline of just over 33%. As this book went to press, the S&P 500 had fallen more than 40% from its peak back in October 2007, showing that this bear comes from the grizzlier side of the forest.

That said, it also means—at least from a historical perspective—that, by now, we are probably most of the way through this particular bear market. And the average bull market that rumbles in afterward usually lasts for five years and yields 166% in cumulative gains. **So avoid the urge to sell your stocks recklessly.**

Better still, bear markets have a tendency to create serious bargain prices in top quality stocks. After all, the business of

most public companies has nothing to do with real estate speculation, and there are loads of companies that have no leverage
whatsoever. Why, we ask, should a company like Netflix see its
stock fall 50 percent just because bankers and a small population of land speculators ruined their financial lives through
short-term greed?

In our opinion, if you're making regular contributions to your
brokerage portfolio or retirement account, you're now picking up
good stocks on the cheap. If retirement is still more than a decade away, and you've got extra cash on the sidelines that you
won't need for the next three years or so, allocate even more
money to stocks during these tough times. Above all else, **stick
with a plan and *keep* investing**.

And while you're at it, stay far away from companies that are
lining up for their piece of the government's bailout package.
While companies like AIG and Citigroup spend valuable time
soaking up taxpayer money—de-leveraging their tattered balance sheets and deluding shareholders—good companies can reinvest in their business, gobble up weakened competitors, and
grow their market share. These are the companies that will deliver huge rewards once the market turns and the economy gets
back on its feet.

Finally, Fools looking to make money in both bull *and* bear
markets should check out our *Motley Fool Pro* service. Using
long-short strategies and options for protection, *Pro* is designed
to boost your returns in up, down, flat, and topsy-turvy markets
like 2008. You can take a look at that entire service by visiting
motleyfoolpro.com.

LOOKING AHEAD: HOW CAN THE FOOLISH INVESTOR AVOID THE NEXT FINANCIAL COLLAPSE?

First, it's important to acknowledge that there will be more credit crises and more bear markets in our future. But there are some important warning signs and crucial steps we can take to prepare our portfolios for the eventual calamities.

Focus on living within your means. Most of the people who found themselves in the direst of straits in 2008 are those who spent themselves silly and ended up with too much credit card debt and mortgages worth more than the value of their homes. Setting a reasonable budget and keeping a rainy-day savings account handy will keep you investing in the market and prevent you from having to dip into your retirement accounts at the worst possible times.

Watch out for excessive leverage. Right before its collapse, Lehman Brothers' assets-to-equity ratio (a common measure of leverage for financial companies) was 25 to 1. AIG's was 11 to 1. Compare that to Berkshire Hathaway's ratio of 2 to 1. Stick to companies that have low assets-to-equity and low debt-to-equity ratios, and high interest-coverage ratios.

Be skeptical of long periods of low volatility. How volatile has 2008 been in the markets? Think back to the most terrifying roller coaster ride you've ever been on. Now multiply that experience by 10. So far, there have been a total of 37 days when the market closed up or down by more than 2%—and that doesn't count intraday moves of that magnitude. In 2007, there were just 17 such days. In 2006, there were only *two* such days. Like the calm before a storm, persistently low volatility markets are strong signals of complacency among investors and markets. That's usually a signal that stormy waters might be just around the bend.

Look out for bubbles. Market bubbles are crystal clear in hindsight, but difficult to spot when inflating. Yet you might have had at least an inkling that things had reached silly proportions when profitless dot-com companies were awarded billion-dollar valuations in the late '90s, or when hundreds of people camped outside during the real estate boom just to get a shot at the latest luxury condo offering. When your next door neighbor or coworker starts boasting about the latest can't-lose, get-rich-quick scheme, it's time to get skeptical. Stick to a steady investment plan and don't chase hype.

Stick with great companies with little to no leverage. Great companies will survive and thrive through any market cycle. This book will help you find them.

And now, let's start assembling your portfolio for the future!

The Motley Fool

MILLION DOLLAR DOLLAR PORTFOLIO

CHAPTER 1

GETTING STARTED

Americans make three primary investment mistakes.

A startlingly large portion of our populace stands on the market's sidelines forever, missing out on the greatest builder of wealth available to the average (law-abiding) citizen. Many Americans just never save—or invest—anything. This is the greatest mistake of all. No matter your age, the best time to start investing is now.

The second biggest investment mistake is waiting too long to start. It turns out that financial independence can't be achieved as quickly as everything else in our lives: 90 seconds in the microwave oven, one-click buying on a Web site, or speed dial on our mobile phone.

The third biggest investment mistake is the subject of this book. People with this affliction might have money put away and may have purchased some mutual funds and even a few stocks. They've recognized the value of getting started, allowing the returns to compound over time. They make us proud. But they often have one tragic flaw: They are wildly unsuccessful pickers of stocks.

PICKING *GOOD* STOCKS

Investors often pick the wrong stocks and build the wrong kind of portfolio. They lack any coherent strategy. When the stocks they buy inevitably drop—at least temporarily—these folks cash out their shares and take a loss, running from the market altogether. Or they invest in bad stocks and stay with them for too long, "just hoping to get back to even." These strategies combine the damaging elements of desperation, blind optimism, and greed.

But even the most comically inept investor is in a far better situation than the non-investor or the late-comer. Because while the first two groups need to undergo a near-religious conversion before they see the light, a bad investor just needs a bit of strategy and guidance to accompany an existing practice and passion. This stuff is eminently teachable. It's what this book is for.

Think about how hard it is for many of us to get past those first two mistakes. The odds are stacked against an early start at successful investing. Most Americans begin their professional careers saddled with credit card debt and student loans while trying to pay for all that life entails, often on a relatively small starting wage. There's not a lot of cash floating around.

And even in the unlikely event that their couch cushions were overflowing with $20 bills, most people wouldn't know how to properly put the found money to the best possible use. Our high schools and universities have failed miserably to educate their students about how or why to invest. For the most part, no one has stressed the importance of saving and the value of investing, so they wander relatively blindly (or at least shortsightedly).

These are thorny, sometimes seemingly insurmountable issues and we by no means intend to belittle or gloss over them. In fact, previous Motley Fool books and countless Fool.com articles have provided advice and step-by-step guidance on how to work through them. That's our mission.

Once you're ready, we're here to inspire you to not only invest, but to invest *well*. There are two components to investing well:

First, you have to choose the right stocks and second, you need a strategy for putting those stocks together in a smart, balanced way. This book shows you how to do both.

Before we get to that, though, there's one principle you must embrace.

NO ONE'S PERFECT

In order to succeed, you must first accept that you will fail. Great investors pick stocks that lose to the market at least one time out of five. It's a lot like basketball free throws—Michael Jordan, arguably the game's greatest player of all time, shot just a bit over 80% from the line over his career.

Chances are, you're not the Michael Jordan of the investing world, at least not just yet, so it's essential to set realistic expectations, to know ahead of time that you're regularly going to miss—especially at the outset. Expect that even if you get to be very good, and that's if you're very, *very* good, you'll still be wrong 20% of the time. If you're just starting out, plan on being wrong half the time as a simple baseline from which to improve.

Yes, that's right, *half* the time. But don't be discouraged. To mix our sports metaphors, you'll be batting .500. That would get you your very own wing in the Hall of Fame!

12 STOCKS

This book is about picking great stocks. We're writing it in order to improve your ability to pick winners and avoid losers. But perhaps even more important, it's about how to put those stocks together in a portfolio that will see you through good times and bad, a portfolio that will grow. And grow and grow. Our goal is simple—we want to help you to develop your own $1 million portfolio.

To that end, we'd like to start our journey together with a

challenge: Buy at least 12 stocks. That's right. Not just one stock that your uncle claims can't miss. Not a couple bets on two numbers at Atlantic City. Not three equities for your IRA, four tech stocks, or five Dow Jones Industrials heavyweights. At least 12.

Why 12?

First, you are diversifying meaningfully. You are conditioning yourself from the shock of a few losers. And you *will* have a few losers. But you'll have a few winners, too, and in many cases, your winners will more than make up for your losers. Why? Because stocks can only lose 100%, yet there's no limit to how high they can climb. As you spread your dollars across a manageable number of your best ideas, you will plink down your money, watch your stocks, learn more about them as you monitor their performance, and enjoy a first-year gain or loss comparable to the market averages. You will probably not double your money right away. (Sorry.) You will also not lose most or all of what you invested.

What we guarantee you *will* do by buying and holding 12 stocks for a minimum of one year is condition yourself to be patient. And by watching and learning, you will have cleared the first hurdle that truly bedevils first-time investors. You will have actually invested. If you don't know where to start—how to open a brokerage account, how to buy a stock, how to get over that wave of nausea when you are trying to commit to that first purchase—visit us at mdpbook.com, a special area of our site just for readers of this book. We'll be happy to answer your questions on our message boards and do whatever we can to guide you through the world of investing. Above all, we want you to consider yourself an investor for life.

THE 12-STOCK ASSIGNMENT

Obviously, it's not about guesswork, or just buying stock in the company whose ticker happens to share your initials. Investing is a sometimes successful, occasionally confounding, continuously fascinating exercise in learning about yourself. By diversifying and learning from your successes and failures, you will discover the investing strategy that best suits you. You might find more than one.

This book is organized around a series of distinct investment strategies, and some companies that exemplify each approach. We'll start by showing you how to choose your first stock. (If you're already investing, feel free to skip ahead to Chapter 4 and dive in to our first strategy.) Then we'll move on to how to invest in dividend-paying stocks—companies that send us a check just for buying shares. Next we'll turn our attention to the blue-chip companies that reside in the calm waters of value investing, where we aim to buy great companies on sale. We'll devote a chapter to small caps, the little wonders that hopefully will turn into the monster companies of tomorrow. We'll look at Rule Breakers, those businesses that are challenging the conventional wisdom and changing the way we live. And we'll travel the globe to look at the international investing arena, an incredibly rich and diverse collection of stocks that includes representatives from each of the strategies.

Each one, practiced well, can and does beat the market. But each also uniquely attracts and repels different investors with their varying psychologies, tolerances for risk and loss, time horizons, and degrees of interest and engagement. As you read through the chapters, it's quite possible that one approach will seem more compelling, and one may just not seem to fit with your temperament, time line, or financial goals.

We encourage you to read with an open mind. While you might think you're one sort of an investor, as a wise man once wrote, there's no better way to figure out the color of your parachute than by doing lots of skydiving.

For some of you, this book will act as the beginning of your journey in investing. For those who are already experienced investors, it will enhance your understanding of investing, and perhaps open your eyes to new strategies to deploy in your portfolio.

BEYOND THESE PAGES

If this isn't the first investment book you've read, you've probably noticed how the subject matter of the books that live on these shelves in the bookstore (or, more likely, on the same tab of the online shopping outlet) stays the same. If you happen to pick up the book two years later, it's going to focus on the same stock, provide the same analysis, and reach the same conclusions.

Paper as a medium enjoys a certain permanence and dependability that is not really the friend of the investor. We love Peter Lynch (a prominent member of the investing world's Mt. Rushmore) and his books as much as the next Fool, but even we admit that his superb stories about his lucrative investment in the Pep Boys (Manny, Moe, and Jack) get a bit less helpful with each passing year. We wonder, for instance, what Lynch might have thought of former CEO Jeff Rachor, who in 2007 was paid more than $17 million in total compensation before leaving the company after only a year. As of this writing, the market value of Pep Boys sits at less than $500 million, which means that Rachor extracted more than 3% of the company's total value just in his annual executive take. Would Lynch still like that stock? We'd guess not. Yet it's still featured in his great book.

We've written a few investment books ourselves, and don't want to put readers in this same state of nostalgic confusion anymore.

Thankfully, there's this thing called the Internet. There's this Web site called The Motley Fool at fool.com. And now there's a special part of our Web site—mdpbook.com—accessible only to readers of this book, where we will provide updated information as well as our favorite stock ideas from each strategy in this book on an ongoing basis.

This book may look like just a book, but we promise you that it is far more. No matter how experienced an investor you are, it represents one giant step down the lifelong, lucrative path of successful investing. We plan to walk beside you as you go, in these pages and online.

CHAPTER 2

WHY GREAT
INVESTORS ARE ODD

The temptation at this point is to start talking stocks.

We hunger to ask if you think Netflix will become a dominant media company or technology roadkill. Can Apple flourish if Steve Jobs isn't at its helm? How will Howard Schultz fix his beloved Starbucks? What's the future for alternative energy?

Our homes have been filled for decades with debates over which industries will flourish and falter, which companies will succeed and fail, which leaders are gods or goats, which stocks will win or lose. It's in our nature to get right into it all now, to initiate the debate. The problem is that if we don't first offer up a warning, all that talk won't lead to great investment results. In fact, it could lead to despair.

So, here's the warning, which Motley Fool investment experts Tim Hanson and Buck Hartzell spend much of their time studying, teaching, and writing about for us.

WARNING: Your brain is likely to make it very difficult for you to succeed as an investor.

That's right. The very brain that's going to help you process this book could be the force that undoes your portfolio. The brain that will be analyzing companies, strategies, management teams, and financial statements could also lead you to subpar investment results. Unchecked, your brain will cause you to:

1. Buy and sell stocks at the wrong times
2. Overestimate your ability to beat the market
3. Trade maniacally in search of the big winner
4. Focus on the evidence that supports your conclusions
5. Discard evidence that does not

Each of these faults is hardwired into our intellects, a fact that has been revealed by recent studies in a fascinating new field called behavioral finance. There are entire books devoted to the topic (we recommend Jason Zweig's *Your Money & Your Brain*, Nassim Taleb's *Fooled By Randomness*, and Gary Belsky's *Why Smart People Make Big Money Mistakes—and How to Correct Them*). But the purpose of this interlude is to help you work on your investing *temperament* as much as you do your investing philosophy and stock selection.

THE LOGIC OF PATIENCE

You may be wondering, if you reliably pick winning stocks, why it would matter *when* you buy and sell them or when you add new money to the market? Maybe you've also read ad nauseam that you should buy to hold, keep the frictional costs of taxes and trading to a minimum, be willing to buy more (rather than sell) when your favorite stocks decline in price, and focus on long-term fundamentals rather than short-term market machinations. But can you actually do it?

It's an important question. When master investor Warren Buffett was asked by a group of business school students early in 2008 why so few people have been able to emulate his success—despite the tomes that have been written dissecting his investing philosophy—Buffett responded, "The reason gets down to temperament. People want to make money fast, but it doesn't happen that way."

Put simply, there is no way—not one described in this book, not one you can order from a television infomercial, and certainly not one color-coded in a presentation at your local airport Hilton—to get rich quick in the stock market. When the greatest investor in American history says, "it doesn't happen that way," it's smart to listen. Successful investing takes time. Years and years. Even decades. That's why one of the most important lessons we can teach you (before we get to any of the strategies that have helped us beat the market for years) is the lesson of patience.

THE ECSTASY OF THE AGONY

The problem is that we human beings are not predisposed to being patient. What's more, thanks to legacy behaviors from our cave-dwelling days, we're also naturally loss-averse and more inclined to shoot first and ask questions later.

These are not the traits of a world-class investor.

Of course, this all makes sense in context. Early humans didn't have long life spans. We were lucky to live from day to day. And we were rewarded (through survival) for running from threats rather than sticking around to investigate their intricacies. It didn't matter how many teeth a tiger had, how sharp they were, or how deep an incision they might make if you weren't around to tell anyone about it. Of course, we no longer live in that world. And when it comes to stock investing, these primal tendencies create enormous headwinds against our success.

Consider this. Psychologists Amos Tversky and Daniel Kahneman (who later won a Nobel Prize for their groundbreaking work) proved that monetary losses hurt us emotionally to a far greater magnitude than monetary gains please us. Now add to those findings what Jason Zweig wrote in *Your Money & Your*

Brain: "Your investing brain comes equipped with a biological mechanism that is more aroused when you anticipate a profit than when you actually get one."

Put these remarkable truths together and what you'll discover about most investors is that we're predisposed to chasing the next big thing. We fear losing, so we recklessly trade out of positions. And yet this suboptimal strategy satisfies our psyche because it allows us to both forget about losers (by selling them) and then to take frequent pleasures in buying new stocks that we believe will be big winners. Sadly, it doesn't matter to our brains if these stocks subsequently rise or fall 50%. Our brain enjoyed a chemical jolt of happiness simply by buying them. And it will do so each time we repeat the process.

Market data bears out this conclusion. Berkeley finance professor Terrance Odean found in a study of trading patterns that investors today have a median holding period of just 113 days. That's short—really short. (Remember that Warren Buffett's preferred holding period is "forever.") That 113 days is 90% shorter than the minimum three- to-five-year holding period you'll see us recommending over and over again in this book and at Fool.com.

The effect of all that active trading is to meaningfully reduce the total returns of your portfolio. The only people who will reliably make money here are the trading houses who get paid per transaction (and who, not coincidentally, will give you all sorts of rewards to lure you into that active trading!). Tragically, all of those mistaken actions were supported by the most powerful muscle in your body: your brain.

ON BEING FOOLISH

The longer that you invest, the more you will come to see that the most profitable way to buy stocks is to do so with a long view. It can be tough. It goes against the very chemistry of your brain. When you actually have money in the market, you will—because of your noggin—find yourself doubting your research conclusions when your stocks fall. After all, in the stock market as in the schoolyard, it's far easier to take the consensus position. And here comes your second problem. Your brain will feel far better if it yields to the general consensus. You won't be called odd, you won't be singled out as a failure, and perhaps most importantly, if you do end up being wrong, you won't have to exclusively blame yourself. This can cause real problems.

It's critical to know that the consensus sentiment surrounding a stock does not always reflect the value of the share of the business. Our friend, money manager Ron Muhlenkamp, is fond of pointing out that high-profile stocks like General Electric will trade for a hundred or more different prices on any given day. Did the company's value really change that often in one day? Of course not. And it's by tuning out the noise of those frequent transactions that you can separate the "game of the stock market" from the "business of investing." It's the latter where you find people like Warren Buffett, who has made serious money by buying great businesses at fair prices for 5–15 years or more.

This, however, ain't easy. And that's why history has so few truly great investors despite the enormous sums of money that are invested in the stock market. Those who are truly great are able to go against the tendencies of their brain to conform their temperaments to the demands of the stock market. These folks are aberrations. They are, for lack of a better word, *odd*—or as we prefer to say, *Foolish*.

One of those oddballs, Seth Klarman of investment firm Baupost Group, told a room of MIT students in a recent speech that "Investors unfortunately face enormous pressure—both real pressure from their anxious clients and their consultants as well as imagined pressure emanating from their own adrenaline, ego, and fear—to deliver strong near-term results. Even though this pressure greatly distracts investors from a long-term orientation and may, in fact, be anathema to good long-term performance, there is no easy way to reduce it."

If Mr. Klarman feels these pressures despite his sterling, decades-long track record, then there's little chance individual investors will instantly master the temperament needed to handle them. Again, this stuff isn't easy. It demands deliberate effort. It demands discipline. It demands that you take the long view.

Teach yourself to rely on reason and logic rather than emotion and reaction.

LET REALITY SET IN

As we now move toward chapters in which we unveil our entire investment approach—across multiple strategies, and in pursuit of superior returns around the world—you must let the reality settle in that your brain, untrained, can get you into a good deal of investing trouble.

Don't misunderstand this. We are firm in our belief that the clearest route to your financial independence—to a million-dollar portfolio and beyond!—is through the patient analysis and repeated purchase of common stocks. But you—and we—must continually work on the brain, disciplining it against its base instincts. Because even if you're an individual investor with only two clients—you and your spouse—you will face internal and external pressures similar to those Seth Klarman talked about with the MIT students. You have the same mental make-up, which means your brain will constantly want you to cut your losses, pursue new and bigger opportunities, and let emotion influence your research. While that's normal, remember that you want to be *abnormal*. To succeed, you must go contrary to your nature. To be great, you need to be odd.

These are just a few of the mental challenges you'll face as an individual investor. Rest assured, there are many more. So commit now to working as diligently on managing your temperament as you do on picking stocks. That means reading articles on the subject and maybe a few of the books we noted above, as well as those in our reference section. It means being passionate about being dispassionate, as well as making good mental notes about your biases, feelings, and the frequency with which you buy and sell stocks in real time. That's because the best counter to your brain, memory, and emotion is data uncolored by eventual outcomes.

Finally, know that even if you do reliably pick great stocks, you can undermine all of your hard work by buying and selling them too often. That's why we've placed this chapter as a speed bump before we head out onto the highway of investing together.

We now will explore the timeless principles of superior investing that will lead us toward the greatest companies and stocks to own for the future. With your temperament in training, let's get cracking!

CHAPTER 3

YOUR FIRST STOCK

If you have the time, ability, and interest, individual stock investing is the single best way to build your own million-dollar portfolio. You're the best person to build a portfolio that most accurately reflects your time line and risk tolerance. What's more, stock investing, because it's active, forces you to track your performance, measure it, and adjust your savings and investing plan from time to time in order to meet your long-term goals.

The old—yet applicable—saw here is "Out of sight, out of mind." If you don't stay on top of your investments, you will lose sight of them. You won't know if you're saving too much, or not enough, or if your investment dollars are drastically underperforming your expectations.

Now, that does not mean you should be an active stock trader. Far from it. The best way to earn a fortune in the stock market is to be a patient long-term owner of high-quality companies. Warren Buffett has said that he'd be a richer man today if he'd never sold a single share of stock—and he started investing at age 11! That's not only because the market moves in fits and starts and can take years to ascribe to even the highest-quality companies their fair value, but also because buying to hold reduces the frictional costs of taxes and trading that can severely hamper long-term returns.

Some basic math here is illustrative. Let's say you start with $1,000 and it costs you $10 to invest it all in a single company. The stock you choose then goes on to earn a mediocre 7% per year for the next 30 years. When you sell three decades later, your $1,000 will have become $7,043, and you'll pocket $6,137 after paying Uncle Sam your long-term capital gains tax bill, which for most investors is 15%.

Now let's say you pay $10 to invest that same $1,000 in a stock that returns 12% in its first year. But then you decide to sell (paying another $10 plus higher short-term capital gains taxes) and buy another stock (paying another $10 to trade). It too earns 12% per year. But then you decide to sell and buy again.

Keep up this activity for the next 30 years, and remarkably, you will have turned your $1,000 into just $3,073 for an effective 3.8% annual return even though you *thought* you were outperforming that mediocre stock by 5 percentage points annually. That's an example of how much taxes and trading costs can hurt, and it's one of the main reasons we advise all investors to buy to hold. Besides, you are much more likely to find one stock that averages a 7% per year return for 30 years than you are to find 30 stocks that each return 12% in the year that you own them.

You'd need to find a stock that does way better than 12% to make any sort of rapid trading strategy worth your time and effort. In fact, according to a 2006 research report from Charles Schwab, an investor who sells a stock and pays short-term capital gains taxes must find a stock that outperforms the old stock by 21.2 percentage points just to offset the taxes! In our example above, you'd have to earn approximately *48% annually* to match the 30-year returns of our seemingly mediocre—yet tax- and trading-cost-efficient—7% annual gainer. To put that in perspective, if you can keep up 30% annual returns for three decades, you will be lauded as the greatest investor who has ever lived.

Is that you?

If it isn't—and there's no shame in not being the greatest investor who has ever lived—then you should buy to hold for an average holding period of three to five years.

FINDING YOUR FIRST STOCK

We've found that the best advice for someone getting started investing is Peter Lynch's famous maxim to "Buy what you know"—even if it is often misquoted, taken out of context, and altogether flawed. Because here's the thing about your first stock pick: It doesn't have to go up in order to have been a success.

Sound crazy? It isn't.

The primary goal of your first stock is to get you started and learning about investing. Above all, this first stock must:

1. Be interesting to you
2. Have financials and a business strategy you understand
3. Be a company you'll enjoy following and talking about with fellow investors

You're going to be spending a lot of time getting to know your first stock pick, so you might as well enjoy it.

So back to "buy what you know."

If you don't know Peter Lynch, he's probably the world's second-most famous investor (behind the aforementioned Warren Buffett). As the manager of Fidelity's Magellan fund from 1977 to 1990, he earned 29% annual returns (which is why we said earlier that if you could keep up 30% for 30 years you'd be the greatest investor who has ever lived). He's also written several fantastic books on investing, is a nice guy, and continues to work for Fidelity as a research consultant.

One of his most famous stock purchases—and one that he writes about in his book *One Up on Wall Street*—was Hanes. He found the company when his wife, Carolyn, raved about its new panty-hose, L'eggs, which were department-store quality but available in the supermarket. Thanks to this idea and many others, Lynch calls Carolyn one of his best sources for investing ideas.

Lynch refers to this "buy what you know" tack as "the power of common knowledge," and he believes it's one of the most significant advantages individual investors have over Wall Street investors who spend way too much time at the office and why our online community is so powerful.

While we agree with that 100%, it's important to note that Lynch didn't just buy Hanes because it had a hot product. After getting the tip from Carolyn, he did thorough fundamental research to determine the financial strength, growth potential, quality of management, and so on of the underlying company.

While many folks remember how Lynch stumbled across Hanes, they don't know *all* of the reasons he decided to buy. It's for this reason that he updated *One Up on Wall Street* with an introduction that warns "Peter Lynch doesn't advise you to buy stock in your favorite store just because you like shopping in the store. . . . Never invest in any company before you've done the homework."

We agree with that, too.

In other words, start with "buy what you know," but *don't stop there*. With your first stock—with every stock—do whatever research is necessary to understand what you're buying, why you're buying it, how much you're paying, and what could cause you to sell.

That's getting somewhat ahead of ourselves, so let's start with a critical question: What do you know?

Think of the public companies you encounter every day. Make a mental list. If you're like most normal people, you'll immediately start thinking of retailers, restaurants, and Web sites such as Wal-Mart, McDonald's, and Google. If you're like David, your list will also include video game makers such as Activision. If you're not sure if a company you know is public or not, look up its

Web site. If it is a public company, it will provide a link to its stock price and investor relations Web site.

Now, although David's Activision pick may seem strange to non-gamers, it's actually a great example of a company you can "know" that Wall Street won't. Unlike the others mentioned, when David recommended Activision back in September 2002, it was small and unknown to many investors. But—and this is the important point—its Tony Hawk, Doom, and Spiderman video game franchises were *known to him*.

Activision has since more than tripled and David did even better (to the tune of 600% returns) by buying more shares of the stock after the market oversold it six months later.

That's the real power in buying what *you* know. So rather than making a quick list of obvious companies that pop into your head, consider keeping a pad with you for a few days and recording all of the companies you encounter *each time* you encounter them. A day could start something like this:

MONDAY MORNING

Woke up. Ate a *Nutrigrain* bar. My child asked for a glass of *Tropicana* orange juice. Brushed my teeth with *Colgate* toothpaste. Got dressed in *Anthropologie* shirt and *Hollister* jeans. Got in my *Toyota* Camry and drove to work, stopping for breakfast at *McDonald's* along the way. Got to work, where I used *Microsoft* Windows on a *Dell* computer. Thought again about getting a *BlackBerry* because everyone has them!

That may seem excessive, but if you stick with it, some good ideas will materialize. In this example, you'll trace Nutrigrain back to Kellogg, Tropicana to PepsiCo, Colgate to Colgate-Palmolive, Hollister to Abercrombie & Fitch, BlackBerry to Research In Motion, and Toyota, Starbucks, Microsoft, and Dell to their namesake companies.

What's more, if you had done this exercise and come up with

this list five years ago—a reasonable possibility for any consumer—and decided on BlackBerry-maker Research In Motion because your fellow employees were all early adopters, you'd be up roughly 5,000%. That would have turned a $5,000 investment into roughly $250,000—taking you a long way toward a $1 million portfolio right there. That said, if you'd picked Dell, you'd be down 40%. In other words, "buy what you know" won't necessarily get you anywhere . . . which is why there are more chapters to this book. But to identify the best ideas, you need to keep track. And if something keeps popping up again and again, make a special note of that. You might be on to something big.

Now, there will be cases where a product or store concept isn't public itself, but is owned by a parent company that is. These lineages can be more difficult to trace, though a quick Google search will usually point you in the right direction. Many "hip" brands may shiver at the thought of disclosing to their customers that they are actually owned by a cadre of wing tip–wearing old men. Take Anthropologie, for example, which is a favorite retailer of many of the women in our office. Its site doesn't provide any clue that it's owned and operated by publicly traded Urban Outfitters. Perhaps unsurprisingly, neither does Urban Outfitters's retail site.

You need to find your way to a separate URL, urbanoutfitters inc.com, to get shareholder information on the company—which also owns Free People and Terrain.

There's also no sign on the Vitamin Water Web site that its manufacturer, Glacéau, is a subsidiary of Coca-Cola, and Blue Moon Brewing doesn't exactly announce that it is owned by conglomerate Molson Coors. In fact, the Blue Moon Web site goes out of its way to give the impression that Blue Moon Brewing is actually an independent craft brewer.

Alas, to invest successfully, you must be a detective. Just as some companies work to hide their ownership of brands designed to appeal to more independent-minded consumers, those same companies may often work to hide from shareholders their operational difficulties, the details of their compensation plans, or their strategies for the future. That's an unfortunate fact of investing, but one that rewards the diligent investor.

The good news is that everything you need to know is readily available online. One simple step is to try plugging the company's name and the term "investor relations" into your Google search. Check beyond the first page of search results if nothing good materializes right away.

When you've finished finding some candidates for investments you know, your list could look something like this:

COMPANY	TICKER	IR WEB SITE
Wal-Mart	WMT	http://walmartstores.com/Investors
McDonald's	MCD	http://www.mcdonalds.com/corp/invest.html
Google	GOOG	http://investor.google.com/
Urban Outfitters	URBN	http://www.urbanoutfittersinc.com/investor/index.jsp
Coca-Cola	KO	http://www.thecoca-colacompany.com/investors/index.html
Molson Coors	TAP	http://phx.corporate-ir.net/phoenix.zhtml?c=101929&p=irol-irhome
Whole Foods	WFMI	http://www.wholefoodsmarket.com/investor/index.html
Home Depot	HD	http://ir.homedepot.com/
Bank of America	BAC	http://investor.bankofamerica.com/phoenix.zhtml?c=71595&p=irol-irhome
Krispy Kreme	KKD	http://www.krispykreme.com/investorrelations.html

Right off the bat, we'd advise you to stay away from financial institutions like Bank of America—at least for your first stock pick. Though they may possess a sound management team and many have been long-term winners, they are notoriously hard to value. As the recent subprime mortgage default crisis has made clear, a bank's assets may not be as valuable as they're stated to be on the company's balance sheet. That type of unknowable risk can sabotage even the most experienced investors, so stay away for now.

Lest this sink your ego, know that even the universally admired Warren Buffett has what he calls a "too hard" pile. Anything he doesn't understand, can't analyze, or can't trust goes in there, and he's said that that's one of the reasons he didn't participate in the Internet stock boom of the late 1990s (or the resulting bust).

After sticking Bank of America or any other financial institution in our own "too hard" pile, we're left with nine fairly friendly and consumer-facing firms. Excellent.

PICKING YOUR FIRST STOCK

You are going to read a lot in this book about ways to analyze different types of companies—big ones and small ones, retailers and banks, money losers and money makers, and foreign and domestic stocks. When it comes to picking your first stock, the key is to limit your downside surprises. Hopefully, this section will give you a few important points of reference and some tools to analyze them.

Our methodology is governed by another pearl of wisdom from the exceptionally quotable Warren Buffett. He said, "It's far better to buy a wonderful company at a fair price than a fair company at a wonderful price." In other words, focus on finding a wonderful company for your first stock rather than a ridiculously cheap stock.

Now, in some sense, this dichotomy is false. In the stock market, you're occasionally able to buy wonderful companies at wonderful prices. For example, Apple, a company you most definitely "know," was selling for $7 per share in December 2002. At that time, the company had nearly $6 per share in cash. That means you were buying the business—a business that would go on to enormous success with the iPod and iPhone—for just $1 per share. Even if you don't know a lick about valuation, you can tell that was a pretty good price. Today, Apple trades for around $100 per share.

Given that enormous return potential, we should all be on the lookout for wonderful companies at wonderful prices. But opportunities like those aren't necessarily available on a daily basis. And while Ron Muhlenkamp has said you can turn even the best company into a bad investment by paying the wrong price, we're going to start with a few ways to find a wonderful company regardless of the price. It's a good place to start and, at the very least, half the battle of investing.

So what makes for a wonderful company? If we're going to borrow from Warren Buffett's ideology, we might as well start with his parameters. Though Buffett is loath to disclose individual stock picks, he is happy to share his methodologies.

For example, in his 2007 Berkshire Hathaway annual report, Buffett wrote about the traits he looks for in any acquisition. They are:

1. At least $75 million in pre-tax earnings
2. Consistent earnings growth
3. Good return on equity
4. Manageable or no debt
5. Quality management that's committed to the company
6. A simple business model

Let's break them down one by one. If at any time in this chapter—or anywhere else in this book—you encounter a term you don't recognize, simply visit www.flossary.com for our glossary of financial, business, and investing terms.

1. AT LEAST $75 MILLION IN PRE-TAX EARNINGS

Here, Buffett is looking simply for size. Given that Berkshire Hathaway is an enormous conglomerate, it's not worth his time to purchase any firm that won't have a meaningful impact on his bottom line. As an individual investor, you don't necessarily need to demand at least $75 million in pre-tax earnings, but we'd suggest you require at the very least a positive number and, going a half-step further, earnings that have been positive for some time.

Like Buffett, you don't need to waste your time with companies that "hope" to be successful—particularly since this is your first stock. Profitability—even better is *consistent* profitability—means that you're already dealing with a proven business.

And how do our nine remaining companies stack up against the profitability test?

COMPANY	TICKER	IS IT PROFITABLE?
Wal-Mart	WMT	Yes
McDonald's	MCD	Yes
Google	GOOG	Yes
Urban Outfitters	URBN	Yes
Coca-Cola	KO	Yes
Molson Coors	TAP	Yes
Whole Foods	WFMI	Yes
Home Depot	HD	Yes
Krispy Kreme	KKD	No

In fact, Krispy Kreme lost more than $60 million in 2007. No thanks.

2. CONSISTENT EARNINGS GROWTH

With this requirement, Buffett is looking for confirmation of a profitable track record over many years. All things being equal, a higher growth rate is better than a lower growth rate, since if you pay fair value for a stock, your return should climb right along with that company's organic growth. Buffett, however, does not suggest a minimum growth rate. Rather, he says that earnings should be consistent. It's up to us to decide what that means, so we'll rank our companies by their earnings growth rates over the past five years.

How do they stack up?

COMPANY	TICKER	HAS IT BEEN PROFITABLE IN EACH OF THE PAST FIVE YEARS?	WHAT IS THE FIVE-YEAR ANNUALIZED EARNINGS GROWTH RATE?
Google	GOOG	Yes	111.4%
Urban Outfitters	URBN	Yes	42.4%
Molson Coors	TAP	Yes	25.2%
McDonald's	MCD	Yes	21.8%
Coca-Cola	KO	Yes	14.4%
Whole Foods	WFMI	Yes	13.3%
Wal-Mart	WMT	Yes	9.9%
Home Depot	HD	Yes	3.7%

Data as of 12/31/07`

Google is far and away the fastest grower here. Home Depot is the clear laggard. To our mind, that's enough to get Home Depot tossed off this list. Although you'll find many investors calling the company a buy at current prices, it is more of a turnaround story than a consistent powerhouse. With more research expertise, Home Depot is worth some study. But since this is our first stock pick, we'll stick with more proven performers. (Home Depot also recently underwent a management change, so that would have gotten it jettisoned a couple steps down the line anyway.)

3. GOOD RETURN ON EQUITY

What constitutes a "good" return on equity varies from business to business, but "good" can roughly be defined as anything better than 10%. A good return on equity is important because it indicates a company that can make a lot of money without a lot of continued investment. This metric generally indicates a company with a strong brand or dominance in its market, and it should mean that the company will hold up well if economic times get tough.

Here's how our remaining candidates stack up:

COMPANY	TICKER	RETURN ON EQUITY, TRAILING 12 MONTHS (TTM)
Coca-Cola	KO	30.9%
Google	GOOG	21.2%
Urban Outfitters	URBN	21.0%
Wal-Mart	WMT	20.4%
McDonald's	MCD	15.2%
Whole Foods	WFMI	11.5%
Molson Coors	TAP	7.9%

Data as of 12/31/07

There's undoubtedly some danger in comparing companies in different industries, but for our purposes here, we'll get rid of Molson Coors, given its mediocre returns to shareholders. (Incidentally, the company also has more than $2.3 billion in debt.)

4. MANAGEABLE OR NO DEBT

A company is obligated to pay its debt holders *before* it pays its stockholders (terrible news for Fannie Mae shareholders). That extra layer of security is one reason debt holders—by buying bonds—generally earn lower returns (they're earning lower interest rates in exchange for taking on less risk). When a company has little to no debt, stockholders don't need to worry about debt holders extracting money from the company when those bonds come due. This gives companies added flexibility, particularly if the economy sours. When there are no debt holders to pay, a company doesn't have to worry about going bankrupt. Generally, a company without debt can fund its own growth from operations. All of the companies left on our list here have been pretty solid growers, and their businesses generate lots of cash to fund all that growth. That's a very good thing.

So, let's see who has debt and who doesn't by looking on the company's balance sheet.

COMPANY	TICKER	LONG-TERM DEBT
Coca-Cola	KO	$3.3 billion
Google	GOOG	None
Urban Outfitters	URBN	None
Wal-Mart	WMT	$29.8 billion
McDonald's	MCD	$7.3 billion
Whole Foods	WFMI	$769.6 million

Data as of 12/31/07

While Wal-Mart's nearly $30 billion debt load may look like a lot, know that we should talk about debt only in the context of the company's ability to carry it. Two common ratios help in this regard: the debt-to-equity ratio and the interest coverage ratio.

The debt-to-equity ratio measures how much debt a company holds as a percentage of its total shareholder equity (divide debt by equity). If the ratio is 2 to 1 or more, it means the business is capital-intensive—a scenario Buffett seeks to avoid. Despite having $30 billion in debt, Wal-Mart's debt-to-equity ratio is less than 0.7, and Coca-Cola, McDonald's, and Whole Foods all check in at less than that. So no red flags here.

The interest coverage ratio measures the relationship between how much cash a company earns from its business versus how much cash it must pay its creditors. It's also commonly thought of as being the number of times over a company could make its interest payments. In most cases, we'd demand a ratio of at least 1, though the bigger the better.

COMPANY	TICKER	INTEREST COVERAGE RATIO
Coca-Cola	KO	16.5
Google	GOOG	Debt-free
Urban Outfitters	URBN	Debt-free
Wal-Mart	WMT	10.5
McDonald's	MCD	13.5
Whole Foods	WFMI	18.2

Data as of 12/31/07

All of these firms look to have sufficient flexibility when it comes to managing their debt (if they have any), so it doesn't look like any company has to be thrown overboard at this step. On your own list, however, if you see a company with a debt-to-equity ratio greater than 1 and an interest coverage ratio less than 2, consider putting that on the chopping block—particularly if you have other first stock candidates with balance sheets that look more like the ones we've investigated here. General Motors, for example, is struggling to adapt to changing consumer tastes and a more competitive automotive marketplace. The fact that the company is saddled with more than $34 billion in debt means there is little margin for error before creditors come calling. Stay away from General Motors.

5. QUALITY MANAGEMENT THAT'S COMMITTED TO THE COMPANY

Here's where we think stock analysis starts getting fun—and by fun we mean more qualitative and less quantitative. You're going to read a lot in this book, and particularly in the small-cap section, about the importance of a dedicated and entrepreneurial CEO, board of directors, and senior management staff that are all aligned with outside shareholders. We think this core trait of great investments is among the most overlooked by institutional and Wall Street research.

This senior leadership is also, according to documentation in a number of fascinating studies, critical to a company's performance. One of the best of these studies—"Where Are the Shareholders' Mansions? CEOs' Home Purchases, Stock Sales, and Subsequent Company Performance" by Professor Crocker Liu of Arizona State University and Professor David Yermack of New York University—found that "Future company performance deteriorates when CEOs acquire extremely large or costly mansions and estates." The same is true of fancy headquarters. The working explanation for this correlation is that a transaction of this nature signals entrenchment and distraction—someone ready to enjoy the fruits of their labors rather than labor for more fruit.

This circumstance contrasts unfavorably, Liu and Yermack point out, with someone like Warren Buffett. Buffett, who has built Berkshire into an empire and was recently worth more than $60 billion, still lives in the same Omaha, Nebraska, house he purchased for $31,500 in 1958.

Admittedly, Buffett's house is no shack, but his behavior is an anomaly, given the capital available to him and as compared to the actions of his peers such as former Tyco CEO Dennis Kozlowski—who you may remember threw his wife a $2.1 million Ancient Rome–themed birthday party in Sardinia a few years ago complete with an ice sculpture of Michelangelo's David that whizzed high-end vodka. That guy's in jail now.

But while separating Buffett from someone like Kozlowski is easy in hindsight, how can we identify superior management teams in real time across thousands of publicly traded companies? It's an admittedly squishy subject, and one that we deal with by putting a leadership team through these five core questions:

1. Is the founder still active in the company? Is he or she building a legacy of leadership on sound core values?
2. Do insiders have an ownership stake in the company?

How much? Have they been buying or selling shares recently?

3. What's their compensation? Is it reasonable? How is it determined?

4. How long is their tenure, and how good is the track record?

5. Are they smart?

While that's just five questions, those are pretty substantial questions to tackle. If you answer all of them, then you're going to know and trust the management team very much at the end of the day.

Twenty or so years ago, getting after these questions would have been an enormous undertaking. It would have involved hours at the library, scores of phone calls, and an avalanche of careful detective work. Today, it's a fun way to spend a Sunday afternoon . . . so long as your Google-fu is strong.

Unless we have met with a company's CEO, Google is where we start. And Google is pretty good at its job. Type Whole Foods CEO John Mackey's name into your search field and you'll find out that he was a star tight end at Syracuse University, played for the Baltimore Colts with Johnny Unitas, won a Super Bowl, and was inducted into the Pro Football Hall of Fame in lovely Canton, Ohio.

OK, so that's the wrong John Mackey.

Type a more precise search string like "John Mackey Whole Foods" into Google and you'll discover a lot of interesting stuff about this founder/CEO. He, for example, is "the Bill Gates of organic foods," a vegetarian, a libertarian, and an environmentalist who is simultaneously loved and loathed by others in the green movement, and he "no longer wants to work for money."

Sounds pretty interesting.

You'll also discover that Mackey posted anonymously on an Internet stock discussion board to argue with other posters and tout the merits of his company . . . a revelation that got him into some hot water both with the media and with authorities (though he was ultimately cleared of legal wrongdoing by the Securities and Exchange Commission).

That's a tiny fraction of the raw data that's out there on this successful entrepreneur, but as a sample, it gives you an idea of the qualitative gymnastics that you face as a stock investor.

For example, the Whole Foods brand is predicated on social and environmental responsibility, support for local and sustainable agriculture, and care for its employees. But as critics point out, through its expansion and attempts to earn mass appeal, the company has put local businesses out of business and perhaps compromised its core beliefs by stocking certain "conventional" products in its stores. It's also a non-union business—a decision that draws both admiration and ire.

Then there are Mackey's Internet message board shenanigans. Are they evidence of a passionate entrepreneur or someone who talks integrity but doesn't act with it?

As a prospective investor, it's up to you to weigh the facts and decide. That's where the framework above comes into play. Of course, there's a caveat: While it should help you organize your thoughts, it won't make a clear-cut final decision for you. No leadership team at any company will pass all of the tests with flying colors. But if you can find folks who yield satisfactory answers to most of the questions, you're off to a fantastic start.

What are the satisfactory answers? You may come up with your own parameters now or eventually, but here's what we think:

1. Is the Founder Still Active in the Company? Is He or She Building a Legacy of Leadership on Sound Core Values?

We love to see founders who are still active in their companies. While we obviously wouldn't penalize a company like Wal-Mart where founder Sam Walton was active until his death and left a strong senior management team to build on his legacy, we believe that the motivating fire a founding entrepreneur brings to his or her business is a rare and valuable trait when it comes to winning in the business world. That's particularly true at a time when the tenure of the average public company CEO has dropped to less than five years. Five years is hardly enough time to get oriented, study the company, decide on a clear strategic direction, institute that strategy, and then measure and reflect on the results.

In the absence of a founder, we at least like to see long-tenured leaders who have presided over a sustained growth story. We also like to see a company that has a truly independent board of directors.

While it's hard to know exactly how a board interacts with a company's executives, you can make an educated guess by studying the biographies of the board members. The Google board, for example, includes people such as Intel's Paul Otellini, Genentech's Arthur Levinson, and famous venture capitalist John Doerr, all of whom have been successful independently of Google. They don't need their board seats, and they're not the types of people who would be intimidated by founders Sergey Brin and Larry Page.

That's a solid board with technology expertise, leadership expertise, research expertise, and the credentials to speak truth to power.

Contrast that with what you find on the board at XM Satellite Radio—a company that's done nothing but disappoint investors. There isn't one member with immediate name recognition, and there's no clearly established or independent voice with media expertise. That sort of deficiency is what we're looking for when we try to decide whether a board of directors is adding value to a company and if it is tasking its CEO with building the right sort of company for the long term.

Finally, you can learn a lot just by listening to a company's conference calls (easily done over the Internet) and applying your own common sense. When you hear the CEO talk, do you get a good or a bad feeling? Is he or she candid or more prone to covering up bad news and forcing analysts to ask detailed questions in order to extract information? We prefer leaders who share the credit and take the blame, rather than vice versa.

As Warren Buffett said, there are no "called strikes" in investing. So if you sense something wrong or something makes you uncomfortable, just don't invest. It's your money, after all.

As for our first investment finalists, Google, Whole Foods, and Urban Outfitters are all still run by founders. Wal-Mart gets a pass here because Lee Scott has been a lifer at the company and seems to share founder Sam Walton's passion.

As for conduct and the quality of the boards, a company the size of Whole Foods should have a better board than it does. None of the current members seem to have the credentials to challenge Mackey. The same seems to be the case at Urban Outfitters, where founders Scott Belair and Richard Hayne and CEO Glen Senk share the board with two investment bankers and a lawyer. Where's the independent retail expertise?

That leaves us with Google and Wal-Mart.

2. Do Insiders Have an Ownership Stake in the Company? How Much? Have They Been Buying or Selling Shares Recently?

We like to see managers with an ownership stake in the business they lead because it indicates vested interest. Of course, we'd like to believe that anyone who draws a salary from a company has a vested interest in seeing it succeed, but there have been too many horror stories over the past two decades to have us accept that as fact (plus the bothersome statistic about CEOs drawing enormous salaries and then jumping ship after a relatively short stay at the helm). If you're not a shareholder, we simply can't assume that you're looking out for *long-term* shareholder interests.

It's here where John Mackey again falls a little bit short. His

$26 million stake in Whole Foods represents just a 0.8% ownership stake in the company. And despite his confident proclamations of the company's future, he hasn't bought any additional shares on the open market recently even as the stock price dropped 55% from January 2006 through April 2008. At some point, we'd prefer to see him step up to the plate.

We also like to see insiders buying more of their own stock because we believe that it is a bullish signal. We agree with an old bit of Wall Street wisdom that reads, "There are thousands of reasons for insiders to sell stock, but there's only one reason they'll buy: They think the stock is going to go up."

After all, insiders (we hope) know more about their company than outside investors ever could. If they're buying, there's probably a pretty good reason for it.

Studies bear this reasoning out. A Morgan Stanley report on insider buys between 2003 and 2006 showed that these stocks outperformed the S&P 500 index by more than 13 percentage points. Another report from Thomson examined insider buying since 1990 and found that the S&P 500 advanced more than 40% in the two years following widespread insider buying sprees. Both are enormous margins of victory over "average" returns and, in aggregate, show that insider buying is a bullish signal at both the company-specific and macro-market levels.

The good news is that insiders need to report their stock transactions to the Securities and Exchange Commission via the publicly filed Form 4. Those filings are available on the SEC Web site, and there are a number of pay services that will track them for you. And while insider transactions won't in and of themselves persuade or dissuade us from buying any individual equity, we do always check to see what the insiders have been doing.

One caveat here is that it's much easier to own a large percentage of a small company than a large percentage of a large company. But if you stack up the insider ownership statistics of a few of our companies, you'll see some stark differences:

COMPANY	PERCENTAGE OF TOTAL INSIDER OWNERSHIP
Coca-Cola	5.1%
Google	22.8%
Urban Outfitters	28.6%
Wal-Mart	43.4%
McDonald's	0.1%
Whole Foods	1.1%

Data as of 12/31/07

The insider holding percentages at Coke, Google, Urban Out-fitters, and Wal-Mart are much higher than what you'll generally find in the stock market. That's a positive sign that the folks who own these shares continue to believe in their companies. It's worth noting, however, that many of the insider holdings at Wal-Mart are owned by Sam Walton's children—who aren't in-volved in the day-to-day operations of the company. But they're still major holders who could have cashed out their fortunes long ago—and that says something.

3. What's Their Compensation? Is It Reasonable? How Is It Determined?

While insider transactions can be easy to judge, judging the dif-ference between fair and egregious executive compensation can be difficult. After all, most executive salaries will dwarf the me-dian U.S. household income of roughly $50,000, making it seem like *all* CEOs are paid excessively. Then there's the added com-pensation CEOs receive such as annual bonuses, stock options, and use of resources such as company-owned private cars and jets. It adds up.

According to data from The Corporate Library, the average total compensation package for an S&P 500 CEO was more than $14 million in 2007, and the median compensation was $8.8 mil-lion. That's eye-popping.

Without question, there are CEOs who make far more than they're worth. Two that come to mind are former Merrill Lynch head Stan O'Neal and former Home Depot CEO Bob Nardelli. During their tenures, both made questionable decisions that ultimately undermined the quality of the companies they ran. These decisions destroyed shareholder value (O'Neal's by condoning aggressive participation in the subprime mortgage market, Nardelli's by reducing Home Depot's emphasis on superior customer service). Yet both made serious bank. In addition to the multimillion-dollar salaries they enjoyed as CEO, O'Neal walked away with a $161 million severance package and Nardelli received a $210 million parting gift. This is a problem, and one that corporate America has to solve in order for our country to have faith in its business and investment community.

We also believe, however, that great leadership is hard to find. Great CEOs are significant (though not always sustainable) competitive advantages in the business world, so generous compensation packages can be reasonable as long as a CEO's performance and long-term track record warrant such pay.

It's that dichotomy that informs the overarching judgment we make when it comes to CEO compensation. That is to make sure that the CEO is not using the company primarily as a vehicle for personal enrichment. It doesn't matter what a CEO makes as long as long-term shareholder interest is a priority. Performance reviews should be tied to the proper benchmarks and all elements of the compensation package should be transparent and fully disclosed.

This was the problem with the compensation plans at Home Depot and Merrill Lynch. Neither, it turned out, ended up being tied to benchmarks that mattered. O'Neal, for example, should have been judged by the ultimate outcome of the company's subprime investments (which have largely flopped and were written down by $8 billion), rather than by the paper profits it booked at the time the deals were made (which were significant).

The compensation plan at any company you're interested in investing in is disclosed in a company's annual proxy statement.

Make sure that you're comfortable with it and that it aligns with your interest as a shareholder. Pay very close attention to a CEO's incentives. After all, these are the metrics he or she is going to manage toward.

One common CEO incentive that we *don't* like to see is when a CEO's compensation package is tied too closely to the performance of a company's stock. Remember, the stock market is often irrational. Any CEO who tries to control it is delusional. But a CEO can try to manage his or her stock price through all sorts of accounting shenanigans, such as booking revenue early in order to meet quarterly analyst expectations.

These shenanigans generally keep the CEO's focus on increasing a stock's price in the short term rather than on where it should be: building a company's value for the long term. As a shareholder, you want someone who is focused on, and being rewarded for, building long-term value.

What metrics *are* worthwhile for inclusion in incentive plans? There are many, and they can vary from stock to stock and industry to industry. But for a general guideline, just refer back to the traits that Warren Buffett likes to see in a business and that we've been going through in this chapter.

Again, they are:

1. At least $75 million in pre-tax earnings
2. Consistent earnings growth
3. Good return on equity
4. Manageable or no debt
5. Quality management that's committed to the company
6. A simple business model

At least four of those (consistent growth, good return on equity, manageable or no debt, and a committed management team) are easy to incent for. So look for compensation plans that reward those benchmarks and not other, more short-term strategies.

4. How Long Is Their Tenure, and How Good Is the Track Record?

This is an easy one. Long tenures are better than short ones and, of course, managers who have presided over success are superior to those who have presided over failure. Indeed, one study we did at the Fool found that of the 100 top-performing small companies from 1996 to 2005, 84 benefited from committed and long-tenured leadership teams. Of those, 66 were founders or CEOs who had at least five years experience at the company at the start of the timeframe.

That frequency of clearly committed leadership is far greater than in the broader market, and it's another reason why we make management assessment such an integral part of our investment research process.

It's also worth noting that track records don't necessarily have to be made at a CEO's current company. One of our favorite investment tacks is to "follow the entrepreneur." Keep track of people who have founded and built successful companies in the past and see what they come up with next—and when it goes public. Netflix CEO Reed Hastings, for example, has built several successful companies. Before his current project, he founded Pure Software in 1991, took it public in 1995, and made it one of the 50 largest software firms in the world by 1997, when it was acquired by Rational Software (since acquired by IBM) for $515 million.

The key, though, is for you to judge success by the proper metrics—sustained growth and good returns on equity—rather than by a company's stock price. Stock price, as you'll read time and time again in this book and hear from many smart investors, is not always a reflection of a company's quality or value.

5. Are They Smart?

This question is another easy and fun, though subjective, test. We judge a management team's relative intelligence by looking for a few core traits. It's easy to find any of the information below with a quick Google search.

First, are they good communicators? We agree with hedge fund manager Mark Sellers (who gave a riveting speech on this topic at Harvard Business School) that smart businesspeople have both sides of their brain working. They're good with both numbers and language. As Sellers noted in that speech, "If you can't write clearly . . . you don't think very clearly. And if you don't think clearly, you're in trouble." So listen to a company's conference calls and read its CEO's annual letter to shareholders. Both will let you know if your CEO is a clear thinker.

Second, are the senior leaders experts in their fields? This would mean that they're routinely invited to serve on other companies' boards of directors as well as on government and university committees, research teams, or panels. Heck, it's also a good sign if your CEO is invited every year to give commencement addresses. Keep track of those things. They're little, but they count—and they'll give you a better idea of the person who's determining the fate of your hard-earned investment dollars.

Third, do they serve on other sorts of boards or work with charity or government? If they do, it's evidence that they're well respected by their peers. That's about as much as you can do to affirm someone's qualifications without knowing them personally.

Finally, what's their educational background? We write this here with the caveat that a college or even high school degree does not necessarily confer smarts or common sense. Some of our country's most successful business leaders—such as Microsoft's Bill Gates, Oracle's Larry Ellison, and even Facebook's Mark Zuckerberg—were all college dropouts (though they did all drop out from Harvard). But all else being equal, we prefer leaders who have demonstrated a passion for learning. That can be done by dropping out of an Ivy League school to pursue a business idea (as Gates did) or by working one's way through community college (as Ross Perot and Tom Golisano, CEO of Paychex, did).

One smart guy is Google CEO Eric Schmidt. He has an under-graduate degree from Princeton, a PhD from Cal-Berkley, experience at Bell Labs, Novell, and the Palo Alto Research Center, and is also on the boards at Apple and Carnegie Mellon University. Oh, and he's also a member of the National Academy of Engineering, a fellow at the American Academy of Arts and Sciences, and chairman of the non-profit New America Foundation.

6. A SIMPLE BUSINESS MODEL

Here's the thing about simple business models: They're not necessarily better at making money than complicated business models. Yet there's a great reason Warren Buffett loves them: they're much easier to understand. Everything else should go in that "too hard" pile.

That doesn't mean that down the line you shouldn't rescue some names from your "too hard" pile or invest in a company with lots of moving parts. But don't start there. Start with a company where you understand how it makes money. That way you'll understand when it's doing well (making more money) and doing poorly (making less or even losing money).

One exercise we like is to try to describe a company in one sentence. If we can—and can do so compellingly—then it's passed the test. "Great stocks," David will often proclaim, "don't make you think!"

If, however, you find yourself hemming and hawing and droning on in a run-on sentence with multiple commas, ellipses, bulleted lists, and so on, then stop right there. This is not a good first stock. It's complicated and unclear, and you likely won't enjoy following it.

So, can we describe Google and Wal-Mart each in a sentence?

Google makes most of its money by selling targeted advertisements alongside its top-notch Internet search results. Wal-Mart makes money by being the low-cost retailer of an incredible variety of goods.

Both sentences clearly explain how these companies make money and what their competitive advantage is in the space. Google has the best technology; Wal-Mart has the best prices. Those are simple business models, and you'll know very quickly if either is faltering (Google ceases to have the best search capabilities or Wal-Mart ceases to have the best prices).

So Who Wins?

Not surprisingly, both Wal-Mart and Google, our two first stock finalists in this exercise, are favorites of Warren Buffett's. In fact, Buffett himself owns shares of Wal-Mart through Berkshire Hathaway, and he wrote in his 2008 letter to shareholders that Google embodies his dream company that has "an ever-increasing stream of earnings with virtually no capital requirements."

So, while we don't think you can go wrong buying either Wal-Mart or Google today based on this short study of their businesses, don't just go out and make either your first stock. Go through this entire process from scratch. You'll not only learn how to do it and become a more seasoned investor in the process, you may also find a company that will outperform both Wal-Mart and Google from here.

What Can Go Wrong?

If you bought a consumer-facing company like Wal-Mart or Google that you knew well and that you felt comfortable buying, chances are you overpaid for it, at least in the short term. We don't necessarily know if that's true, but consumer-facing companies in good times tend to have lots of growth expectations priced into them.

This book is going to get much more in-depth about valuation later, so we won't bore you with the details here, but if your first stock declines or drops suddenly on earnings, the culprit is likely valuation. Google, for example, trades for a price-to-earnings ratio (the famed P/E) of 39. Wal-Mart's is 19. The market average today is close to 13. That means that investors are willing to pay a premium to own both Google and Wal-Mart because—as we've already seen—they are excellent businesses. When you pay a premium, whether it's for a stock, a bottle of wine, or an article of clothing, you have higher expectations. As a result, if you open an expensive bottle of wine only to discover that it's become vinegar, you will be upset. You may even return it to the store and demand your money back.

This is exactly what happens when a company posts quarterly results that disappoint investors. These investors get upset and some may demand their money back by selling the stock and causing its stock price to drop. This is not the end of the world.

Remember, the purpose of your first stock is not necessarily to make a fortune. It is to help you become a better investor. If you made a mistake with your first stock and that mistake was based on the valuation, well, then you know what you have to work on. The remaining chapters in this book will help you do just that.

Also keep in mind that the stock market is often irrational and that it might test your patience (and stomach) on a daily basis. If you own a great company like Wal-Mart or Google, it's generally worth holding through good times and bad. If you remember our example from earlier in this chapter, it's much easier to do better as an investor by doing less. That means minimizing your tax burden and trading costs, and the only way to do that is to buy to hold.

The stock market, however, is not *always* irrational. If your stock drops substantially, it is always worth revisiting your research. You may discover that you were wrong about your assessment of the quality of a business. You may also discover, later on, that a fundamental part of your investment thesis was based on inaccurate or no longer accurate information (the CEO resigns over a previously undisclosed scandal, the accounting turns out to have been fraudulent, or a competitive advantage—like Google's search technology—has eroded). In either of these scenarios, it is time to consider selling.

We recommend that investors keep good notes about *why* they bought a stock. Only by knowing that—and being able to refer to it—will you know when something has gone wrong.

WHAT YOU SHOULD LEARN FROM YOUR FIRST STOCK

If your stock goes up right off the bat, you may become a victim of dreaded confirmation bias. You'll convince yourself that your analysis was flawless, that you have all the makings of a top investor, and that this Warren Buffett we keep referencing isn't all he's cracked up to be. If you're not careful, such a mind-set can lead to sloppy research processes and excessive risk-taking.

You may actually become a better investor in the long run if your first stock drops in the days following your purchase. Such a scenario would be a gut-check, and it would help you to develop the emotional makeup to be a great stock investor.

But if you find yourself drilling down on your assumptions, reassessing the effectiveness of your process, and looking for what you missed or did not miss, then you have the potential to be a successful stock investor. If you really focus on the business and decide that although the stock price has dropped, the quality of the underlying investment remains the same and you want to *buy more*, then you have the makings of a *superior* stock investor.

In other words, if your first stock can teach you to have an even temperament about the market, that's a major victory. If it goes down because you missed a crucial piece of information, then you've also benefited. Presumably, you'll not make the same mistake twice.

Your first stock should only be a small slice of your portfolio—even just a few hundred dollars. Never invest more money in stocks than you can afford to lose. If you're a beginning stock investor, your portfolio should be built upon a sound asset allocation plan and a set of carefully chosen mutual funds. (See Appendix A for a detailed guide to mutual fund investing.)

Above all, we view your first stock as a learning tool. Some of you may learn that investing on your own is too time-consuming, too stressful, or just not much fun. And that's OK, too. At The Motley Fool, we invest alongside you in our newsletter services. Come join us!

Finally, when you're having fun following your first stock and regaling cocktail party attendees with tales of your research, your first stock should also have taught you what Warren Buffett has called one of the most important lessons that he learned about investing: You should have started sooner.

Motley Fool Advisor Tim Hanson contributed to this chapter. Tim spent a few years digging into the fundamentals of small-cap companies for our Hidden Gems *and* Pay Dirt *newsletter services, and now serves as co-advisor to* Global Gains. *The first stock Tim bought was Whole Foods.*

Visit us at mdpbook.com to get some of our current favorite stocks—free! You might find the perfect candidate for your first stock purchase.

CHAPTER 4

DIVIDEND DYNASTY

At this point, you're probably thinking, "I get it. High-quality stocks are my route to a million-dollar portfolio." But now you'd like more guidance on what types of equities to buy.

You may already know the classifications of stocks—value, high-growth, small-cap, blue-chip, high-yielders, international stocks, and so on. But that taxonomy, while useful, has overlaps that can be confusing. After all, aren't there such things as high-growth dividend stocks? What about blue-chip value stocks?

Over the next several chapters, we'll give you specific guidance on how to build your portfolio around the most useful stock-picking strategies. We'll move beyond the black and white into the grey areas of classification, where most of the best long-term investments find their hiding places. But let's start with one of the most fundamental principles, both theoretically and practically, at your disposal—the dividend. Investing in companies that pay dividends has let our *Income Investor* newsletter service beat the market by about 8 percentage points.

GET PAID TO INVEST

Rewind the clock to your childhood, back to your average Saturday morning. If you're like us, you had chores around the house. Weeding the brickwork out front. Cleaning up board games from the floor of your room. Cutting lawns, hosing flowerbeds, clipping hedges. Your reward—a few dollars of allowance—was as good as gold.

We can reclaim that childhood glory together by investing in companies that pay dividends, the business world's allowance. When we invest long in public companies, there are two ways to profit: stock appreciation and dividend payments. Each makes up a part of what we call the "return equation." The first, stock appreciation—or capital gains—is straightforward. We buy stock in Whole Foods Market or Apple, and then we root them on, hoping years from now to sell those shares at a higher price.

Dividends are the second part of the return equation. A dividend is a quarterly, annual, or one-time special payment back to the shareholders. Household and personal care giant Procter & Gamble, for example, has paid a dividend to its shareholders for more than 100 years. The company currently pays out around 40% of its earnings each year in dividends. Even if Procter & Gamble's stock goes down one year or the next, or remains flat for a three-year period, all's not lost. Stockholders can earn money during flat periods in the form of dividend payments. And those payments are made out of the company's annual flow of earnings.

For that reason, dividend investors need to keep their eyes trained to the bottom line.

THE BOTTOM LINE

The primary way that a public company delivers investment returns—as capital gains or via dividends—is by generating profit. It's the raison d'être of incorporation. Of course, there are many accompanying reasons to be in business. Public companies fill consumer needs in the marketplace, provide tens of millions of jobs, compete to lower prices for buyers, and strive to help humanity use its resources more efficiently. But the bottom line is *the bottom line*. Profit is necessary for every public company's operations—from the world's largest oil company, ExxonMobil, to other flourishing companies like Copenhagen's Vestas Wind Systems, with the grand mission of building and maintaining wind power systems to produce electricity.

Companies need to make money to survive and to reward their shareholders for shouldering the risk of investment.

Of course, given the natural limitations of accounting, "profit" can take many forms. In our 15-year history at The Motley Fool, we've had courtside seats to view public companies as they've flourished and faltered. And we've watched closely enough to know that there are both healthy *and* unhealthy forms of profit. The former includes gains won by delighting customers, renewing long-standing business partnerships, innovating to create sustained competitive advantages, and making prudent investments. But not all stated profit is healthy! Always remember that not every company's chief executive is committed to building a great business for the long term. Short-term greed, fostered by flawed compensation plans, can lead certain CEOs to furiously bend and twist accounting rules to create phantom profits. By doing so, they can mislead their board of directors, the marketplace of investors, and sometimes even themselves into thinking they've succeeded. That can enable them to take home millions in compensation for a job poorly done.

The beauty of dividend investing, as you'll see in a moment, is that when practiced Foolishly, it can help you steer clear of scoundrels.

Let's start in on this problem by defining profit as *the money remaining after all expenses are subtracted from the sale of products and services*. That's the "bottom line" to a company's income statement, with revenues at the top, material expenses below it, followed by the cost of labor and marketing, through to interest expenses and taxes. Here's a simple, imaginary example:

THE FOOTBALL CLUB OF ALEXANDRIA
Fiscal Year: 2008

Revenues:	$100,000,000
Cost of Goods:	–$20,000,000
Gross Profit:	$80,000,000

Operating Expenses	
Salaries:	–$20,000,000
General & Admin:	–$10,000,000
Marketing:	–$5,000,000
Rent:	–$2,000,000
Total Operating Expenses:	–$37,000,000
Operating Profit:	$43,000,000
Debt Expense:	–$3,000,000
Taxes:	–$14,000,000
Net Income:	$26,000,000

In this case, FOOT's bottom line for 2008 is $26 million. After we account for all the year's operating costs, interest expense (from debts), and taxes, we're left with $26 million for the company's owners. For publicly traded companies, all of the shareholders are owners, all with a legal claim on the earnings a company generates each year.

Yet that's really all we have, a *claim* on the earnings. That claim does not extend to the company's assets, like its buildings or computer equipment or the brand name or the stunning Picasso hanging in the foyer of corporate headquarters. Shareholders are due only whatever the company earns each year alongside our voting rights as owners of the corporation. For that reason, the profit direction of any company whose stock you own should be a very high priority to you.

All else being equal, the stocks of companies that continue to earn more money year in and year out will rise in value. They'll also have more money to pay out to their shareholders in the form of dividends. There's that return equation again. Let's say you own one tenth of 1% of the Football Club of Alexandria. At the end of 2008, your claim on FOOT's $26 million in earnings is about $260. Now, while you have a claim on those earnings, you're probably not going to receive a check in that amount in the mail. A company's board of directors and its CEO choose what to do with those earnings. Essentially, they have five choices, not all of which are mutually exclusive.

1. Bank the earnings
2. Reinvest in the company
3. Make an acquisition
4. Buy back company stock (this increases each owner's share of the pie)
5. Pay out dividends to shareholders

As we noted above, a dividend is simply a slice of a company's earnings that the board decides to pay to its owners. Not all companies choose to pay them. Fast-growing companies, which you'll learn about in Chapters 6 and 7, typically need to reinvest all of their earnings to fuel growth. They live by the old mantra "You gotta spend money to make money!" These companies tend to be smaller, with less stable earnings but higher potential growth rates. In most of these cases, it would be ill-advised for them to promise a regular dividend. The canary in the coal mine for investors is when management overpromises and underdelivers, thereby having to reduce or eliminate dividend payments in down periods. That's a no-no.

Let's look again at Google—one of the most innovative and remarkable companies in history. In just its tenth year of existence, the online search powerhouse earned more than $4 billion in profit. That's an unmatched pace in the history of business. What does Google do with all that cash? Today, it spends about a third on research and development with the aim of growing its market share over the long term. Its management team reinvests the earnings aiming to benefit shareholders for years and decades to come. So in our return equation, Google is fully focused on the first variable—stock appreciation. And there's nothing inherently wrong with that.

But other large companies, like Campbell Soup and Norfolk Southern, which operate in slower-growth industries, don't have the luxury of reinvesting their earnings at consistently high rates of return. Yet they too generate gobs of earnings each year. So what should they do with all that excess cash, absent the attractive opportunities for substantial reinvestment in their business? They could stick it in the bank to earn piddling interest, but that's not very inspiring. They could make game-changing acquisitions, but those typically sound fascinating upon announcement then prove disastrous upon integration. Think America Online and Time Warner, Compaq and Hewlett-Packard, Sprint and Nextel.

So along with making the necessary reinvestments of earnings back into their operations, many large, established companies pay out quarterly or annual dividends. Benjamin Graham, the father of security analysis and co-author of the seminal investing work *Security Analysis*, put it best when he said, "The prime purpose of a business corporation is to pay dividends to its owners. A successful company is one which can pay dividends regularly and presumably increase the rate as time goes on."

Let's take a look at the 20 largest companies in the S&P 500.

COMPANY	TICKER	DIVIDEND PER SHARE	YIELD (DIVIDEND/ PRICE)
Pfizer	PFE	$1.19	6.70%
AT&T	T	$1.51	4.63%
General Electric	GE	$1.18	4.38%
JPMorgan Chase	JPM	$1.52	4.30%
Philip Morris	PM	$1.84	3.57%
Coca-Cola	KO	$1.40	2.72%
Johnson & Johnson	JNJ	$1.66	2.55%

continued

COMPANY	TICKER	DIVIDEND PER SHARE	YIELD (DIVIDEND/ PRICE
Chevron	CVX	$2.32	2.35%
Intel	INTC	$0.47	2.27%
Procter & Gamble	PG	$1.40	2.20%
ConocoPhillips	COP	$1.70	1.85%
Microsoft	MSFT	$0.43	1.66%
ExxonMobil	XOM	$1.40	1.59%
Wal-Mart	WMT	$0.90	1.59%
IBM	IBM	$1.60	1.34%
Schlumberger	SLB	$0.91	0.89%
Hewlett Packard	HPQ	$0.32	0.74%
Apple	AAPL	$—	0.00%
Cisco Systems	CSCO	$—	0.00%
Google	GOOG	$—	0.00%

List from http://www.indexarb.com/indexComponentWtsSP500.html.
Data from CapitalIQ (7/4/2008).

You'll notice right away that the last three companies pay no dividend—Apple, Cisco, and Google. That should come as no shock. These are high-growth companies in dynamic industries, demanding additional investments for growth. Just think about the time, effort, and money that Apple invested in creating the iPod, iPhone, and MacBook Air. Innovation requires investment—for which there is, of course, no guarantee of continuing success.

And so here's one key takeaway: Dividend-paying companies are surer bets as investments since, on average, they operate in mature industries and enjoy steady flows of earnings. There is a reason why we have launched our book's examination of investment strategies by focusing first on dividends—this is the safest way to invest in equities.

THE DIVIDEND YIELD

To master dividend investing, you'll have to start with a grasp of the dividend yield and its importance. Nothing tough here. The yield represents the yearly dividend a company pays out divided by its current share price, then expressed as a percentage. So if the annual dividend is $1 and the current stock price is $50, the dividend yield is simply ($1/$50) * 100 = 2%.

Investors use the dividend yield to gauge how much they'll get paid relative to the cost for each share of stock. We often compare the dividend yield between companies within the same industry as well as across other investment types, like savings accounts and bond yields.

The dividend yield should be considered as an interest rate earned for owning a company's stock. The average yield of the 20 stocks in our chart above, including the three that don't pay dividends, is 2.27%, which is just a tad higher than the 2.23% average for all S&P 500 stocks. That makes sense. The 20 companies above are some of the largest corporations in the world. Many operate in established industries, leaving them few places to intelligently invest their enormous piles of profit. Paying a dividend to their shareholders is the best alternative.

THE PAYOUT RATIO

A second critical dividend metric is the payout ratio, a simple calculation to determine how much of a company's earnings are returned to shareholders each year. Why calculate this? Well, how anxious would you be if one of your investments paid out more in dividends than the company earned each year? We'd be pretty anxious. That's not a sustainable program.

Here's how to calculate the payout ratio. Simply divide total dividends by total earnings. Often the easiest way to do this is to take the per-share calculations in a company's financial filings. This ratio is also expressed as a percentage.

Put simply, the lower the payout ratio, the better. That would indicate that management has room to increase its dividend even if earnings don't grow. Here's where the statistic gets even more interesting. There is empirical evidence to show that low-payout companies perform better than their high-payout counterparts. Investment firm Credit Suisse has proved that a portfolio of high-yielding, low-payout-ratio stocks of the S&P 1500 (a bigger universe than the more common S&P 500 benchmark) delivered annualized returns of 19.2% between 1990 and 2006 versus 11.2% for the S&P 500. Just as important, the study found that stocks with low dividend yields and high payout ratios generated subpar annualized returns of just 8.6% (performance below the S&P 500 and below companies that paid no dividends at all).

For obvious reasons, you cannot make informed investment decisions based solely on the dividend yield. This second factor— the payout ratio—has been a key to our continuing success buying dividend stocks in *Income Investor*.

A PENNY INVESTED IS MANY PENNIES EARNED

A truckload of academic studies has shown that investing in companies that pay dividends is just about the best way to earn huge returns over time. Yet it can get far better still. As authors Elroy Dimson, Paul Marsh, and Mike Staunton proved in *Triumph of the Optimists: 101 Years of Global Investment Returns*, a portfolio in which we *reinvest* dividends—using the dividend to then buy more shares of stock—generates almost 85 times the value of a portfolio that relies solely on stock appreciation.

Let's take it one step further. According to money management firm Eaton Vance, more than 50% of the annualized returns of the S&P 500 since 1960 has come from dividends. Translation: Between 1960 and 2005, $1,000 invested in the S&P 500 index would have grown to more than $108,000 including reinvested dividends, but only $23,681 without dividends.

Still not convinced? Try this. According to Ned Davis research, between 1972 and 2006, S&P 500 stocks not paying a dividend returned a measly 4.1% annualized. Dividend payers, meanwhile, blew the hinges off the doors with a 10.1% annual return. The numbers speak for themselves: Dividend investing works.

DIVIDENDS HERE, THERE, BUT NOT EVERYWHERE

However, of the almost 7,000 publicly traded companies on the major U.S. stock exchanges, only about 40% paid a dividend over the past year. You'll come to learn that only the best, most stable companies with earnings power can afford to establish a dividend policy and keep it up indefinitely. Promising to pay a slice of your earnings each quarter or year is not for the faint of heart.

For a company to pay a dividend consistently each year, it should have:

1. Consistent and proven cash earnings power that can grow over time
2. A stable business in an industry that won't experience massive disruptions that could negatively affect dividends
3. Shareholder-friendly management dedicated to treating shareholders as owners
4. A business model that doesn't require massive amounts of capital outlays relative to its earnings power

At this point, it goes without saying that cash earnings are crucial since dividends are real cash outlays made by management. If the earnings vanish, the financial officers will either have to cut the dividend or raise capital by issuing debt. Neither is acceptable. And so here's a great way to understand the effects that dividend paying can have on the business practices of a corporation. Dividends act as Wonder Woman's magic lasso; they force the truth out of a company's financial statements.

The accounting sleights of hand that we mentioned earlier—where CEOs wrestle accounting standards to the mat to juice their short-term compensation—are a very serious problem in the public markets. These dastardly acts can mask devastating operational problems even as executives rake in enormous bonuses. Those are absolute worst-case scenarios for investors. But, for obvious reasons, these are pretty rare occurrences at public companies that feature a long-standing and rising dividend. No accounting trick is going to shield the company from having to either make or break its dividend payment. Dividends are a "barometer of a corporation's health," as Eaton Vance puts it.

It's important that we not overgeneralize, though. There are certainly remarkable companies that would make a mistake by paying a dividend. Take a smaller company like Buffalo Wild Wings, one of our favorites in *Hidden Gems*, our small-cap newsletter at The Motley Fool. Through its hundreds of restaurants, it earns millions in profit each year that it *could* kick back to shareholders in the form of a dividend. But management has made a deliberate decision to spend twice its annual earnings on store improvements and expansions. Buffalo Wild Wings is in supergrowth mode, where it lacks the flexibility to pay a consistent dividend. Its shareholders expect to be rewarded in the years ahead through capital gains, not dividend payments.

Perhaps one day, when Buffalo Wild Wings eateries are in every major urban area, we'll see management pay a dividend. But with the business profitably growing at rates in excess of 25% per year, cash payouts would be a misallocation of funds. A larger company like McDonald's, of course, is in quite a different position. As a $70 billion company that earns nearly $3 billion per year, its years of supergrowth have waned. Beyond making the occasional brilliant investment, as it did in taking a controlling stake in Chipotle before the turn of the century, McDonald's is smart to make dividend payments. It has done so without interruption since 1976. And during that period, McDonald's has grown more than 60 times in value (dividends included) versus around 12 times for the S&P 500.

DIVIDENDS ON THE S&P 500

Earlier we noted that 40% of all publicly traded stocks in America pay regular dividends. That number goes way up—nearly doubling—when you narrow the universe to just the S&P 500, an index of 500 of the largest companies in America. Of the 500 companies that make up the index today, 388 pay a dividend, or 78%. That's not surprising when you consider that the S&P's smallest company, Jones Apparel, still carries a market cap above $1 billion.

Looking over the list of these 388 companies, we see industry classifications that we'd expect—capital goods, energy, utilities, financials, pharmaceuticals, real estate. Just as interesting are the industries we don't see high on the list—high tech, Internet, software, computers. These industries are still relatively young and growing quickly. They require constant innovation and reinvestment of earnings. They don't have the stability seen in industries like energy, food, and capital goods.

INDUSTRY	NUMBER OF COMPANIES	EXAMPLES
Capital Goods	34	General Electric, 3M, Caterpillar
Energy	33	ExxonMobil, Schlumberger, Chevron
Utilities	29	Duke Energy, Southern Co, PG&E
Materials	28	Dow Chemical, DuPont, Monsanto
Diversified Financials	26	American Express, Moody's, Goldman Sachs
Insurance	23	Allstate, Aflac, Progressive
Food, Beverage, and Tobacco	22	Coca-Cola, Pepsi, Anheuser-Busch
Consumer Durables and Apparel	21	Mattel, Nike, Whirlpool
Banks	22	Wells Fargo, PNC Financial, US Bancorp

continued

INDUSTRY	NUMBER OF COMPANIES	EXAMPLES
Retailing	18	Gap, Nordstrom, Tiffany
Real Estate (REITs)*	14	Vornado, Host Hotels, Simon Property
Healthcare Equipment and Services	14	UnitedHealth, Aetna, Stryker
Media	12	Walt Disney, CBS, Gannett
Pharmaceuticals and Life Sciences	12	Pfizer, Johnson & Johnson, Merck
Transportation	10	FedEx, Southwest Airlines, CSX
Consumer Services	10	McDonald's, Marriot, Carnival
Semiconductors and Semiconductor Equipment	10	Intel, Texas Instruments, Applied Materials
Technology Hardware and Equipment	9	IBM, Motorola, Hewlett-Packard
Food and Staples Retailing	8	Wal-Mart, Whole Foods, Kroger
Software and Services	8	Microsoft, Paychex, Western Union
Commercial Services and Supplies	8	Waste Management, Cintas, Equifax
Telecommunication Services	8	AT&T, Verizon, Qwest
Household and Personal Products	6	Procter & Gamble, Kimberly-Clark, Clorox
Automobiles and Components	3	Harley-Davidson, General Motors, Johnson Controls

* REIT=real estate investment trust. A corporate entity designed to invest in commercial real estate properties. In return for tax-free status it must pay out 90% of its earnings each year in dividends. Source: Capital IQ, data as of 7/4/2008.

At this point, if you think dividend payments are mostly for behemoth companies, you're right. But here's where you can find one of the hiding places for great investments—among slightly smaller companies that pay dividends. Check out a dividend dynasty like $6 billion Genuine Parts, a wholesale distributor of electrical and car parts (NAPA Parts is a piece of this company). Genuine Parts is a formal recommendation in *Income Investor*.

The company has increased its dividend payout a freakish 52 years in a row, putting it near the top of U.S. companies in that respect and ahead of larger names like Coca-Cola, 3M, and Johnson & Johnson, all great companies in their own right.

These smaller, dividend-paying companies are often overlooked by investors, giving us opportunities to buy them on the cheap.

ROLLER COASTERS BELONG IN AMUSEMENT PARKS, NOT YOUR PORTFOLIO

In total, Americans spend millions of dollars and thousands of hours each year waiting to get tossed and turned on giant wood-steel roller coasters. We seek them out for the excitement, thrills, and danger that we don't experience in our mundane daily lives. But in investing, most of us shun the topsy-turvy. Studies show that investors far prefer the merry go-round (consistent path with consistent speed) than the Nitro at Six Flags. Our brains and stomachs aren't programmed to handle stock volatility. When the turns get too sharp, most investors are soon crying to get off the ride (and at the wrong time).

Dividends can help settle the nerves. Not only do dividend-paying stocks provide regular income streams to reinvest in more shares, but they also carry less volatility than non-dividend payers and the general market. This a critical point to remember: Dividend investing offers very good returns with lower volatility. Never forget it.

Now, in case some of you worry that dividend investing means buying boring utility companies, fear not. As we pointed out in the S&P 500 table on the previous page, there is a wide range of dividend payers, some of which sell products or services you use each and every day. Just look at the following:

COMPANY NAME	PRODUCTS	YIELD
Best Buy	Best Buy electronic stores	1.4%
Costco	Costco discount warehouses	0.9%
Heinz	Heinz 57, Ore-Ida, Smartones	3.5%
Home Depot	Home Depot DIY stores	4.0%
Kraft Foods	Oreos, Planters, Oscar Mayer	3.7%
Macy's	Macy's and Bloomingdale's	2.9%
Nike	Nike athletic apparel	1.6%
Pepsi	Pepsi cola, Frito-Lay, Aquafina	2.5%
Procter & Gamble	Charmin, Tide, Iams pet food	2.5%
Staples	Staples office supply stores	1.4%

Source: Capital IQ, data as of 7/4/2008

This is just a sampling of the thousands of companies that pay a dividend. If you're planning on building a diversified portfolio— and that should be your goal—you'll want to load it up with dividend stocks, and you can start by looking at the products you use every day.

HUNTING THE DIVIDEND BAGGER

Last chapter, we learned about Peter Lynch and his "buy what you know" strategy, but that and his majestic returns are not all he's contributed to the investing landscape. Far more important to the stock jock's chatter is the Lynch-coined term "multi-bagger," a shorthand for a stock that's appreciated many times above the original purchase price. If you purchased a stock for $10 per share and it now trades at $80 per share, you can brag to your friends (or your spouse) that you have an eight-bagger ($80/$10 = 8). It's a beautiful thing to see those kinds of returns in your portfolio.

With dividends, we're hunting the elusive "dividend bagger."

This is what happens when you hold dividend-paying stocks for years, letting your dividends reinvest and compound over time. A dividend bagger comes about when the shares purchased by your reinvested dividends are worth more than your original purchase amount. (Quickly re-read this paragraph to be sure you understand how amazing this is!)

Now, let's take PepsiCo as an example. Assume you bought 100 shares of Pepsi back in 1988 for a split-adjusted $5.79 per share, or a $579 outlay. If you reinvested all your dividends over the past 20 years, you would now have just over 150 shares of the company, valued at more than $10,000. Those 50 additional shares that your reinvested dividends bought are today worth around $3,400, giving us a near six-dividend-bagger (nearly six times your original $579). And all that for just holding on and redeploying dividends back into more and more shares.

SECRETS OF OUR STRATEGY

While not every company is going to share Pepsi's long-term success, our *Income Investor* team is armed with some strict criteria that help us determine whether a company is a true dividend champ or just a pretender. Here are our core criteria:

1. **Dividend and payout ratio.** We look for companies that pay a dividend with a clear ability to keep paying it. For us, that means companies with payout ratios less than 65%.

2. **Capital gain potential.** We want stocks that will appreciate in value while also paying a steady dividend. As we saw in the Pepsi example, those massive gains come from the combination of growth and income. A rich dividend yield is nice, but if we don't think there is much upside to the stock outside of the yield, we'll stay away.

3. **Financial fortitude.** We're not interested in investing in unproven business models or companies that have paid a dividend

once or twice. We're looking for the best of the best, companies that will continue to return cash to owners, through good times and bad. Balance sheet strength is important and we like to see high returns on equity and capital for us to jump aboard.

4. Competitive advantages. We want the best of breed. We want the last man standing in a corporate bar fight. Companies with winning business models are the ones that last. We are very specifically looking for businesses with very loyal customers, uniquely strong brands, insignificant uses of leverage, and competent leadership with tenure. There's a lot of qualitative work that goes on here, but companies like Campbell Soup, American Express, and Nordstrom stand out.

5. Smart, shareholder-friendly management. This begins with intangibles like integrity—not to mention a winning game plan. As we discussed in the last chapter, we study up on the background, corporate governance plans, and ownership stakes of the executive officers of the company. The leaders are ultimately the drivers of operational returns. We're looking for a management team like we see at Sherwin-Williams, a group that has been at the company for years and has delivered spectacular shareholder returns for decades.

6. Size. Risky little pipsqueak companies can be fun, but we typically want stocks large enough not to get tossed around by turbulent market waves. We like to invest in companies with market value greater than $1 billion. We will dip lower if we find a particularly strong candidate, but it must be *particularly* strong.

Let's take a closer look at a company that meets our six criteria.

PACCAR – A TRUCKLOAD OF DIVIDEND RETURNS

Through this chapter we've pointed to numerous companies that have been wonderful long-term dividend performers. Many are household names like Pepsi, Procter & Gamble, and Johnson & Johnson. But dividends come in all shapes and sizes, and from all types of industries. Sometimes the wonderful company that Warren Buffett wants to buy at a fair price is one that we may not necessarily know much about.

Tom tapped Paccar as an official recommendation in our general equity newsletter, *Stock Advisor*, in July 2005. If you've never heard of this truck and parts manufacturer, don't be alarmed. Most active investors don't recognize the name. But for years, it's been a dividend beauty delivering market-smashing returns. Since 1988, two years after it hit the public markets, Paccar has generated 16% annualized returns. Through a combination of capital gains, regular dividends, and special end-of-year dividends, Paccar shareholders who invested $5,000 in 1988 at a split-adjusted $2.50 are now sitting on a treasure of over $100,000 as of June 2008. That's another big step toward that $1 million portfolio.

Who said truckers aren't sexy?

We got on board this company late during its prolific ride, yet we've still earned nearly twice our money in barely three years. And it's not because Tom found a company destined to be the next Microsoft or because every analyst on Wall Street was touting it as the top stock of the decade. Paccar is a simple story of a family-run business that focuses on what it does best—designing, producing, and marketing the bodies of commercial trucks and aftermarket parts. And doling out cash to its owners through dividends.

Paccar has been around for more than a century, long before trucks roared down U.S. highways. In 1905, William Pigott started the Seattle Car Manufacturing Company to manufacturer logging and railway equipment. In 1934, under William's son Paul's leadership, the company—then known as Pacific Car and Foundry—entered the industrial winch business for crawler tractors, which later served as the foundation for Paccar's winch division (still around today).

After manufacturing Sherman tanks for the U.S. military during World War II, Paccar entered the heavy-duty truck market in 1945 by buying the Kenworth Motor Truck company. A decade later, it added Peterbilt Motors and Dart Truck to its family. Since then it has become a worldwide leader in supplying Kenworth, Peterbilt, and DAF high-quality diesel trucks around the globe. Today around two-thirds of its revenues come from foreign countries.

Let's run Paccar through our dividend criteria to see what Tom saw three years ago.

1. It Pays a Dividend

Paccar shares started trading hands during the summer of 1986. By November 1987, just a few weeks after the October 1987 crash and with its shares down 15%, Paccar declared its first dividend—a little more than a penny per share. Since then it has gone on to pay out more than $10 in per-share dividends. And while it has lowered the dividend from time to time—during the recessionary period of 1991, for instance—it has paid out dividends each and every year. It helps when you've produced nearly 70 consecutive years of profitability. Starting in 1998 it began paying an end-of-the-year special dividend in addition to its quarterly payouts.

So as dividend payers go, Paccar has demonstrated that it is committed to returning cash to shareholders and that it has the financial and operational model in place to keep it going.

2. Capital Gain Potential

When Tom looked at Paccar, he saw a market-leading company run by the great-grandson of the founder, selling at around 13 times earnings and yielding about 4%. He kicked the tires (figuratively, that is), analyzed the growth potential, and studied the sleepy nature of the business: building trucks. But the truck manufacturing industry was just starting to catch the increasing tailwinds of stricter U.S. emission requirements for trucks. Buyers had to update their fleets by 2007 or else face stiff fines. So along with a relatively cheap earnings multiple, there was a catalyst to spark earnings growth and therefore the stock price. Tom predicted the market cap would more than double by 2010.

A healthy dividend and a stock that could double? That's a return equation that adds up quite nicely.

3. Financial Fortitude

At the time of Tom's recommendation, Paccar was a $12.5 billion company selling more than $12 billion worth of trucks and winches, and earning nearly $1 billion in cash earnings. The balance sheet carried almost $2 billion in cash and short-term investments and barely any long-term debt (although it had some debt for its financing operations—a natural byproduct of that business). And, impressively, it had paid an uninterrupted dividend since 1987. Tom wrote then, "I have no concerns about its [Paccar's] financial position."

With this financial picture and its industry-leading position, Paccar possessed the strength to rumble through the inevitable ups and downs of the cyclical trucking business. We're not interested in fly-by-night dividend-newbies that may or may not be around down the road to pay us. We're looking for those 300-pound linemen who can handle any kind of blitz coverage. Paccar was an All-Pro.

4. Competitive Advantage

You may not be able to tell one 18-wheeler from another, but truckers and freight haulers can. If your take-home pay depended on trucking thousands of miles up and down the eastern seaboard, you would want the most reliable truck on the market. That's what truckers get in Kenworth, Peterbilt, and DAF. The company's trucks consistently win customer satisfaction awards and carry the latest technologies.

Supporting these brands is a dedication to innovation in both research and development and information technology that would make a tech company envious. These reinvestments allow Paccar to stay ahead of the curve in designing the next great trucking product. Paccar's integrated global supply chain is a leader in the industry, allowing it to shorten truck production scheduling to mere minutes.

Strong brand names and excellent operational performance allow Paccar to deliver returns on equity north of 20%—and close to 30% when demand is kicking. The cash conversion cycle is less than zero, which means that Paccar is paid by its customers well before it has to pay its suppliers, giving management cash leverage to earn higher returns.

5. Smart and Shareholder-Friendly Management

Individual investors are almost always best served when management and the board of directors own meaningful amounts of stock in their company. We trust them to keep their priorities in line with our priorities. At the Fool, we like to see management teams that own lots of stock in their companies—and even better, are buying shares. That's a clear indication that management considers the stock undervalued.

Mark Pigott, chairman and CEO of Paccar, has trucking in his blood. He is the great-grandson of Paccar founder William Pigott and has been sitting in the executive driver's seat for more than ten years. Since taking over, he has delivered an eight-bagger, or 20% annualized returns, making shareholders—and himself since he owns nearly 2% of the company—wealthy. Mark's uncle James Pigott, a board member since the early 1970s and an owner of 5% of the company, is also on the board. Uncle James collects more than $13 million in dividend checks each year.

With a deep legacy that has no interest in letting down the

family name, intimate knowledge of the business, and a vested interest in earning high shareholder returns, Paccar's leadership team appealed to Tom.

6. Size

Paccar's market cap when Tom recommended it was $12.5 billion—well above our $1 billion guideline.

Not every dividend investment is going to fit so nicely with our six criteria, but we always evaluate each company according to this checklist. It's no surprise that Paccar has been such a big winner for us—returning 34% versus the S&P's return of –2%.

PITFALLS TO DIVIDEND INVESTING

As we hope you now grasp, dividends are one of the best ways to accumulate wealth and beat the market. But buying a bunch of companies that pay dividends is no guarantee of investing success. Applied incorrectly, dividend investing can produce sub-par results. Here are the primary pitfalls of dividend investing, and what you can do to avoid them.

1. Dividend Bear Traps

Be careful of investing in a company that carries a large dividend yield but doesn't meet our other criteria. These "dividend traps" are typically too good to be true. Not that we have anything against high-yielding stocks, it's just that the current yield may actually reflect a severely troubled company. Its stock may have been beaten down (for good reason), and the financials may show an elevated payout ratio. Those can be very ominous signs. Often these companies have fundamental problems that will lead to dividend cuts down the road.

Think back to the 2008 credit crisis that wreaked havoc on many U.S. banks. As the stocks fell precipitously, their yields moved up, some to double-digits. But as the companies' balance sheets weakened, the banks couldn't sustain the payouts. And so, alongside collapsing stock prices, investors agonized through falling dividend yields. Be sure not to focus exclusively—or even primarily—on the dividend yield. The payout ratio is a critical factor as well.

2. Dividend Overloading

Let's say you already love dividend-paying companies. That's great, so do we. But even if you find solid companies with rich yields, low payout ratios, and stocks selling at a discount, you shouldn't build your entire portfolio around dividend payers. You'll want diversification in your portfolio, which means stocks with attractive yields alongside small- and large-cap stocks, value plays and fast-growers, backed by mutual-fund investments. You need to protect yourself from the downside that may ravage one particular group or industry. Too much of a good thing is actually a bad thing.

Also, dividend stocks are more stable and more likely to deliver singles and doubles than home runs. They don't grow nearly as fast as companies that re-deploy all their earnings back into the business. Think here of a telecom business like Citizens Communications. It's a rock-solid company that pays a consistently high dividend. But it doesn't grow much. Of course, our singles and doubles tend to come with less volatility. Nevertheless, it's healthy for the average investor to take a few home run swings on companies that don't pay a dividend. We'll show you how to find the best of these in Chapters 6 and 7.

3. Overconcentration

As you research and track dividend stocks, you'll notice that they tend to fall within a cluster of industries. We listed the primary ones within the S&P 500—capital goods, energy, utilities, and so on. So if you invest purely in dividend companies, you run the risk of too much industry concentration, which is not a good idea. You'll want to make sure you spread your dividend investing across industries and countries. There are some wonderful foreign dividend-paying companies trading on the U.S. markets, which our *Global Gains* newsletter focuses on.

4. The Tax Man Cometh

Alas, there is one downside to getting paid each year—you have to pay taxes on those earnings when you receive them.

ONE FINAL DIVIDEND DEEP DIVE

By digging deeper into the decision-making process behind some of the recommendations in our dividend newsletter, *Income Investor*, you can get an even better sense of what we look for. Here are three short snapshots of dividend-paying, lesson-providing examples. The first two might even make nice additions to your portfolio today.

Petrobras—Booming in Brazil

Income Investor advisor James Early snagged shares of Petrobras not once, but twice, in back-to-back months no less, because he was so excited about the prospects for the company and its stock. *Income Investor* subscribers who heeded his advice earned a double in less than a year. A double? Those types of returns are more commonly seen on our small-cap *Hidden Gems* scorecard. But Petrobras was the world's eighth-largest oil company at the time with a market cap of almost $120 billion—not exactly a speedy little small cap. What did James see that other investors may have missed? Let's drill a little deeper.

Petrobras, the former oil monopoly of Brazil, has an ingrained competitive advantage in its deep-water drilling capabilities unmatched among its oil brethren. Plus, its huge oil reserve assets gave it enough of a cushion to run for more than a decade without ever drilling for another barrel of oil. These reserves, some of the richest on the planet, went unappreciated by the market. Toss in its huge distribution system of gas stations in its home market and nearly 100% of Brazil's production and refining capacity, and we're looking at an operational position that can't be beat.

But James also calculated that this cash flow machine was selling at a huge discount to its true value, and still paying a healthy 3.5% yield. The incoming profits suggested to him that Petrobras could increase its dividend over time because its payout ratio was just 35%, nicely below our cutoff of 60%. Furthermore, the oil consumption rate in Brazil was expected to grow more than double the world's average, so there was plenty of room to run. The return equation was adding up nicely.

Of course the increases in the price of oil have certainly helped, and we won't always be so fortunate to hit this kind of "perfect storm." But fortune favors the brave and James realized that the market was not giving Petrobras its due. His two recommendations have returned 37% and 65% above the S&P.

Diageo — Taste the Magic

Keeping our passport out, we headed next to England to belly up to the bar for some shares of Diageo, the largest producer and distributor of alcoholic beverages in the world. You might not recognize the corporate name, formed from the Latin word *dia* (day) and Greek word *geo* (world), but if you appreciate a fine drink at the end of a hard day, you will recognize some of the company's brands. They include Guinness stout, Johnny Walker scotch, Smirnoff vodka, Tanqueray gin, Seagram's 7 whiskey, and Jose Cuervo tequila. *Income Investor* subscribers have enjoyed market-besting returns of 40% since we added Diageo to our scorecard in May of 2004, yet we believe there are still better days ahead.

After spending years as a bit of a conglomerate—it owned everything from Burger King to Pillsbury—Diageo sold off its non-core businesses and focused solely on the spirits game. Nowadays, Diageo's brand portfolio is one of the tastiest around, containing more top 20 brands than its next five competitors combined. This brand equity gives it an edge with distributors around the world, who push cases of spirits to restaurants, bars, and The Motley Fool for our holiday parties. The Diageo brands sell.

These top-selling brands drive operating margins of near 30% (tops in the industry), returns on equity of around 36%, and more than $3 billion in earnings, which management uses to pay a healthy, and growing, dividend. When we picked it, the yield was around 3.4% and the shares were trading around 14 times earnings. Reasonable, if not drop-dead cheap, for a company of this quality.

Looking through our list of criteria, Diageo scored close to perfect, with the exception of management owning few shares. Yet the executive team is packed with loads of talent. They have been with the company for years and have a specific vision of where they are going. Additionally, they are determined to return cash to shareholders through dividends and billions of dollars worth of share repurchases. Cheers, mate.

Entercom — Radio Killed the Portfolio Star?

We're certainly not immune to mistakes. While we've had more successes than failures, Entercom stands out as one we wish we could take back.

Entercom is one of the largest radio station owners in the country, with more than 100 stations spread across 23 U.S. markets. The big miss here was that we overestimated the company's competitive position. We thought it was stronger not only in the local radio space, but also against the plethora of substitute forces like satellite radio, iPods, and Internet radio. Now, in a world where advertisers have many ways to reach potential buyers, local radio no longer measures up as it once did. The lack of a deep and growing competitive moat was our first oversight.

Our second mistake was overlooking the company's weak financial picture, consisting of more debt than cash. It also was a rookie dividend payer, having started distributing cash to its shareholders just a few months before we recommended it. Adding some salt to the wound was the dual-class share structure that put voting control in the hands of the founding family. While their economic interest aligned well with shareholders, their lock on voting control quieted outside voices. In retrospect, it was obviously a mistake to recommend Entercom—what were we thinking? But this is how you become a great investor—by revisiting your winners and losers with equal intellectual vigor.

In this case, we underestimated the competitive forces facing Entercom and its radio cousins. Earnings dried up, debt levels grew, and a once-cheap stock got cheaper. Ultimately we decided to sign off at a near 50% loss. That's very painful—made less so, though, by our commitment to diversification. We've learned the lesson: Stick to growing businesses that have defensible competitive advantages.

THE PIECE OF YOUR PORTFOLIO

As an investor, you should build a diversified portfolio including all kinds of stocks—stable dividend payers, small-cap unknowns, fast-growing rockets, and large-cap value plays. There is a place for all of them in your holdings. This is a driving principle of our book.

Think carefully about how much volatility your brain can stomach. Well-regarded portfolio management author William Bernstein labels this finding your "sleeping point." That's the point at which you start worrying about your stock exposure. If you're the type who will be pacing the living room in a bathrobe at 2 a.m. at the thought of a 15% single-day drop, you'll probably want to skimp on the small-cap portion of your portfolio and load up on large-cap dividend stalwarts that you know, understand, and can follow.

You will have to determine what the right breakdown of stocks in your portfolio should be. We can help you in later chapters and with our tools and community online at mdpbook.com. But we hope we've gone a long way toward convincing you that dividend-paying stocks are an integral part of winning portfolios. An average investor with plenty of years ahead can have anywhere between 30% and 50% in solid dividend-paying stocks, which include large-, mid-, and small-caps as well as foreign companies. This range is rough, but we think it makes sense given the typical investor's risk profile.

Due to the tax consequences of receiving dividend checks each year, you should consider placing some of your dividend payers in a tax-advantaged account like a Roth IRA or a self-directed 401k, if you qualify. Thanks to the 2003 tax change, dividends in the U.S. are taxed at 15%, the same rate as capital gains. A Roth would shield you from the tax man each year. In a tax-deferred account, however, at withdrawal time you may end up paying a higher tax rate if your ordinary income tax rate is higher than 15%. So make sure you chat with your tax advisor before you start flooding your IRA with dividend payers.

BUILDING YOUR DIVIDEND DYNASTY

Dividend-paying stocks can work for you, no matter who you are or what your investing experience. Whether you're a newbie, seasoned hand, empty-nester, or education saver, dividends should fill an important role in your stock portfolio. The best news is that it's not difficult to start. You don't have to understand high finance, charting hocus-pocus, or discounted cash flow models to enjoy the compounding returns dividends offer.

By investing in a handful of the best-run, highest-quality companies operating in growing industries and with sustainable competitive positions, you're well on your way to creating real wealth that will compound at higher returns year after year. You won't have to worry about the daily gyrations of your stock prices, if the general stock market is up or down, or if the company's latest one-hit wonder is taking off. There is a time and a place for that kind of investing, but it's not part of the deal when we invest in dividend stalwarts.

We are not advocating buy-and-forget investing here, but dividend investing is about as close as you can get. It's been demonstrated that dividends are just about the perfect way to generate winning returns over years if not decades. Your mailbox and your portfolio are waiting for those dividends to start rolling in.

Motley Fool Advisor Andy Cross contributed to this chapter. A Fool since 1995 and a current or past advisor to our Income Investor, Stock Advisor, *and* Hidden Gems *newsletter services, Andy has been a fan of dividends ever since his father taught him the ABCs of compound interest with stocks such as Pepsi, Home Depot, and Johnson & Johnson.*

Visit us at mdpbook.com to get our top dividend stock pick for your portfolio.

CHAPTER 5

BLUE-CHIP BARGAINS

There's certainly something to be said for stocks that pay you to own them. They are vaguely reminiscent of the Sherman tanks that Paccar built during World War II: strong, secure, plodding steadily forward. But for those looking for a little more upside potential, the next step up the risk-reward ladder is value investing.

Value stocks—companies trading for less than they're worth—have a lot in common with dividend-paying companies, and they often pay dividends themselves. But for value investors, the dividend is a happy bonus, the icing on the high-performance cake, the olive in the value martini, the colorful analogy on top of an already clear explanation.

Buying great companies at a good price is even better than a quarterly check. Following the value investing principle of paying 80 cents for the proverbial dollar, it only makes sense that as a group, value stocks have been more rewarding than any other group of equities since the dawn of investing. At The Motley Fool, our value investing newsletter service, *Inside Value,* is beating the market by more than 4 percentage points.

WHO WOULDN'T TRADE 80 CENTS FOR ONE DOLLAR?

Value investing pays. There are lots of studies measuring the extent to which value stocks beat the market's average returns, owing to the many different ways one can define "value" or "growth." One of the most recent, by noted professors Eugene Fama and Kenneth French, determined that large-cap value stocks returned 11.82% per year from 1927 through 2006, compared to 10.03% for the broader market of large-cap stocks. If that doesn't sound like much to you, think of it this way: $10,000 compounded at 10.03% for those 80 years would grow to just under $21 million. At 11.82%, it would grow to a little over $76 million.

Beyond the compelling data is the plain, old-fashioned, common-sense logic behind value investing. By definition, value stocks are businesses that are worth more than their stock price indicates. By focusing on these bargain businesses, you're following in the footsteps of the previously mentioned Benjamin Graham, the man who taught Warren Buffett how to invest and who invented the practice of valuing stocks in the first place—and that's where we begin our story.

In the beginning, there were stocks. But there was no particular way to value the worth of individual stocks—no mathematically proven way to determine what a company or a company's stock was worth. There were plenty of people buying and selling stocks, but they were basing their decisions on a cryptic combination of dividends and rumors. We still see this same combination today in emerging foreign markets, which creates plenty of opportunities for investors, as we'll discuss in Chapter 8.

Back then, businesses published the results of their operations, but investors often had to write to the company to request that information or search for it at the library. It certainly wasn't a couple of keystrokes away on the Internet. But Benjamin Graham, a business professor at Columbia and a renaissance man of extraordinary accomplishment, studied the types of companies that most rewarded shareholders and at what prices. He developed a formal methodology for determining the "intrinsic value" of a company, padded it with what he referred to as a "margin of safety," and made a fortune.

Before we get to the fortune, we should understand the concepts. Value investing starts with the intrinsic value of a company—the value that a company is worth based on what you can rationally expect it to earn and the cash it will be able to distribute to its investors after paying all of its bills. And here's the key to all investing: The value of a stock *is often completely independent of the daily price that a stock trades for*. That's a profound concept, but one that is often forgotten. Consider the degree to which it is still ignored in most coverage of stocks.

To an alarming degree, the chatter that makes up stock "analysis" focuses on what the price of a stock is and where it's going next. Tune in to any financial network, and you'll find talking head after talking head telling you "don't fight the tape," "the trend is your friend," or "this stock is dead money." Any one of these "insights" is nothing more than a prediction about where the stock is headed in the short term. The value investor couldn't care less where a stock is headed or has been. Rather, the question is: What should a rational private investor pay for the whole company?

The answer to that question is the stock's intrinsic value, and knowing whether a particular stock is worth buying or selling by comparing its price to its intrinsic value sets the value investor apart.

VALUE HUNTERS

Benjamin Graham concentrated on what a company had in liquid or near liquid assets: cash on hand and those assets closest to cash, such as inventories and accounts receivable. Back in Graham's day (the 1920s to 1950s), the market was so inefficient at gathering and digesting information that you could make an easy fortune simply buying companies that were trading at a market value lower than what they had in net cash. Those were the days!

Alas, now it is well known that companies trading for less than their cash and liquid securities on hand are typically great investments. You've got to dig a bit further today, but the search is more than worth it.

The difference between price and value is at the heart of the value investor's approach. As Warren Buffett said, "Price is what you pay. Value is what you get."

The market yields hundreds of different quotes for the price of a stock every day. If you track every tick up and down throughout the day, the actual number of prices for a popular stock will be in the thousands. Those are all real prices that you can choose—or not choose—to pay for a stock. But that doesn't mean that the value of a company is changing every couple of seconds. Instead, the intrinsic value of a company can well be increasing at the same time that the price of its stock is falling.

But if the price of a stock isn't a correct valuation of the business, what should give an investor confidence that buying a company for a price below its intrinsic value makes for an investment that can be sold for the actual—and higher—price later on? Why do we expect the market to come to its collective senses and see the value that we see? The answer to that question is in a famous quote from Benjamin Graham: "In the short term, the market is a voting machine. In the long term, the market is a weighing machine."

Key to making money in the stock market—particularly in value stocks, which are often not appreciated for significant periods of time—is to have the right temperament. You must have confidence that the market will ultimately recognize the value of a company over time. The market price at any given moment reflects the flavor of the month and the whims of buyers and sellers. When headlines shout that gas prices are skyrocketing, droves of traders sell the shares of companies affected by gasoline. Any business with the word "financial" in its name took a tumble with the subprime crisis, even if it was only tangentially related to the mess. When there's a headline about a potential new cure for a disease, shares of the company making the drug take off . . . even though the company is likely years and many levels of unpredictable hurdles away from reaching the market.

The market's extreme focus on the near term creates opportunities. Companies that don't make headlines, companies that miss earnings estimates by a penny or two, and those that are engaged in some form of business that isn't "sexy" are the companies that make the best value investments.

THREE KEYS TO VALUE

Bruce Greenwald now teaches the value investing course at Columbia that Graham created, and his book, *Value Investing: From Graham to Buffett and Beyond*, provides teachings that master Graham would surely appreciate. Greenwald says that there are three things a good value investor must do.

1. Look Closely at the Assets

Start with the balance sheet. How much cash does the company have? It's always nice to see companies with piles of cash on hand because that'll serve them well when things get a bit rough. You also want to know what else the company owns—the value of its buildings, its property, plants, and equipment. What are its patents and other assets worth? Luckily, all the information you need is contained on the balance sheet.

The "book value" of the company—everything the company has minus its liabilities—is the most reliable information you'll have. As Greenwald says, "Low market to book all over the world—every place—has outperformed the market in every extended period at least by 3% to 5% per year."

To clarify, that means that companies with very, very low ratios of market price to book value—those where the market values the stock at a fraction of the book value of the company—are stunning outperformers. Such bargains aren't easy to come by. Where true blue chips are concerned, you're unlikely to find big, well-known stocks trading at a fraction of their book value. Companies with prices that far out of whack are usually unloved for a reason. They are more often the spinoffs, the turnarounds, the bankruptcies, and the other messy situations that classify as riskier deep-value investments, which is an entirely different book. (In fact, it's the subject of a wonderful book entitled *You Can Be a Stock Market Genius*, by Joel Greenblatt.)

But by toning that principle down a couple notches, you can definitely find value among the market's big boys. Blue-chip companies are more likely to have a lot of their value tied to their brands and other intangible items that don't necessarily contribute to book value. They don't need as much equipment as some old-line industrials to make massive profits. Companies like Coca-Cola, Kraft Foods, or Pfizer are comparatively "light" companies in terms of assets, yet at the right price still qualify as value investments.

2. Know the Present Earnings of the Company

The second most reliable factor is what the company is earning right now—not what it earned when things were unusually and temporarily good in the past, and not an estimate of what the company could earn in some delightfully optimistic version of the future. We're optimists ourselves, but we're not just going to assume that companies will increase their earnings year after year at astronomical rates. On average, companies only increase their earnings by about 3% to 6% per year.

The present gives the best idea of a company's earnings power. There will be time to make estimates about the company's future, but the value investor has to be a bit curmudgeonly compared to the typical growth investor.

3. Last and Least, Consider Growth

Many people divide the investing world into two opposing categories—value and growth. The value investor cares only about
book value and a low P/E multiple; the growth investor scoffs at
these things, investing in companies that rapidly grow their sales
and earnings.

But as Warren Buffett has said, there is no true division between value and growth investing. The growth of a company is
always factored into the intrinsic value of an investment. You
cannot determine the intrinsic value of a company without esti-
mating what its future cash flows might be. Instead, what distin-
guishes the classic value investor from the growth investor is
that the value investor is looking for a large chunk of the value in
the present. The growth investor is looking for most of the value to
be developed in the future.

Outside of the value framework, most investing strategies
take growth as a given for any company and incorrectly assume
that all growth is good. In reality, a lot of growth can be detri-
mental. Too often, companies are fixated on growth for growth's
sake—or worse, for the sake of a management team that rewards
itself with bonuses on the basis of a company's short-term stock
price or how many acquisitions it can make. But the reality is
that growth often does not benefit the investor nearly as much as
it enriches the company's employees and management.

All that growth in sales has to be funded by greater expenses,
whether it's increases in equipment or more hiring. To fund that
growth, a company either has to funnel much of its earnings into
its own operations or raise additional capital by issuing more
shares or taking on more debt. Either way, that cuts into profits.

While growing profits leads to winning investments—no great
company of the past century stayed tiny—value investors care
much more about how management *uses* the company's assets.
The majority of the time, that means returning money to investors either by buying back shares (and thus increasing the value
of each existing share) or by increasing the dividend.

AND THREE LITTLE WORDS

Warren Buffett's favorite three words are "margin of safety."

This phrase refers to buying stocks of companies that not only are underpriced by the market, but are substantially below your calculated intrinsic value. If investing were as easy as coming up with your own valuation for a stock and then seeing it proven out, it would make sense to buy all the stocks you could find that are 10% below what you've calculated to be their intrinsic value. But we're all fallible. We all make mistakes about a company's true worth because we don't have perfect vision into the future.

For that reason, even Buffett isn't satisfied with a 10% or even a 20% margin of safety, and he's pretty darned good at applying a value to a company. He's going to hold out for ones that are 30%, 40%, or even 50% or more below his fair value calculation. To give yourself some room for error, wait for companies trading well below their intrinsic value, ones where the margin of safety between a conservatively calculated intrinsic value and the market price reaches 30% or more. For blue chips, a margin of safety of 30% is rare; for a high-quality business, 20% may be a better guide.

Once you've conducted the valuation, be patient. Wait for a good price. Then, when a good price comes around, keep waiting. Because you're waiting for a great price.

DIGGING THROUGH THE BLUE-CHIP BARGAIN BASEMENT

In a famous speech given by Warren Buffett in 1984 at the Columbia University School of Business, he stated that it was no coincidence that so many successful investors studied under Benjamin Graham. Buffett said the reason that these investors decisively beat the market was that they were singularly focused on finding companies trading at prices on the stock market below what a private investor would pay. Ultimately the approach works because it depends on the discipline to ignore the market's fluctuations. Many other investing strategies are focused on charts and trading techniques. These buyers and sellers of stock chart readings create opportunities for the disciplined value investor.

But value investing also works because, by definition, it must. If you are acquiring stocks below their intrinsic value, the market will eventually recognize that value. Or, if not the market itself, some company or group of investors will decide to acquire the company at a premium. Companies available for below their intrinsic value will always rise in share price . . . *except when they don't.*

BEWARE THE VALUE TRAP

Not all companies that sport some, most, or even all value indicators will be winning investments. Many a company has revealed itself to be a "value trap"—a company with a low book value or low P/E ratio that remains in that bin for a long, long time, as seemingly transitory problems reveal themselves to be permanent.

Take Eastman Kodak. It managed the seemingly impossible task of returning essentially nothing to investors for 40 years. Its management issued an endless parade of quarterly reports, annual reports, and profit warnings explaining that its most recent problems were now behind it. The company was pointed toward a brighter kind of future that you'd want to take a whole roll of pictures of, they would promise—but it hasn't yet developed.

Not every company that's going through a rough patch is destined to come back. But if you're looking at large, high-quality companies with lengthy histories of success, the odds are in your favor that the winners will outnumber the losers. And even if you get a couple bad apples that slowly lose value over time, a portfolio diversified among many blue chips will assuredly yield enough big winners that will, over the long haul, cover for your disappointments. After all, a loser can only cost you 100% of your investment, but there's no ceiling to the upside.

When trying to distinguish the potential winners from the losers, value investors use many approaches to reach their magic answer. In a nutshell, however, the classic value investing strategy is to find companies that are unloved. It's the companies that are underappreciated based on their assets, their current earnings, and their opportunities for growth that turn up the corners of the curmudgeonly value investor's smile. After all, the stock market is just an auction, and we like to buy merchandise that few are bidding on. Typically, it will be priced cheaper than its true value.

BEHIND BIG BLUE

Although we agree with Buffett that the division of the world into growth and value stocks is somewhat arbitrary, the investing community persists in neatly dividing it this way. Take the Russell 1000, an index of what are roughly the 1,000 largest publicly traded companies. Russell divides the index strictly along that split, with the value half comprising those companies that have lower price-to-book values and lower expected growth rates. The value names include many companies from the oil and financial sectors, well-known businesses that have a lot of assets: the biggest companies as of early 2008 are ExxonMobil, General Electric, AT&T, Chevron, Bank of America, JPMorgan Chase, Pfizer, ConocoPhillips, Citigroup, and Procter & Gamble.

In the "growth" half of the Russell 1000, the biggest companies were Microsoft, Cisco, Apple, Google, IBM, Intel, Schlumberger, Hewlett-Packard, PepsiCo, and Wal-Mart. That's obviously a list primarily of tech companies, plus a few well-known names that have either decent growth or less in the way of tangible assets.

The value investor can profit from both sides of the great investment divide. That's because value comes not only in the world of solid assets, but—on less common but still plentiful occasions— from great companies that have a strong horizon of reasonable growth.

Although IBM might currently be classified as a growth investment, that wasn't always the case. If you turn back the clock to 1993, the once-proud leader in technology was stalled in a decade-long period of stagnation, having ceded leadership in computers to younger, faster-moving hotshots like Microsoft. The stock was stuck at a split-adjusted price of less than $11 per share, no higher than it had been in—get this—1967.

Sure, the company didn't seem to have a good story going for it. It was no longer the technology innovator that it had once been. But wasn't there something to like there? To the astute value investor, there was: an easy-to-discern book value, tangible assets galore, and actual earnings.

For a good chunk of the year, IBM traded at less than the worth of its assets. It had a book value below 1, meaning you could buy the whole company for less than the "book" value of its assets. It also had begun scraping together some earnings, as long as you looked past a couple of large non-recurring and non-cash charges. But looking just a little bit past those stated earnings, IBM's business was beginning to produce cash again. The company was trading at the end of the year for less than 15 times earnings adjusted for the one-time charges, below the market's average historical multiple, and well below IBM's historical multiple.

Most investors had had it with IBM, having watched the company do nothing for them over the balance of the previous quarter century except pay some dividends—and then suddenly the dividend was slashed in early 1993. The company looked to be on the brink, and the market priced it accordingly.

But a few value investors saw opportunity. The company had new management in the form of CEO Lou Gerstner as of April 1993, and new management can often be the catalyst that turns a moribund company around. There were plenty of tangible assets, cash being one of them, but also property, plants, and equipment, and the many patents that the company had developed over the decades.

It turned out to be a classic value opportunity, and the credit goes mostly to CEO Gerstner. However, you hardly needed to bet on the company the moment he came into office. Sure, IBM doubled in price between its 1993 lows and 1995, but there was still plenty of value left. From January 1995, when the price was at a split-adjusted $20 per share, to the end of 2007, the stock again increased 556%, making it an 11-bagger from late July 1993.

Certainly IBM could go straight down the drain, though companies as big as IBM with sales in the tens of billions of dollars are much more likely to bounce back. The rewards here were a reasonable bet, given the assets of the company and its earnings. You could have made this bet and won handsomely, even if you did poorly on many other investments. The spectacular rewards with IBM were not discovered by investors interested strictly in the growth of the company, as there was no growth to measure.

HIGH ON THE HOG

That's not to say a company has to be on the scrap heap to get a value investor's heart pumping. Let's say you love motorcycles. When it comes to motorcycles, the best-known name around is Harley-Davidson, a company so popular that customers tattoo themselves with the name to show their devotion. This company exemplifies value investing on a number of levels. First, it was one of the truly great value investments of the 1980s and 1990s, rising from a split-adjusted price of $0.33 a share in 1987 to $40 a share in 2000—that's more than a 100-bagger. Even if you'd waited until 1992 when it was at a split-adjusted price of $4 a share, there was still a lot of fuel left in the tank. It was still good for a tenfold increase in price over the next eight years—one of America's great business stories. Let's look at why it remained such a strong value buy for so many years and how you could have spotted it.

In 1901, 21-year-old William Harley designed a motor to put onto a bicycle. He was soon joined by his good friend Arthur Davidson, and together they started a company that would eventually build motorcycles. Over the next 70 years, the company was private, surviving the ups and downs of the American economy, with major contributions to the war efforts of both World War I and World War II. By the 1950s and 1960s, though, the company saw its reputation diminished, as it was associated with the Hell's Angels and other less savory characters.

In 1967, the company was bought out by American Machinery and Foundry (AMF), which produced leisure equipment such as snow skis, golf clubs, and bowling balls. AMF mismanaged the company to the point of near death, and sold it for $80 million in 1981 to a group of private investors, including Willie Davidson, a descendant of the original Davidson family. They rebuilt the company, placing a new emphasis on quality that had gotten away from them for decades. Customers returned. In 1987, Davidson and friends took the company public.

That was the beginning of a spectacular ride. Shares of Harley at the end of 2007 were worth roughly 110 times what they traded for when the makers of the Fat Boy first went public. And that's with a product that's right under everyone's nose.

From the time that it went public to today, Harley-Davidson has never appeared to be a value stock on the basis of its asset base. It's never traded at a particularly enticing price-to-book ratio. While it has solid assets in the form of its plants, equipment, inventories, and cash, its value came not from to-the-moon estimates of the company's future, but from the ability to grow at a measured but prolonged pace while improving its profits from each bike sold (the profit margin) and sticking to its core business.

And that's exactly the way a company that truly belongs in this style of investing typically goes about creating value. It's generally not by expanding outside its core competencies. You might recall that Coca-Cola tried to grow by branching into motion pictures, a value-destroying move epitomized by what is now the poster child for Hollywood flops. From 1982 to 1987, Coke owned Columbia Pictures, the masterminds behind *Ishtar*.

That's the type of growth you want to avoid at all costs, and not just because the movie was painful to watch. Yes, Coca-Cola became a great value investment for Warren Buffett . . . but only in 1987, after it had rid itself of Columbia pictures. Coincidence? Hardly.

Which brings us back to Harley, which makes motorcycles. For the better part of two decades, Harley had the opportunity to do the right thing with its profits—sink them back into the business, making new and better products, and reaching out to loyal customers. In fact, the true glory years for Harley's stock were those when management limited how fast the company made bikes. Rather than make all the hogs it could sell, Harley increased production at a rate of only about 10% a year, lower than what the marketplace could bear. The ensuing scarcity of bikes raised the value of those machines that did make it to the market. For the better part of a decade, customers were willing to pay more than the manufacturer's recommended price. In fact, many were willing to pay more for used bikes than new ones, just so they didn't have to stay on a waiting list.

Harley-Davidson made for an excellent value investment from the time it came public until at least 12 years later, as the market continually underestimated the company's ability to generate cash for its shareholders. During the seven years between 1988 and 1995, Harley grew sales from $709 million to $1.35 billion—strong but hardly overwhelming growth. This represents only 9.6% sales growth per year, and less than that when you factor in inflation. But while those numbers are nothing to sneeze at, what was truly amazing was that Harley's share price went from an adjusted price of $0.68 per share on December 31, 1988, to $6.38 on December 31, 1995, a total return of 838%, and a stunning compounded return of 36% per year. During those glory years for Harley shareholders, the growth in sales hardly began to tell the entire story.

How did the shares increase in value during a time in which sales were not especially exciting? For one thing, the company was becoming more and more profitable on every dollar of sales. These expanding margins proved that the company was becoming much more efficient in its operations, and instead of focusing on growth, it was more concerned with running its business better.

At the same time, there was real growth in the operations. Harley-Davidson had to raise money to grow, but it did so without issuing loads of new shares and diluting existing shareholders. Over those seven years, the company only increased shares 20%, and then kept its share count steady for the next decade. In 2004, it started buying back its own shares. At the beginning of 2008, the company actually had fewer shares outstanding than it did 20 years before, a remarkable achievement for a company selling more than eight times as much product as it was back then.

Earnings growing faster than sales is definitely a marker to watch for in the value realm. Sales simply can't grow at levels approaching 20% per year for long. As Harley proved over that time period, growing sales below double-digit percentage rates can be plenty, as long as the business is becoming more efficient. Harley didn't need to get reckless and start buying up other operations. It didn't start selling Hog Beer or Harley-Davidson hot dogs. It grew internally—patiently, consistently, and intelligently. In other words, it grew just like a value company should.

THE CHALLENGE OF PATIENCE

Almost everybody can find a classically defined value stock right for them. Whether you like cereal or banks, cola or motorcycles, medicine or kitty litter (who are you?), you're bound to find a company that makes products you know, understand, and enjoy following. And the results of value investing speak for themselves, as we've consistently beaten the market in *Inside Value*.

Any established path to beating the market's returns—and with less volatility than the market's averages—appeals to the vast majority of investors.

While it seems obvious that the approach should be appealing, this strategy just doesn't take hold for some investors. Warren Buffett put it this way: "[I]t is extraordinary to me that the idea of buying dollar bills for 40 cents takes immediately with people or it doesn't take at all. It's like an inoculation. If it doesn't grab a person right away, I find that you can talk to him for years and show him records, and it doesn't make any difference. They just don't seem able to grasp the concept, simple as it is."

What Buffett means is that not everybody "gets" the concept of investing in companies at a deep discount if it means they have to wait a while, maybe even years, for the market to agree with their assessment. Many people like the daily action the market provides, and enjoy guessing the next move—even though frequent trading has been shown to deliver very poor returns. More than anything else, the value approach demands patience and a willingness to stay disciplined without an upward move in share price to confirm your thinking. You have to be willing to wait for as long as it takes for the market to recognize the value of your dollar, even as it stubbornly remains at "40 cents."

The best time to buy value stocks is when nobody else wants them. If everyone "knows" that they are producing the next big thing, changing the world, or reinventing life as we know it, shares aren't going to come cheap. Value stocks, almost by definition, are not the ones grabbing the headlines for their outstanding performance or for joining the ranks on the 52-week-high lists. Value investing will also not work for frequent stock traders. These are the kinds of stocks that don't give you a lot of quick pops and drops. The excitement behind blue-chip value investing doesn't reside in life-changing tales of a stock that moved up 800% in a year or two. Those stories were common during the late 1990s with Internet stocks, but as we saw in 2001 and 2002, what rises dramatically and rapidly often falls with equal fury.

The excitement of blue-chip value investing comes from looking at long-term charts of what value stocks do as a group over a period of decades—or what they have done for Warren Buffett. That extra 2% or 3% a year in returns, multiplied over a lifetime of investing, makes for some heart-pounding piles of cash down the line. It will give you your million-dollar portfolio—and much more.

ADDING VALUE TO YOUR PORTFOLIO

The value approach encompasses an enormously wide range of styles, which can lead to very different types of stocks in a portfolio. In the case of Warren Buffett, a large part of his equity holdings are formed by Coca-Cola, The Washington Post Company, American Express, and GEICO. These are all companies that saw more of their value tied to the growth properties of their franchises than in a strict book value approach. Some, such as "vulture investor" Wilbur Ross, have made billions by diving into extreme situations such as bankrupt or near-bankrupt steel, coal, and textile companies. The approach of value investing is flexible enough to permit investors to buy stocks from nearly any sector as long as it is accompanied by a strict discipline of valuing the security first, and waiting for a sufficient margin of safety.

How do you build the value portion of your portfolio? Without getting down too deep into the weeds, you should always remember that every valuation of a company hinges on an accurate estimate of all the future cash flows of the business, properly discounted. You need to estimate how much the company is going to be making next year, and the year after that, and for all the years that follow. This is exactly what we teach in detail in *Inside Value*.

In the December 2004 issue, advisor Philip Durell recommended toothpaste and soap provider Colgate-Palmolive, pointing to its excellent balance sheet, high debt rating, shareholder-friendly policies, and exceptional brand value. At the time, the company did not have huge levels of cash lying around, nor did it have tons of hard assets. Most of the company's value comes from its ability to charge a premium for its brands, coupled with a superlative world-wide distribution system.

Sticklers for companies with price-to-book ratios below 2 would have skipped out on this company, as its metric then was close to 20. But, as Philip points out, this company's brand recognition provides a substantial moat, the advantage that keeps competitors at bay. And as the great value investors have demonstrated time and again through outstanding investing returns, products and services that offer wide and sustainable moats are the ones that reap the biggest rewards.

Philip's valuation of Colgate-Palmolive was premised mostly on the company's proven ability to create cash with its operations. We're looking at a company that's been cleaning our teeth for around 200 years. There's a lot of data available on how well this company typically does over time in terms of growth, and its current earnings are easy to compare to previous years.

In this case, we have Philip's estimate of what the growth of earnings would be—a cool 9% per year. Consider how much more conservative that estimate is than the more common estimates you'll see from Wall Street analysts, which tend to start around 10% to 12% for the most moribund company, and work their way up from there. Remember that one of the keys to getting it right as a value investor is not to be too aggressive.

Philip saw the company increasing earnings at 9% a year from 2004. Between the end of 2004 and 2007, Colgate actually increased its earnings 9.4%, so over that period at least, the estimate was accurate and conservative. The stock fairly quickly met the $58 value that Philip had assigned to the company.

Did that mean that it was time to move on? Not at all. The value of a company is not static. As a company delivers on its operations, the value of both the cash it has accrued and the new opportunities that it has identified must be reintroduced into the computation of the company's intrinsic value. Throughout the time that *Inside Value* has followed the company, the analysts working on the service have taken the quarterly results, re-run them through the Motley Fool HQ supercomputer (actually an Excel spreadsheet), and have redetermined the value. As of May 2008, the calculated value had moved up to $72.

Somewhat coincidentally, so had the price of a share of Colgate-Palmolive. For the moment, at least, the newsletter and the market were on the same page about the value of one stock. A rare exception to the rule that value and price are two different things.

The realization by the market of Colgate-Palmolive's value means that as of May 2008, there was no margin of safety for the purchase of shares. That's what happens when a stock moves up over 60% in a little over three years. However, that isn't reason enough to sell shares. It's better to hold on to securities that are fairly valued rather than trade in and out of them. Any new money should be added to other companies that instead are trading at sufficient margins of safety below their own fair value. Constantly following more companies every month allows the *Inside Value* team to invest with that happy margin of safety, which has helped us earn market-beating returns.

THE PIECE OF YOUR PORTFOLIO

Blue-chip value stocks have made up all or nearly all of the portfolios of many legendary investors, and for good reason. With their stability, they don't require the same level of vigilance by investors. They aren't going to be as volatile as riskier fare. Shares rarely plummet when growth projections are missed. And, as we've mentioned, they usually increase in value over time. We're quite fond of blue-chip value stocks.

But that's not to say you should load up on blue chips to the exclusion of other asset classes. (And we're not saying that just because there are a lot of chapters left to go.) We absolutely think that blue-chip value stocks and dividend payers are extremely attractive and provide a foundation of a fully diversified Foolish portfolio, but they're just the start.

As much as we like stability, we also see the value of high returns. By taking on the extra risk in small caps, international stocks, and select growth companies, you give your portfolio a better chance of phenomenal results as opposed to a steady march upward. But if you make blue-chip value and dividend stocks the core of your portfolio—especially for beginning investors—you will be able to make a lot of wrong calls on risky stocks before they cause too much damage. Great companies selling at a discount provide a solid base that can defend your portfolio against the worst the market has to offer.

Motley Fool Senior Analyst—and former SEC attorney—Bill Barker contributed to this chapter. While his focus at the Motley Fool has been on the Pay Dirt *and* Hidden Gems *services, Bill is a value guy at heart who searches for bargains in all aspects of his life, especially when it comes to tennis shoes.*

Visit us at mdpbook.com, where you can get our current top value stock idea.

CHAPTER 6

THE TREASURES OF SMALL-CAP INVESTING

At this point in your journey of investing, we hope we've been able to convince you that the single greatest way to increase wealth is via the stock market. Nothing—not Treasury bills, not municipal bonds, not even home ownership—outperforms the returns available through the stock market.

Sort of.

Over any given year, it doesn't matter all that much whether you own bonds, stocks, CDs, or a decorative spoon collection. The returns from each on a $10,000 investment during any one average year amounts to a couple hundred bucks. You're not going to get rich on one-year returns.

Sorry 'bout that.

But when you study the outcomes over decades, it becomes clear that owning stocks is the greatest wealth-generating action you can take.

The news only gets better as we glide down the market cap range into the lesser-known room-to-grow world of small-cap stocks, the companies that we at The Motley Fool call "Hidden Gems." When most people think of stock market investments, they think of companies like the ones we've already discussed: Wal-Mart, Google, Coca-Cola, IBM, and other easily identifiable monsters. Especially for the newbie investor who's looking for a little stability, these giant companies seem to offer the safest ways to invest money in common stocks. Without question, they do that, and there's a place for quality large-cap businesses like these in every portfolio.

The problem is that many of these companies are already too large to grow substantially over the next three to ten years. And they're too well-followed on Wall Street for any investor to gain a serious pricing edge in the auction market of stocks. Warren Buffett has warned investors that his returns at Berkshire Hathaway will necessarily slacken, as he has no choice but to allocate more and more of his $40 billion in cash into large-capitalization companies. As much as it pains him, he simply has too much money to invest in small companies, an area of the market where he once said he could earn 50% per year. His dilemma is that in order to invest enough in a small company for it to make any difference at all to the Berkshire bottom line, he'd have to buy it outright—a few times over.

If you're like most individual investors, you don't have Buffett's problem. So you have a built-in advantage—an ability to negotiate into the tiny, inefficient crevasses of the market. And because of that edge, small caps—which we define as those companies valued between $200 million and $2 billion in market capitalization—offer individuals the greatest shot at superior returns and independent wealth.

At our *Hidden Gems* newsletter service, small caps are our playground. Given the choice between, say, Wal-Mart and the leading producer of deer repellent—American Vanguard—you can probably guess which is the larger company. As of this writing, Wal-Mart's market capitalization is $200 billion. American Vanguard's is just $400 million. Wal-Mart is 500 times larger.

But which is the better investment opportunity? On average, the small-cap world of deer repellent, coin counting machines, chicken wings, and funeral homes is more lucrative for investors. There are thousands of publicly traded Hidden Gems, and the aggregate returns of this group are impressive.

Let's turn once again to Dartmouth College finance professor Kenneth French (you might remember him from Chapter 5). He carried out a study encompassing all U.S. stock market returns between 1926 and 2000, graphing the theoretical returns of a single dollar invested in 1926. He found that if he invested that dollar in large-company stocks, he'd get to $2,128. That's outstanding. But when he invested that same dollar over the same period in small-company stocks, it grew to $5,522. More than double the returns! And while the extra $3,394 is nice, you're going to be investing more than a single buck. When you apply those same returns to far more substantial investments throughout your investing career, you'll find yourself on the road to lasting wealth.

To check his work, French conducted the same study looking at stock returns from the United Kingdom, Japan, and several other countries. His findings were unambiguous: in the UK, small-cap stocks returned an average of 2.6% better than large caps per year.

Take a gander at what 2.6 percentage points of excess returns per year do to your investments over a quarter century:

25-YEAR INVESTMENT HORIZON

INVESTMENT	T-BILLS	BONDS	REAL ESTATE	STOCKS	HIDDEN GEMS
$5,000	$16,931	$27,137	$43,115	$60,677	**$108,526**
$5,000/yr	$250,567	$338,382	$461,620	$585,938	**$893,804**

To maximize the potential for gains, go where the money is—to small caps, the Hidden Gems of the stock market. With help from our *Hidden Gems* team—which is beating the market by nearly 24 percentage points!—we'll show you how.

BUYING THE SEED INSTEAD OF THE PLANT

Small-company stocks offer tremendous opportunity in part because, relative to large-company stocks, these securities represent part-ownership in businesses that tend to have a lot more room to grow. If a software company with $50 million in annual revenues grows to $500 million, that would transform that business and likely enrich investors . . . yet its revenues would equal just 1% of Microsoft's sales base. Conversely, for Microsoft to grow its sales by ten times, it would need to increase its total revenues from $50 billion to $500 billion, and that would mean absolute and utter domination of the world of technology.

While we're sure Microsoft has considered the possibility, in all likelihood, you won't land a ten-bagger owning Microsoft anytime soon. That tremendous growth is in the past for Microsoft. Today, the law of large numbers—and anti-trust regulators who fight business monopolies—get in the way. Though not impossible, it is going to take a very, very, very long time before Microsoft returns ten times its present value to shareholders.

The likelihood of scoring a 10-bagger is enhanced if you focus on the stocks of first-rate small companies that fly below Wall Street's radar—like Microsoft back in 1990. These companies have far more room to grow, and you can find these stocks on the cheap because they aren't being followed closely—if they are followed at all—by the investment banks. Gigantic corporations like General Electric and Pfizer have their every move scrutinized by dozens of professional analysts; their shares are already held by hundreds of money managers and hundreds of thousands of individual investors. Finding meaningfully discounted prices among large-company stocks is daunting.

At *Hidden Gems*, rather than go where the investment crowd already is, we spend our days rustling through the dustbins of the more than 5,000 listed stocks valued under $2 billion, looking for the best investments. Specifically, we look for small companies with:

1. Rising demand for their products
2. Great business models
3. Firm financial foundations
4. Forthright managers who hold a significant ownership stake in their businesses
5. High and rising rates of return on equity
6. Stock prices trading at low multiples to owner earnings
7. Little analyst coverage
8. Scant institutional ownership

BUT FIRST, ONE THING. WELL, ACTUALLY TWO.

Lest we be accused of being too general regarding our affinity for small-cap stocks, let us make two clarifications.

Even within the universe of small-cap stocks, there are investment fads, crazes, and manias. These often form around "obviously great" companies, often referred to as "growth" stocks. They operate in temporarily hot industries, with buyers furiously lining up "not to be left behind" (one of the most devastating phrases in investment history, responsible for more net investment losses than any other five words). We like growth. After all, it's tough for a company's valuation to shrink while sales go from $300 million to $3 billion. But when growth companies are considered "obviously great," everyone already knows about them. That does no favors for potential investors because such universal admiration means a higher price for the stock. In fact, here's a controversial thought borne out by years of investment research:

Obviously great companies tend to make for bad stock investments; obviously horrible companies tend to make for better stock investments.

We prefer to avoid both camps, searching instead for solid small companies, unknown to the general public and priced at a discount.

How does an investment sour when you have an obviously great business in the hottest of industries, carrying a high price tag? In 2000, Cisco Systems was riding high, in the wake of awesome growth in the Internet industry. At a market capitalization of $550 billion, it was definitely not a small cap, but it's a perfect example. For a short time, Cisco Systems was the most valuable company on the planet. When Paul Johnson, an analyst at investment bank Robertson Stephens, wrote Warren Buffett an open letter trying to convince him to buy Cisco, he made his argument using nearly infallible measures such as excellent returns on invested capital, spectacular cash flow generation, and superlative growth rates. Cisco was an obviously great company, he maintained. And it really was. Yet Buffett didn't buy.

So what happened to Cisco?

The stock imploded the moment that the unpredictable yet inevitable downturn in the computer cycle took place. And we—well, Tom—were right in the midst of the action. He held the stock much of the way up and then watched it get clobbered. Cisco's shares tumbled from $82 per share down to a low of $8, an incredible evaporation of nearly $500 billion in shareholder wealth. It happens. Cisco was priced as a growth stock. It was obviously great. And it was already a large-cap company. Be very, very wary of obviously great large companies tagged with a rich valuation. These companies have less room to grow, are already owned and followed broadly, and often see their stocks crumble.

Small-cap value stocks are the flipside to this fascination with growth and obvious greatness. The unloved. The forgotten. The underfollowed. The unknown. For evidence, we return once again to Professor French and his incredible set of data. His work shows that since 1926, small-cap value companies have returned 14.9% per year, while small-cap growth stocks have averaged 9.9%. In fact, while small-cap value stocks thrashed the returns of large-cap companies, small-cap growth stocks actually trailed them! (Re-read that to be sure you just processed it. Not all small companies are attractive investments!)

Let's compare the two in our table format.

25-YEAR INVESTMENT HORIZON

INVESTMENT	SMALL-CAP GROWTH STOCKS	SMALL-CAP VALUE STOCKS
$5,000 (one-time investment)	$52,956	$161,056
$5,000 (annual investment)	$532,356	$1,203,394

Who wants to be a millionaire? As an investor, your best route to millions is via small-cap value stocks. And this leads to an interesting conundrum: We're looking for world-beating small caps, but not the ones that everyone else loves. In order to win with *Hidden Gems,* we have to look for the best and brightest that don't appear to be world-beaters to everyone else. The good news is that there are loads of these stocks. Retailers like Costco, Bed Bath & Beyond, and Best Buy spent years as undiscovered small caps, just waiting to be bought by value-conscious long-term investors.

For us, the sweet spot is when we find good-to-great companies at good-to-great prices. This statement seems intuitive, but allow us to provide a little further definition. The greater the company, the more we can allow the price to slide to the "good." The less great the company, the more we need to demand fantastic prices. But be clear. Many of the best investments we've selected in our *Hidden Gems* newsletter tilted toward the former. We bought truly great companies at decent prices and then watched as the businesses outperformed expectations.

WHY HIDDEN GEMS INVESTING WORKS

Why are small, often unknown companies so attractive for investment? Let's start with liquidity and volume. The market favors liquidity. Lots and lots of it. Institutional investors want to be able to get in and out of stocks in a split second, without worrying that the price they pay will be far off from the one they think they're getting. For large investors, liquidity is essential. They prefer widely held and well-known companies.

But for small, private investors like us, liquidity stinks. We dream of a land where there are lots of sellers and no buyers—*except for us*. Fortunately, if you're not too fussy about semantics, it happens all the time in the small-cap environment.

Think about what it means for a company to trade $200,000 in share volume per day. That sounds like a lot of money. But in the global marketplace, that's significantly less than peanuts. It's not even the shells of peanuts. If you're a fund manager with $10 billion to invest, how long will it take to build a meaningful position if the stock you like is only trading $200,000 per day? And what'll happen to the price as you're doing all the buying? It will go up and up and up. For large institutions, getting into small stocks just isn't practical, and that's the heart of Buffett's lament.

With only $200,000 moving through a stock over an entire day, you can bet that no investment bank in the country is going to offer research coverage, no big mutual fund is going to own it, and only a handful of institutional investors are going to want to mess with it. In effect, none of them want to have to explain to their investment committees, their bosses, or their partners why this itty-bitty stock sits in their portfolio—a stock they couldn't sell in an orderly fashion if necessary. General Electric trades more volume than that *every second*. You could cover that much dollar volume with two shares of Berkshire Hathaway. Why bother with the guppy?

When a big chunk of the market isn't even fishing in the pond where you're casting lines, you can find sound companies at ridiculously cheap prices. That's a beautiful thing. We call it "The Inefficient Pond Theory," and we invite any remaining business school professors or students who think the market is perfectly efficient to fish with us one day. The waterways where small caps swim offer a great deal of inefficiency because there just aren't that many ready buyers.

The big difficulty with small-cap investing is that the companies in this realm tend to be obscure. Everyone has heard of Home Depot, which has 2,200 stores, generates annual revenues of nearly $80 billion, and has a market capitalization of $40 billion. Few people, though, have heard of Duckwall-ALCO, a variety-store chain that has 262 locations in 23 states concentrated in towns with fewer than 5,000 people, has revenues of $500 million, and a market cap of less than $40 million.

Duckwall-ALCO may or may not be a good investment. What we can guarantee you, though, is that the market pricing around Duckwall-ALCO is much less efficient than it is for Home Depot. There are dozens of Wall Street analysts who follow Home Depot. There is one analyst following Duckwall-ALCO. There are thousands of investors paying attention to every move that Home Depot makes. Duckwall-ALCO trades on average just $100,000 per day. Virtually no one is watching. There simply is no big money pushing the shares around; it wouldn't be worth their time.

So while Home Depot's price calibrates quickly on the consensus of thousands of people as to how the firm is doing, Duckwall-ALCO's value on a daily basis may be determined by a single investment club in Dubuque. Point being, there is little attention being paid to these small companies. And in the markets, a lack of attention is a key ingredient for long-term value.

THE MARKET IS WILD

Let's revisit Buffalo Wild Wings, the Minneapolis-based purveyor of chicken wings we mentioned a few chapters back. To illustrate our point in this chapter, we recently pulled some data for the stock:

52-week high:	$44.19
52-week low:	$18.25
Variance:	58.7%

Is the market really suggesting that this business was worth $775 million in July 2007, but only $321 million the following January? Yes, this is exactly what the market is suggesting. The real question we need to answer is "What's the business worth?" Because it ought to be obvious that a fast-growing company cannot be worth $300 million and $800 million at roughly the same time. Our goal as investors is to buy $500 million businesses when the market's charging $300 million. If you think these things don't happen, let us assure you: *They happen all the time.*

We like even better when we can buy a $500 million business for $300 million and watch the company grow into a $3 billion business. It's this effect—the fact that great businesses make themselves more valuable over time—that keeps us from selling a $500 million business when its market cap increases to $600 million. After all, the $500 million valuation is based on our own analysis, and mathematically speaking, it's our single point of highest confidence in a range of values we believe the company *could* be worth. It might be substantially more. If you're disciplined enough to only buy companies when they are priced at the low end of your range of potential values, your returns over time are almost guaranteed to satisfy.

Holding a company when it's in the higher end of your range of values leaves you somewhat susceptible to a stock drop, given the lower margin of safety. But if you've properly identified the company as a superior generator of wealth, the biggest mistake you might ever make is selling it because its shares are a few dollars too high. If you bought Costco back in December 1987, for example, your shares rose 75%, from $23 to $40 in about two months. That's a great return—but over the next 20 years, the stock has risen another seven times in value—*tax-free*. Ultimately, it is nearly impossible to manage superior long-term results by focusing on short-term aims. Costco has evolved from a regional small cap into one of the most important retailers in the world, generating spectacular returns for shareholders in the process.

TIME FOR AN EXAMPLE: DREW INDUSTRIES

Small-cap investing isn't always focused on companies that are as undeniably exciting as chicken wings and deer repellent. Tom recommended Drew Industries for *Hidden Gems* in May 2005. This White Plains, New York–based company operates in the extraordinarily exciting market of parts and accessories for the motor home and recreational vehicle (RV) industry. Please contain your enthusiasm. It's a company that we found fairly late in the game. Between 1990 and 2005, it rose 50 times in value. Is this because the RV market was so explosive that it floated all boats? Were investors so focused on dot-coms that we forgot to pay attention to the proliferation of white whales on our nation's highways?

No. Drew Industries succeeded almost in spite of the sleepy nature of its business because it is run by a couple of motivated, shareholder-friendly geniuses. Leigh Abrams and Fredric Zinn have led this company for four decades and have made a fortune for their shareholders. A visit to Drew Industries' global headquarters gives you a sense of the company's values. We love leaders that are frugal with shareholder money. But nothing prepared us for our visit to Drew.

Their office is in a nondescript building in downtown White Plains. Were you to ask the students at the karate studio that takes up the bottom floor of their building if they knew which company's global headquarters were located just upstairs, likely none of them would have a clue. As we rode the elevator up, each floor seemed to carry us back a decade. The door opened on the fourth floor, and there we were in the 1970s. We half expected the Brady Bunch to come strolling from behind the wood paneling. The executive washroom sat outside the office suite, down the hall, and required a key (which was attached to a heavy piece of wood, so we wouldn't forget to return it). The place was, in short, anti-swank.

And yet from this modest place, Abrams and Zinn turned a

collection of horribly unspectacular businesses into a fantasti-cally rewarding investment. We couldn't be happier as long-term partners with these guys—unless we could have managed to find them closer to 1990 than we did. We'd probably be happier in that case, as $20,000 invested in 1990 is worth around $1 million to-day. That would have given you your entire $1 million portfolio in one fell swoop.

Let's take a look at Drew Industries as it relates to our list of characteristics.

1. A rising demand for products.

In 2002, Drew Industries' revenue stood at $325 million. By the end of 2007, it was $668 million, a clean double. Importantly, earnings per share generally tracked total revenue growth. Many people focus exclusively on the bottom line as a measure of a company's health. We think that when investors focus too much on earnings per share as a measure of a company's health, they miss something fundamental. It's easy to use accounting ruses to grow earnings in the short term. But if a company isn't putting out products that people want to buy, then all that accounting fiction isn't going to make a difference in the long run. Drew Industries has demonstrated excellent long-term growth.

2. A sound—even sleepy—business model.

Drew Industries has focused on two major sectors—mobile homes and RVs. We've already noted that these aren't thrilling sectors. But guess what? A non-exciting sector is unlikely to draw kids into a garage or rally PhDs around the lunch table to whip up ways to form a competing company. Buried treasure is, in fact, buried. These aren't fast-money companies. They're long-term, steady-growth, achingly dull businesses. To that we say, "Fantastic!"

A favorite story: A competitor called up Drew management one day and claimed that Drew was infringing on a patent. CEO

Abrams consulted a patent attorney who said, "Yes, it's probable that you are in fact in violation of their patent." But rather
than settling, Abrams offered to buy the competitor for about
$6 million, which they did. Then Abrams set out to sue everyone
else in the sector, figuring that if his company was unknow-
ingly violating the patent, in all likelihood, other companies
were as well. Drew Industries has generated more than $25 mil-
lion in settlement-related revenues alone from this acquisition,
not to mention the incremental revenues from bringing the company in house—all for just $6 million in acquisition costs.

These guys know everything that's going on in their industry.
They stick to their knitting and they know that the ultimate goal
is to generate cash for their shareholders. The day Drew Industries cavalierly diversifies into a sexier business segment is the
day we look for the exits.

3. A firm financial foundation.

The idea here is to find a company with plenty of cash and no
debt. But we're not doctrinaire about this. Companies sometimes
find that a little debt causes them to act with greater discipline,
as debt repayment requires steady cash flows.

We look for companies with low levels of debt, as debt-ridden
companies have an additional risk factor that works in the same
direction as other market risk factors. You know the old adage
about the best time to borrow being when you don't need the money?
Well, the opposite is also true. If you have a lot of debt that you
need to service and your market suffers a downturn, delaying
that cash payment can push a company into default and bankruptcy. One such disaster happened to the well-known brand
U-Haul. At the moment its business suffered a temporary downturn in 2003, its debt service levels exceeded its cash levels.
Boom. Bankruptcy for an otherwise healthy business enduring its
normal cycles.

Drew Industries carries a low level of debt on its balance sheet,

$27 million as of December 2007, versus $56 million in cash. Our rule of thumb is that a company's debt should be no more than two times its shareholder equity. If it's much higher, the firm is carrying an excessive level of debt, as well as other pernicious forms of leverage.

4. A forthright leadership team.

One knock on many CEOs is that they have a story to tell—er, *sell*. Anything that makes their shares go up today is a good thing; anything that might make them go down tomorrow morning is bad. Of course, over the long term, we want the shares to rise. That's why we're here, putting our money to work. But there's a danger for companies with share prices that rise without commensurate improvements in the underlying business. People who buy in at elevated prices on unrealistic expectations tend to lose, and lose badly. The company's reputation will suffer. And management—who likely were far too focused on short-term performance—may put the organization in permanent competitive danger over the long haul. A realistic share price is always better than a distended one if you're a long-term owner.

At Drew Industries, the insider directors and executives own 13% of outstanding shares. Naturally, then, a high share price is of interest to them. Given that self-interest, the following story may surprise you. Drew Industries' share price skyrocketed following Hurricane Katrina's devastation of the Gulf Coast, as the Federal Emergency Management Agency (FEMA) purchased nearly 25,000 manufactured homes for transitional housing to help those displaced by the storm. For many chief executives, this circumstance would be an ideal time to trumpet the company's growth story—to stoke the fire just a little bit. We phoned Abrams, and he warned us not to read anything into the demand from the federal government. Abrams felt it was likely to be one-time in nature. Federal agencies have a tendency, in his observation, to over-order and then let unused inventory bleed back into the market. As it turns out, Abrams was right. Company revenues in 2007 trailed those of 2006, and the chief culprit was soft demand for manufactured homes.

In every instance, we would rather hear truthful neutral or negative news from our leadership team than manufactured glory stories that might jump the stock over the next few days or weeks. You should adopt this perspective as well.

5. A high rate of return on investments.

As with Drew Industries, we occasionally look at companies that are not at the moment demonstrating earnings growth, or even positive earnings at all. We track earnings histories carefully, and as part of our analysis, we seek to determine whether a company's earnings swoon is temporary, cyclical, or a sign of systemic weakness at the firm. The first is an opportunity, the second is a piece of information, and the third a warning of more pain to come. We look at a few measures here for rates of return (what returns they're getting on the investments they're making). We study the return on assets, return on equity, and return on invested capital at all of our companies and look for signs of improvement. All of these are important in helping us determine the quality of the firm and its earnings, as well as the likelihood of the company generating positive returns into the future.

We seek companies that generate oodles of free cash flow. The stronger a company is, the more it is able to generate excess profit to invest in the future, pay dividends, or buy back its stock. Cash flow is an important measure for all non-financial companies, but it's especially important for small caps that need to reinvest in their operations to grow. A company lacking positive cash flows is unlikely to thrive, as it will consistently need to go to the public markets to fund growth.

6. All at a reasonable price.

Price, of course, is key. There are lots of rough measures that people use, including one of Peter Lynch's favorites, the PEG Ratio. This measure divides the price-to-earnings ratio of the company by its growth rate, with PEGs below 1 being considered cheap. A company with a P/E of 8 that is growing at 5% per year would have a PEG of 1.6 and is therefore expensive. A company trading at a P/E of 40 with a 50% growth rate has a PEG of .8 and is therefore cheap. This measure is often useful, but it also has some problems. Most importantly, PEG fails to take into account changes in growth rate. A company growing at 40% that has captured 10% of its addressable market is a vastly different beast than one that's captured 90%.

A measure we like to use is to think about companies the same way you would real estate. Real estate professionals focus on a number known as a "capitalization rate," which is essentially the company's pre-tax earnings divided by its enterprise value—it's essentially a P/E that takes debt into account.

For Drew Industries, the cap rate breaks down like this:

Fiscal Year 2007
(in millions except for cap rate)

Pre-tax earnings:	$66.0
Market capitalization:	$400.0
(minus) Cash on hand:	−$56.2
(plus) Total debt:	+$27.3
Enterprise value:	$371.1

With Drew, we get 17.8%.

The higher the cap rate, the lower the risk that we're taking regarding a company's valuation. At a minimum, we want to see cap rates exceeding 10%, suggesting a yearly rate of return of 10%.

A cap rate that drops into the low single digits means that the company offers a low current yield for shareholders. While this won't necessarily push us off of a company we believe has extraordinary future earnings power, at the moment the company barely yields better than the risk-free rate offered by U.S. treasuries. The best situation of all is for us to find a company offering a high capitalization rate and extraordinary earnings power or some other characteristic that the market has not yet recognized. At 17.8%, Drew Industries, even after the super long-term gains shareholders have enjoyed to date, offers a compelling investment based on its capitalization rate.

WHEN SMALL CAPS DIE

Right now, you might be wondering why you wouldn't put 100% of your money into small-cap stocks. If the returns are better in small caps, why would a rational investor put a red cent anyplace else? The truth is, we believe that much of what passes for asset allocation wisdom is garbage. (We think we've laid out a better approach in Chapter 10.) And we do believe—depending on your age, income level, and risk temperament—that you could construct a well-diversified portfolio out of just small-capitalization stocks.

But you have to be aware that the outsized climbs in small-cap stocks also happen in reverse. And as we've seen on multiple occasions (and have been seeing), companies in certain segments of the market tend to move together, particularly in times of great volatility. Without knowing anything about any of the constituent companies, we can almost guarantee that a portfolio made up exclusively of small-cap companies is going to be substantially more volatile than the overall market as measured by the S&P 500. During the great times, it's easy to forget what it feels like to see your stocks lose 20% or 30% or more in a single day. In the small-cap sector, these declines can happen in a hurry.

Even sleepy little Drew Industries has been a volatile stock. When we first recommended Drew in May 2005, it was trading for $18.95 per share. Over the next two and a half years, the stock was one of our best performers, reaching a high of $44.18

in October 2007—a 133% gain! However, rising energy costs and declining disposable income combined to crush Drew's share price. As of August 2008, our recommendation was actually slightly in the red. As we said above, we still believe Drew is a great company, but it just goes to show that small-cap investors often must endure sharp declines on the way to outsized gains.

Even if you have the stomach for the potential increased volatility, the fact is that small-cap companies are often far less secure than large caps. Let's face it—behemoths like General Electric may have bad years, but short of extreme situations such as those that occurred with Tyco and Enron, it's unlikely that things will be so bad that shareholders will lose a bundle. Small-cap companies are not in the same boat. They compete against larger firms, they have fewer resources than the big companies, and some of them are pretty speculative. They are also more dependent on their managers, who may or may not be competent. And so, while you're unlikely to see sudden, massive gains in large-cap companies, you can also be pretty confident that you're not going to have your entire investment wiped away. With small-cap companies, you will almost assuredly experience both along the way.

DEFENDING AGAINST THE DANGERS

In our experience, the two greatest risks for small-cap investors are pricing volatility and the threat of defaults. The greatest protection against them is to invest in a broad, diverse array of small-cap companies within your overall portfolio. Investors will hotly argue the relative merits of broad versus concentrated portfolios, and there are convincing arguments on both sides. While broad diversity will temper the outsized results of picking a concentrated number of overwhelmingly successful stocks, the problem, as Peter Lynch wrote, is in knowing in advance which few are going to work out best!

Some of America's greatest investors—Lynch, Walter Schloss,

and Joel Tillinghast—have at any point held hundreds of positions. While this strategy dilutes the gains of your greatest decisions, it lightens the blow from the few stocks that inevitably go wrong, and protects you when the winds of volatility swirl. Further, it increases the likelihood that you'll find the 10- and 20-baggers that will carry your portfolio. To uncover these stocks, you have to find companies you believe the market misunderstands. That's a tough task. While the market is impetuous, it's not stupid. Many times you're going to find out that the market understood a company perfectly. It happens. If your analysis doesn't hold up on one company out of the 100 in your portfolio, you've put 1% of your portfolio at risk. But if it's one stock out of five? Well, a permanent loss of 20% of your invested capital can take years to regain.

And what's worse, there's that beast factor involved with holding very few stocks. The academics call it "risk." We call it "volatility." Have you ever noticed that the daily movements in companies—even big ones—tend to be much more exaggerated than those of the big indexes like the Dow Jones Industrial Average? Name a big company at random and quote its stock. Look at the high and low for the year. For the fun of it, I'll quote one right now.

Starbucks

52-week high:	$28.60
52-week low:	$15.39
Variance:	46.2%

In a single year, the difference from low to high on Starbucks was nearly 50%. If you flip back a few pages, you'll see that a similar quote for Buffalo Wild Wings showed a variation of more than 60%! If you quote even some of the largest companies, you'll find that their share price variance during any random one-year period often exceeds 40%. Those are huge moves! And a lot of it is just the market's own form of kinetic energy.

There are investors who would not bat an eye at their shares moving that much in a concentrated portfolio. These people tend to be sophisticated investors. For most of us, a broadly diversified portfolio composed of carefully chosen stocks is better. Everyone has stock investments that go badly. *Everyone.*

A FEW FINAL HISTORICAL EXAMPLES

Many of today's greatest companies began their publicly traded lives as Hidden Gems: small, obscure, and unloved.

Before Wal-Mart was "Wal-Mart," it was just a chain of 32 unremarkable stores in rural Arkansas. At the company's first annual meeting in 1971, there were six attendees—including the management team. The company was valued at less than $50 million. Today it's worth around $230 *billion.*

Many of today's most successful companies, from Best Buy to Dell to Taco Bell, share similarly humble origins. There were early signs of greatness at these businesses, but for years, the companies were too small to attract Wall Street's attention.

Of course, it's easy to identify Hidden Gems in the rearview mirror ("Dude, I *told* you Taco Bell could support more than 5,800 U.S. locations!"), but separating the real jewels from the small-cap pyrite takes a keen eye.

In this section, we'll profile three of our favorite Hidden Gems, and share the qualities that first drew us to these businesses. And to be fair, we'll provide one disaster for good measure.

Now You're Cooking: Middleby

You've probably never heard of Middleby, but this company may have cooked more of your dinners than you have. Middleby manufactures commercial kitchen equipment—ovens, warmers, fryers, and griddles—for major restaurant chains such as Cheesecake Factory, Ruby Tuesday, Pizza Hut, and Papa John's. The company also provides kitchen equipment for convenience stores, schools, and prisons, and makes food-processing equipment for companies such as Sara Lee, Kraft Foods, and Tyson Foods.

Today, Middleby is a profitable growth machine that generates tremendous return on equity, but that wasn't always the case. The company was plagued by declining sales, poor margins, and a lack of strategic direction until a man named Selim Bassoul grabbed the reins.

Bassoul is exactly the type of leader we like to see at our Hidden Gems companies: passionate, dedicated, and innovative, with a large ownership stake to boot. In the late 1990s, new management, led by Bassoul, radically restructured Middleby's business. Instead of serving the entire kitchen, Bassoul chose to concentrate on the company's core competency. He eliminated less profitable businesses such as sink sanitizers, mixers, and refrigerated deli cases—more than half of the company's products—and threw Middleby's might behind heat.

That was the beginning of a turnaround that has created tremendous value for shareholders. In 2001, Bassoul engineered the acquisition of Middleby's biggest competitor, the Blodgett Oven Company. He also slashed the number of distribution facilities, reduced total headcount by 36%, and began to aggressively repay the company's debt.

At the same time, Bassoul implemented a performance-based culture with the goal of improving sales and operating income per employee. He emphasized customer satisfaction, energy efficiency, and continuous innovation, introducing higher-margin products that could cook healthier food faster.

The results were immediate and impressive. Between 2001 and 2003, Middleby's revenue doubled, while net income increased 11-fold. Margins improved across the board, and the company's return on equity leaped from 4% to 35%. As a result of the Blodgett acquisition, the company now had inroads into the school and public institution markets, and Bassoul was actively seeking additional growth avenues.

By the time we discovered Middleby in October 2003, the stock had already tripled. But at a market cap of just $175 million, it was still far too small to attract Wall Street's attention—only one analyst followed the company. Since that time, Middleby shares have appreciated for us more than 530% (a six-bagger!), but Wall Street remains largely oblivious. Even today, the company is followed by just seven analysts.

You Calling Us Chicken? Buffalo Wild Wings

We know what you're thinking. No, we don't find all our investment ideas while we're eating—just most of them.

Although the first B-Wild opened its doors in 1981, the chicken chain didn't start flapping its wings until 1994, when Miracle Ear founder Kenneth Dahlberg asked his CFO Sally Smith and controller Mary Twinem to clean up his investment in the struggling sports bar. Smith stepped in as CFO and two years later jumped to CEO; Twinem took over as CFO. And the business, with the 90-year-old Dahlberg serving as chairman, has flourished ever since.

B-Wild's new management team gave the business a much-needed kick in the pants. When Smith and Twinem took the helm, B-Wild lacked any semblance of a brand identity. Customers couldn't tell from the exterior whether it was a wing-slinging sports bar or a tire store. The new management team introduced a relentless focus on building the brand and enhancing the customer experience—making sure patrons could count on the same fun, family-friendly atmosphere at every B-Wild location. Smith made it a point to interact with as many customers as possible, soliciting their feedback on every aspect of their dining experience, right down to which of B-Wild's 14 dipping sauces they preferred (we're partial to the Mango Habanero).

B-Wild grew from just 35 locations in 1994 to around 250 restaurants when we recommended the company in July 2004. The company boasted an expanded menu and broader demographic appeal, and it was successfully penetrating new markets. By the time we found B-Wild, it was one of the country's ten fastest-growing restaurant chains, with sales increasing at a

33% annual clip. But at a market cap of a little over $200 million, B-Wild was simply too small for Wall Street's scrutiny. Once again, the Street's loss was our gain: B-Wild shares are up 191% since that point.

Boring Is Beautiful: Sun Hydraulics

Screw-in hydraulic cartridge valves. Ductile iron subplate manifolds. Sun Hydraulics is about as boring as it gets. And that's exactly what drew us to this 38-year-old industrial equipment company.

For the non-engineers out there, Sun Hydraulics manufactures components that help control force, speed, and motion in machine tools, bulldozers, and other large similar devices. The company has been profitable every year since 1972, and has paid out quarterly dividends since it came public in 1997. Sun boasted excellent margins, a strong balance sheet, and tremendous growth potential, both domestically and abroad.

That wasn't even the best part. Sun featured the kind of family-run, insider-ownership culture we love to see at *Hidden Gems*. Sun's founder and former CEO, Robert Koski, sat on the board of directors, and his family held a 30% ownership stake in the company. Koski instituted a unique ownership culture—so unusual, it became the subject of three Harvard Business School case studies.

At Sun, there were no job titles or job descriptions, no hierarchy, no organizational charts, no private offices, and, in fact, no walls inside the building (except for structural purposes). It was the ultimate horizontal organization, with only a few top executives. Employees were cross-trained and encouraged to make suggestions and changes in all areas, so continuous improvement was hardwired into the company.

Sun's success was hardly a secret. From the beginning of 2004 until we recommended it in October 2007, the stock had increased in value nearly eight times! You know how the story ends by now—despite Sun's strong fundamentals, quality management, innovative culture, and history of success, only one analyst followed the company. We couldn't be more thrilled—as of this writing, Sun has returned 20% for us.

Sleep Number Zero: Select Comfort

Select Comfort had much that we look for: a great product, strong financials, a super-efficient business model, and little Wall Street attention. Yet we're using the company as our example of a Hidden Gem gone wrong.

We weren't just wrong about Select Comfort. We were *spectacularly wrong* about Select Comfort. We loved its product—a high-quality mattress with air chambers that allowed different firmness settings for each side of the mattress. The company claimed its "Sleep Number" technology was clinically proven to help people fall asleep faster and to sleep more comfortably. And we were believers—Tom purchased a Select Comfort mattress, and claims he's never slept better.

Select Comfort's efficient business model was also attractive. Select Comfort employed a made-to-order manufacturing process and delivery system, which enabled the company to operate with a negative cash conversion cycle. That means the company collected payment for its mattresses before it even ordered the parts to build the bed! That type of efficiency is quite rare, and it made Select Comfort's operations far more flexible than those of conventional mattress manufacturers like Sealy, Serta, and Simmons.

The company boasted surging revenues, a pristine balance sheet with ample cash and no debt, and phenomenal return on equity. Sound great? We thought so—and that's why we made Select Comfort our first (and only) four-time *Hidden Gems* recommendation.

But shortly after that fourth recommendation, the Select Comfort story started to deflate.

Select Comfort's unfocused marketing campaign had always been a concern (a luxury product being hawked via infomercials at 3 a.m.?), but we were confident that management would craft the right message to connect with its target customer. However, repeated advertising revamps failed to generate the kind of brand awareness enjoyed by arch-rival Tempur-Pedic.

Meanwhile, trouble in the housing market made consumers question whether they could afford a $3,000 mattress, and Select Comfort developed a nasty habit of missing its quarterly earnings guidance. The stock began to slide—slowly at first, but gradually picking up speed as the consumer environment deteriorated. Making matters worse, the company conducted a series of ill-fated stock repurchases that depleted its cash hoard and forced it to take on debt. By the time we finally sold the stock, Select Comfort had lost about 80% of its value.

Yup. 80%.

Select Comfort will forever haunt our scorecard, but the losses we incurred on this investment are inconsequential compared to the value of the lessons we learned. For starters, we now insist on a top-notch management team—no matter how strong the underlying business appears.

Select Comfort's management was waving red flags all along, but we were so enamored with its efficient economic model that we failed to see them. CEO Bill McLaughlin did an admirable job of reviving the business from the brink of bankruptcy in 2001, but it should have been clear that he wasn't the right man to grow a multibillion-dollar mattress brand. McLaughlin didn't love beds. He didn't have any industry experience. He took the Select Comfort job after working at Frito-Lay in Europe in part because Minneapolis seemed like a nice place to raise a family. That's not enough.

A great CEO must demonstrate passion and mastery in the field of business in which the company is engaged. We want our leaders to eat, breathe, and sleep the business, like Selim Bassoul or the dynamic duo at B-Wild—and we want executives and directors to own a lot of stock, which Select Comfort's leaders did not.

In addition, the management team at Select Comfort didn't

demonstrate the Warren Buffett–like partnership mentality that we value so highly. Management was a little too generous with stock option compensation for our liking, and more interested in conducting share repurchase programs than modifying the miserable marketing campaign. We want our CEO, CFO, and board of directors to feel equal alignment with employees, shareholders, and customers of the business.

Secondly, the "brilliant" business model may not have been as brilliant as we originally believed. After all, how often does the typical consumer actually purchase a new mattress? Even the most stalwart Select Comfort shopper only needs a new bed once every ten years. It's awfully tough to build brand loyalty when shoppers are visiting your store once a decade.

And finally, the Select Comfort experience only underscored the importance of a solid balance sheet—especially at a smaller company. When we first found Select Comfort, it had $74 million in cash and zero debt. By the time we finally sold out, Select Comfort carried $43 million in debt and had just $6 million cash on hand. In a short time period, a few questionable management decisions transformed a healthy, growing company into a business in legitimate danger of bankruptcy.

There is one additional lesson that you can learn from our Select Comfort experience, and it has nothing to do with stock selection. Small-cap stocks are risky. Even the most promising company can turn into a giant pumpkin at the stroke of midnight. If you decide to be a small-cap investor, make sure you hold a well-diversified basket of *at least* a dozen small-cap stocks, and never put yourself in a position where your financial and emotional well-being is dependent on the performance of any single company.

THE PIECE OF YOUR PORTFOLIO

We've already said you could allocate 100% of your capital to small-cap stocks and create a well-diversified, market-beating portfolio. However, for the vast majority of investors, that's probably not a prudent approach. We think small caps should constitute at least a portion of your investable assets—probably somewhere between 10% and 40%, depending on your risk tolerance. If you are terrified by the thought of one of your portfolio holdings losing a quarter of its market value over the course of a single day, then you'll probably want to keep that number on the low end of that range. If you're willing to accept greater volatility in exchange for greater potential rewards, then small caps are right up your alley. One benefit to evaluating small-cap companies is that they tend to be somewhat simpler structures than the massive conglomerates with multiple divisions, branches, and subsidiaries. Dow Jones Industrial Average–component United Technologies sells air conditioners, helicopters, elevator fuel cells, and aircraft engines. Analyzing its financials requires knowledge of a wide range of businesses. Dawson Geophysical, a small-cap company, operates seismic services for oil and gas drillers. To know Dawson Geophysical, you must understand the economics of oil and gas drilling. We won't claim this is easy, but it's a far less daunting task than sorting out a huge, complex firm like United Technologies.

Over time, small caps beat large caps because they're unknown to the general public and generally ignored. Yet they tend to be easier to analyze than large caps. Investing is a complex pursuit, involving critical analysis, math, psychology, and even a little soothsaying. But that doesn't mean that it can't be made simpler. Seek out small-cap companies with the characteristics we listed above, do a little thinking about the three most important elements of the business, and get on the road to mastery of small-cap investing. By so doing, you're seeking ownership in companies most people don't know about. And this much we can guarantee—if a company is unknown, it's much, much harder for it to be efficiently priced. If you're looking in places where few others are, you're going to find some bargains. And when those bargains are applied to the stocks of sound and promising small companies, the sky's the limit!

Motley Fool Advisor Bill Mann and analyst Rich Greifner contributed to this chapter. Bill—a longtime Fool who previously reigned as co-advisor on Hidden Gems *and lead advisor on* Global Gains—*once ate an entire plate of Buffalo Wild Wings' hottest wings and lived to tell about it. Rich, a senior writer for our* Million Dollar Portfolio *service, witnessed this feat and lost his appetite for a week.*

Visit us at mdpbook.com for our best small-cap stock right now.

CHAPTER 7

RISK TAKERS
AND RULE BREAKERS

Let's begin our adventure in growth stock investing with a tale—a true one at that. In April of 1770, Captain James Cook and his crew became the first Europeans to land on the east coast of Australia. Rumors of a southern continent in the far Pacific had been circulating since the time of Ptolemy, but no exploratory voyage had ever achieved more than glancing blows off the north and west coasts. By the time of Cook's voyage, there were serious doubts as to whether the southern continent even existed.

When he set off in the *Endeavour* in 1768, Cook's chief mission was to sail to Tahiti and take measurements that would help establish the distance of the sun from the earth. Exploration was an afterthought, but his choice to take the westward route on his homeward voyage changed the course of history.

Cook's journey brought him into contact with the Tahitians and Maori people of New Zealand, but little prepared him for the reaction of the aboriginal Australians, described by Robert Hughes in *The Fatal Shore*, a history of Australia's founding.

It was the largest artifact ever seen on the east coast of Australia, an object so huge, complex and unfamiliar as to defy the natives' understanding. The Tahitians had flocked out to meet her in their bird-winged outriggers, and the Maoris had greeted her with *hakas* and showers of stones; but the Australians took no notice. They displayed neither fear nor interest and went on fishing.

When Cook and three other men landed on shore in a small craft, however, the native Australians reacted with alarm and fear. They had quite simply not seen the huge, high-masted ship pass their fishing boats; its enormity was simply too great and alien for them to mentally process.

Business is full of invisible ships—challenges to the status quo so unexpected that they are imperceptible, sometimes even when they are in plain view. The goal of investing in what we call Rule Breakers—emerging growth companies with some special characteristics—is to join the band of pirates aboard these invisible ships. We want to be there for a share of the booty when a new company emerges to dominate a business niche.

Let's get one thing straight up front: Not all growth companies are Rule Breakers. But all Rule Breakers exhibit, or promise to exhibit, extraordinary growth. Most are small-cap stocks. So while Rule Breakers would generally be lumped into the category of small-cap growth, there are some special characteristics that distinguish them from the herd.

DISRUPTION IS IN ITS DNA

In the late 1970s, common wisdom held that no newcomer could ever join the ranks of the world's largest pharmaceutical companies. Most of the well-known drug companies—household names like Pfizer, Johnson & Johnson, Merck, and others—trace their origins back to the 19th century. They were built over decades, deploying huge amounts of capital to build up imposing infrastructures. That a newcomer could catch up seemed far-fetched. The pharmaceutical R&D process for a single drug can take more than a decade from the lab bench to the pharmacy shelf, and building an organization that thrives under such constraints requires not only a lot of capital, but *patient* capital. Add to that the need for a global apparatus to distribute and sell drugs around the world—it just wasn't something a start-up could reasonably hope to accomplish.

In the midst of that environment, a company called Amgen started exploring the commercial possibilities raised by new genetic engineering technologies. In 1973, for the first time scientists spliced instructions for making a protein into an unrelated host organism. Microscopic cells grown in a vat could become factories for a new kind of medicine: biologic drugs.

It wasn't that Amgen was a stealth organization or that it was working with arcane knowledge. The recombinant DNA technology around which the company was built was the subject of a National Medal of Science. The successful insertion of frog DNA into a bacterial cell in 1973 by Stanley Cohen and Herbert Boyer—one of Amgen's founders—is often cited as the most significant discovery ever to be overlooked by the Nobel Prize committee. But even though anyone involved in biological R&D must have been aware of the discovery, it didn't seem like a commercial, competitive threat to pharmaceutical business-as-usual.

Amgen itself struggled with the possibilities raised by new genetic engineering technologies. In its 1983 IPO prospectus, the company outlined the handful of projects it was working on. One was indigo dye. Another was chicken growth hormone. The entrenched pharmaceutical industry wasn't exactly shaking in its boots.

Yet just two years later, in 1985, another biotech company called Genentech launched a human growth hormone to treat a hereditary condition in children. Four years after that, Amgen launched Epogen, a red blood cell booster that, in a slightly different form, is still the company's chief source of revenue today.

Still the drug companies paid little notice.

Fast forward to 1996, 20 years after the birth of the biotech industry. The aggregate market cap of the entire industry—the value of *every single public biotech company in the world, added together*—was less than that of just one drug company, Merck. Yet that same year, annual sales of Amgen's Epogen and its white blood cell booster, Neupogen, each broke $1 billion for the first time. The first monoclonal antibody, a new class of biologic that has added tens of billions of dollars in value to the industry, had been approved two years before. If the ships on the horizon weren't apparent before, surely they were by now, right?

Well, they were to some people. In 1994, David established the original Rule Breakers portfolio with $50,000, and Amgen as one of the companies in the original roster. That pick helped the portfolio return more than 1,200% over the next five years.

Today, Amgen and fellow biotech Genentech are two of the largest 20 pharmaceutical companies in the world. Through its health-care sales, Amgen outranks venerable companies like Schering-Plough and Procter & Gamble, and trails only a little behind Eli Lilly, a company founded exactly a century before Genentech. Perhaps even more significantly, the biotech industry has become one of the main sources of innovation for the old guard. Though they haven't given up on conventional pills, the mainstream pharmaceutical industry has transformed itself, through acquisition and investment, into a branch of the biotech industry. They throw billions of dollars every year at small biotech companies, looking to license the next big blockbuster drugs, which are proving increasingly elusive to their in-house R&D efforts.

Now *that's* creative disruption for you.

PROFIT, EVEN THROUGH HINDSIGHT

After you finish reading all about small caps and value and mutual funds and retirement, hold on to at least one key point from this chapter. It's easy to look back with hindsight and say, "Look how important this technology turned out to be!" But making massive profits from the advent of the biotechnology industry didn't require being a visionary who saw what few others did in the early 1980s. You could have waited until the leading company in the sector had *multiple billion-dollar products* and still racked up market-crushing returns.

Where are the creative disruptions happening today? Some are undoubtedly just bubbling up now, invisible to all but a few. But others have matured enough to become apparent to investors willing to break a few rules, and still offer great potential returns. Are those opportunities in solar power? In robotics? In something seemingly boring, like soft drinks? Maybe all of the above?

To find these companies is a challenge to your sleuthing abilities. To *buy* them can be a challenge to your well-honed impulses as a cautious investor. Often these companies don't have the qualities we expect to find in a "smart" investment. They may be losing money. They may trade at an exorbitant P/E multiple. A consensus of investment banking analysts may not agree the company is a "buy." In fact, you may not find any analyst that reports on them at all.

But that's not to say that Rule Breaker investing is about taking giant gambles on unproven, blue-sky ideas. Sure, trying to recognize the ramifications of important innovations before others do is part of the approach—and as we'll discuss later, Wall Street hands the individual investor some built-in advantages in that regard. More importantly, it's about recognizing the companies already creating a new niche, and identifying the ones that are going to dominate tomorrow.

In other words, it's the ultimate in growth investing, and using this strategy, David's *Rule Breakers* newsletter service is beating the market by more than 12 percentage points.

WHY BUY GROWTH?

Why are investors obsessed with growth? That's not a riddle. The answer is straightforward: Because growth, more than anything else, drives sustainable increases in earnings and cash flow. And these factors determine a company's real worth and, hence, its stock price.

When we talk about growth, we're basically talking about a company selling more goods and services this year than it did last year, and expecting to sell even more the following year. Increasing sales aren't the only way for a company to grow the bottom line—it could, for a while at least, cut expenses and "do more with less." It could buy back its own stock and decrease the denominator used in the earnings per share calculation (as long as this amount outweighs the loss of interest income from the money used to repurchase the shares). But there's only so much fat to trim, and if a company is going to see its profits—and ultimately its stock-price rise over the long term, it must grow the top line.

But wait a minute. Didn't we just tell you in Chapter 5 that value stocks beat growth stocks? Well, yes, we did . . . and they do . . . broadly speaking.

Unless, that is, you pick the *right* growth companies.

OK, that may sound like a glib answer—*of course* you'll come out ahead if you pick the right stocks! But the fact is that you're not investing in broad concepts; you are investing in carefully selected businesses—and behind this seemingly foolish statement stands a principle that has enriched a lot of Fools. We're not suggesting you search out "hot companies" or high rates of growth in isolation. Rule Breaker investing is about identifying companies that are likely to turn a high growth rate—or an anticipated high growth rate—into a sustainable force to drive future cash flow for a long time. With the right principles and a little discipline, you can pick these stocks, and the payoff can be huge.

EVERYONE'S GOTTA GROW

If we scared you at all about growth earlier in this book, let us put you at ease now: There is nothing about pursuing strong growth that contradicts a value-based approach.

Most value investors, if they are looking to hold a stock for the long term, are ultimately counting on growth to make their investments gain in value. Outside of a few special situations like mergers and acquisitions or spin-outs, value investments only pay off if the company improves operations or increases sales. The small-cap strategy we outlined in Chapter 6 involves finding largely *unnoticed* (and therefore underpriced) growth.

The strategy we're talking about here involves finding *under-appreciated* growth, and that can be trickier because the companies involved are often quite well known and actively traded. We don't necessarily have the liquidity advantages that come with *Hidden Gems*. But we have other advantages. We'll discuss some of those in a moment, but first let's take a look at the big picture. Earlier in the book, we cited research to suggest that value handily beats growth. Let's take a different look at the same question.

A STOCK-PICKER'S GAME

In a May 2002 study, David Kovaleski of SEI Investments looked at the performance of fund managers working in different investment styles and measured them against their relevant benchmarks. Large-cap value funds were weighted against the Russell 1000 Value Index, and large-cap growth fund managers against the Russell 1000 Growth Index.

He found that over a five-year period, just 20% of the value managers managed to beat their benchmark, while 55% of the growth managers did. That's a striking difference. Does it contradict other studies that favor a value strategy?

Not necessarily. It suggests that growth is a strategy in which *stock pickers* may have a better chance of success. Buying growth with a broad-brushed index approach is a formula for underperformance, but some smart choices can lead to outperformance.

And there are reasons that this makes sense. A good value investment will rise in price because the market will eventually take notice of it—either because people become more widely aware of its performance or because they recognize that its problems are being corrected. As the market corrects its earlier impressions, the stock rises, sometimes dramatically. If it is to continue to rise, however, the company has to do more than show it is worthy of recognition. It has to perform . . . and grow.

Some "value" investments actually have great growth potential, while many will at best turn in tepid growth even if all goes well. The best growth companies, however, will achieve phenomenal expansion. And the very best can keep it up for years, letting you grow wealth while deferring taxes. That kind of long-term, high growth is what creates 20-baggers and even 100-baggers. A single investment like that can transform your portfolio—your whole financial future, in fact. And you're unlikely to find such a company without identifying extraordinary growth potential. The businesses we're talking about aren't just looking to succeed in an established industry. They want to shake things up, topple kings, speak truth to power, and all that.

SURE, THERE'S A CATCH

There are two catches. First, rapid growth *usually* doesn't last long. Some companies manage to grow sales at an exponential rate (over 100%) for a year, maybe even several. But maintaining that pace eventually becomes impossible. If they are successful, companies naturally mature to a state of slow growth. They evolve into the kind of large, steady companies that offer steady, but usually not large, returns. Using a growth strategy means finding companies that can sustain extraordinary growth longer than the market realizes or expects, either because you've caught it early in its growth cycle, or because it has such strong structural advantages that it maintains a dominant position in its industry.

The second catch is that the market tries to anticipate the future. You may have heard about companies being "priced" for future events, including an expectation that future earnings will be a lot better than the ones you see today. Sometimes predictions are too rosy; sometimes they underestimate what a company can do. When they are too optimistic, high-priced stocks crash down to earth. When they are too cautious, an "expensive" stock can keep rising, sometimes for years. We want to find the latter.

FINDING BREAKERS, AVOIDING FAKERS

Rapid growth can lead to big returns . . . or painful mistakes that will drag down your portfolio. Just *how* do we find the companies that will win the Darwinian struggle for survival in a hostile and competitive business environment?

First, recognize that this isn't just a numbers game. Screening stocks for high rates of revenue or earnings growth, for instance, may lead you to businesses that have experienced brief spurts for transient reasons. Think back to our example from Chapter 6 of how Drew Industries experienced a spike in demand following Hurricane Katrina and the government's purchase of large numbers of manufactured homes. Drew is a great company, but if you'd bought on expectations that its 2006 rate of growth would continue, you'd have been sorely disappointed. (In fact, those investors who bid the stock up to over $38 a share in the months following the hurricane undoubtedly *were* disappointed when it fell back below $24 by the following summer.)

Indeed, those investors who don't love spreadsheets and math may feel a special affinity for Rule Breakers. These companies are hard to assess by traditional valuation metrics like P/E ratios or discounted cash flow calculations. While all companies are ultimately valued on their ability to produce cash from their operations, Rule Breakers tend to operate in such a state of flux that trying to predict their future with any kind of numerical precision is a questionable prospect.

Think of all those analysts who can't successfully pin down what a company will earn in a given quarter even after the sales are all in . . . yet still think they can predict how much the same company will sell for five years from now out to three decimal points. And the problem gets much worse when the company in question is rapidly gaining market share, creating new demand, and seeing high-double-digit growth—all subject to a lot of volatility. That analysis involves more variables, moving less predictably in larger swings. To paraphrase the statistician John Tukey, you're better off being approximately right than precisely wrong, which is where most numerical analyses will get you with these kinds of companies.

That doesn't mean analysis is unimportant. In fact, it's more important than ever in the world of Rule Breakers, even if it requires less feverish use of your calculator.

Here are six criteria you can use to help identify a Rule Breaker. Not every great growth investment has all these traits, but then again not every growth company is a Rule Breaker. The companies with these characteristics deserve special attention. They are more likely to be the businesses that see extraordinary growth sustained over a long period of time, and defy investors' expectations. They are the companies most likely to lead you to market-beating returns.

1. Top Dog and First Mover in an Important, Emerging Industry

A top dog is a company that has a dominant market share in its industry. Usually that also means it is the largest by market capitalization. A first-mover business was the first to exploit its particular niche—in most cases, it created the market. Think

DVDs by mail and Netflix. Think of Whole Foods Markets in natural and organic groceries, Starbucks in coffee, or Microsoft in world domination . . . and software. You might argue that Starbucks didn't invent the coffee shop, or that Whole Foods wasn't the first to stock its shelves with eggs from free-roaming, gourmet-fed chickens and gluten-free cereal that has saving the rain forests as a goal. But they were the first to conceive of these businesses on a national and international scale, when others didn't recognize the major growth opportunities.

Remember also that your prospective investment should be a top dog, a first mover, *and* operate in an important, emerging industry. You may remember Kozmo.com, a short-lived company that let you order virtually anything over the Internet, from a single candy bar to a Palm Pilot, and have it delivered to your door in under an hour. It was a first mover and, for a time, top dog in this endeavor. But was one-hour delivery of snacks and electronics really an important, emerging industry? Likewise, the ill-fated company Webvan was a first mover in dedicated home delivery of groceries—a business area that could conceivably still someday prove important. But Webvan was never top dog. For a while, market capitalization made it look that way, but its sales were nothing compared to those of the major grocery store chains, which had better infrastructure to compete in the same business. And they did.

2. Sustainable Advantage Gained Through Business Momentum, Patent Protection, Visionary Leadership, or Inept Competitors

In a free market, all successful businesses attract competition. The critical question is how well a company will fend it off.

Patents are one key means of sustaining competitive advantage. In some businesses, like the pharmaceutical industry, patents alone are enough to enforce a lasting competitive advantage. A unique molecule can be patented, and competitors can't count on making a few changes to it and having it work the same way (there are only a few atoms of difference between Ritalin and cocaine, for instance—good luck getting the second one past the Food & Drug Administration!) On the other hand, patent protection can be problematic in the software industry, where protected inventions can often be worked around.

Luckily, there are other ways of protecting a competitive advantage. Companies have trade secrets (the formula for Coke isn't patented, but it is a well-guarded secret known to only a few employees) and expertise can be built over time that others find hard to duplicate. Some businesses require daunting levels of capital investment to establish. Other companies are sustained by their reputation and brand name. Sometimes companies are just smarter than their competitors, and sometimes competitors find they just can't adapt to a changing world. We'll discuss examples of both those situations a little later.

The point here is to find a company's moat—its bulwark against inevitable competitors—and figure out how many alligators are in it.

3. Strong Past Price Appreciation

What we want to know here is if the stock has already been going up. Consider Newton's First Law of Motion, also called the law of inertia: *Corpus omne perseverare in statu suo quiescendi vel movendi uniformiter in directum, nisi quatenus a viribus impressis cogitur statum illum mutare.*

Got it?

Well, OK, we need the translation, too: *"Every body perseveres in its state of being at rest or of moving uniformly straight forward, except insofar as it is compelled to change its state by force impressed."* A translation of the translation is that something in motion tends to remain that way unless an outside force acts on it otherwise.

So it is with the best growth stocks. They continue rising because their advantages allow them to sustain remarkable earnings and cash flow growth, and to win new converts among the ranks of both customers and investors continuously. Don't count on momentum to save your bacon in the absence of other strong fundamentals. But a strong company that is firing on all cylinders can sustain a remarkably extended appreciation in stock price.

Also remember that the market isn't stupid. If the company you're evaluating strikes success or anticipates great things, some of that will find its way into the stock price. The market may underestimate the company's potential, but if it isn't valued much at all in the form of a rising stock price, you need to reevaluate whether this company has the potential you're banking on.

4. Good Management and Smart Backing

Unless you're specifically looking at a turnaround, spin-off, or takeover situation, one rule you never want to break is that good management trumps almost all other concerns. Think of a company like Target, which we would argue is at its core just another discount retailer with few structural advantages over its rivals. Yet by dint of good management, it has returned a lot of value to shareholders over the years. Better a mediocre business with great management than a great business with mediocre management. Over time, the latter group will screw up a free lunch.

Judging the quality of a management team is a bit subjective, but that's because human beings head these companies. Luckily, we're human beings, too, and most of us are equipped with some ability to assess the subjective aspects of personality. As we've suggested in chapters past, listen to conference calls and investor presentations. Even if you can't talk to management directly, the Internet makes it easy to hear how the top brass thinks and how they interact with investors. Are they smart? Visionary? Inspiring? You'll necessarily get an imperfect picture, and you may not be able to put a number on it, but you can get some idea of whom it is you are entrusting with your money. In addition, the heads of Rule Breaker companies are often career entrepreneurs with a track record of business formation you can look to.

5. Strong Consumer Appeal

It's almost impossible to underestimate the power of a strong brand. If a business has mass consumer appeal, sustaining extraordinary growth is that much easier. A brand eventually reinforces itself—that's why a company like Starbucks has never really had to advertise. A brand also becomes associated with an *experience*. We are creatures of habit, and when we have to think less, our lives seem easier. You may know where your next cup of coffee is coming from, or where you'll buy your next computer, or where you'll go to look for your next outfit—without thinking about it. That's the habituation that comes from a strong brand, and it strengthens a company against its competitors immeasurably. Brands also give a company pricing power over rivals—is that Starbucks venti really worth double the cost of a cup of the stuff in the corner convenience store?

One final thought: We'd rather see a company sell a $1 item to a million people than a $1 million item to one person. That may seem counterintuitive, as selling to a million people seems like a lot more work than selling to just one. But repeat business gets a lot easier when a product has mass appeal.

Of course, some great companies are engaged in specialty businesses that are not intended to have mass consumer appeal. That's OK, too, but we want to know that the company's product, name, and reputation constitute a brand among the people who matter. Even if you're looking at some esoteric software business, ask yourself: Could this company price its product 5% or 10% higher than its competitors and still maintain market share because of its reputation?

6. Grossly Overvalued, According to At Least One Significant Constituent in the Financial Media

This criterion might sound like an odd one. Who wants to buy a stock that everyone says is too expensive and poised for a tumble?

But this actually aligns with what we said earlier about avoiding "obviously great" companies. In this case, a major media source is saying they *don't* like the stock. Bravo! Being derided as overvalued is a trait shared by many Rule Breaker companies that "smart" investors avoid and that then go on to double, triple, or quintuple over subsequent years. The "too expensive" label gets thrown around because analysts don't appreciate how powerfully a Rule Breaker can disrupt its industry, displace competitors, and grow over a short period. Fear leaves many on the sidelines, only to come in later and drive the stock up further once the financial media finally gets on board.

These six criteria aren't guaranteed to weed out every dog, or to point you to every winner. But they offer a framework for evaluating fast-growing companies. They can focus your attention on the characteristics most likely to be shared by companies that turn growth into extraordinary performance over a long period.

MAKING MONEY BY BREAKING RULES

We've outlined an approach for finding rule-breaking companies. But these companies often command high stock prices because investors already recognize at least some of their advantages. Winning here means finding companies where investors have recognized, but underestimated, potential growth. Why does the Rule Breakers approach give you a better chance of finding them?

To understand why, let's consider the concept of discounting. We're not talking about marking down last year's jeans, exactly, but rather about applying a present value to future dollars. If someone says they will give you $100 a year from now, what's that worth today? How much money would you take at this instant in lieu of that $100 payment down the road? There's no exact answer because it depends on the kind of returns you demand—what you think you can do with money now versus later. As long as you're reasonably rational, however, you'd be willing to take less than $100 now to avoid waiting a year.

Discounting is the art of finding present values for future scenarios. One of the best means of valuing a company is to predict what its cash flow will be in the future, and discount that back to a present value. But the faster that company is growing, the more the present value depends on increasingly distant future cash flows, and the more unpredictable that kind of analysis becomes. That opens up growth stocks to more uncertainty, risk, and volatility. But it also confers a few advantages.

The first is that most investors are risk-averse. They'd rather take a smaller risk with a lower payoff than a larger risk with a higher payoff. That keeps them on the sidelines until the growth stock that was "too expensive" suddenly becomes the "obviously great" company everyone just has to own. Then, look out.

The second is what is called conservatism bias, which means that people are too slow and too timid to update their beliefs in the face of changing evidence. This scenario is particularly true when exceptional changes are taking place in a business or industry— that is, when rules are being broken.

When we think of the future, we tend to extrapolate in a straight line from the present. Who in the 1980s would have expected that within a decade crime rates would be at their *lowest* levels since the 1950s? No one we know of. We can model probable events with reasonable accuracy, but we are terrible at foreseeing the impact of the improbable.

Medical technology company Intuitive Surgical first turned a profit in 2004. The maker of the da Vinci robotic surgical device earned 67 cents per share. Plenty of analysts were willing to hazard guesses on what the company would earn several years hence, but not one dared to suggest it could pull in $3.70 a share by 2007.

That would be to suggest that over the following three years, earnings would climb at an annual rate of 77%! To publish such an outlandish prediction would be to risk ridicule, to appear like a biased cheerleader more interested in pumping the stock than in providing a sober estimate of the future.

In fact, Intuitive Surgical did grow that fast. Some analysts even recognized that Intuitive represented a paradigm shift in the field of surgery, yet they couldn't bring themselves to envision a future so different from the present.

In our 1999 book *Rule Breakers, Rule Makers*, David hazarded a guess on what the market capitalization of Amazon.com would be in 2009. At the time David was writing, Amazon was worth about $6 billion. The point was not to predict the future, but rather to illustrate how futile such long-term projections were in a fast-changing business. His "mostly, if not completely, ridiculous" estimate: $18 billion. Amazon's actual market cap as of this writing in 2008: $32 billion.

That's not too bad for a wild, 10-year-old guesstimate. But just consider that someone who was very bullish on the possibilities of the Internet and the prospects of Amazon.com, writing at a time when investors were feverishly pushing the valuations of Internet companies into a speculative bubble of historic proportions, still undershot the mark by almost 50%.

AN INTUITIVE BET

So, are there really any companies out there that satisfy all these criteria?

Absolutely. We live in a free market society with (relatively) abundant capital that richly rewards innovation. In an average year, more than 350 new companies enter the stock market for the first time, each one claiming something competitive to offer the world. Few of these are Rule Breakers, but you'll never run out of hunting opportunities.

One great example flitted past just a couple of paragraphs ago.

Like many great technologies, the magic behind Intuitive Surgical was born from military funding. In the late 1980s, researchers at the Stanford Research Institute, working under contract to the U.S. Army, created a prototype of a robot that could act as the hands of a surgeon. The idea was that a skilled surgeon could operate controls in one location while a robot mimicked those precise manipulations elsewhere. On the battlefield, that meant that skilled surgeons—always in short supply—didn't have to be in the same place as a wounded soldier. The robot just had to be there.

And while the battlefield applications were impressive, Intuitive Surgical was founded in 1995 by a team of entrepreneurs and scientists who believed civilian applications weren't far behind. Procedures conducted by the robot they developed were far less invasive than conventional surgery—an entire operation could be performed through a tiny 1-cm "port," eliminating the need for large, open incisions. The company's founders believed the technology would shorten hospital stays, reduce healing time, and improve post-surgical health.

But not many others shared this vision. With little attention from the outside world, Intuitive refined what it called the da Vinci system, and in 2000 gained FDA marketing approval. The company went public in the same year. It racked up less than $27 million in sales that year, and the stock traded between a split-adjusted $10.76 and $38.12 a share.

Intuitive Surgical was added to the *Rule Breakers* portfolio in April 2005, at a price of $44.17 a share. The stock had more than doubled from its debut price, while sales had more than quintupled. Despite a lot of evidence that surgeons were open to the benefits of robotic surgery, investors hadn't woken up.

Let's look at how Intuitive Surgical stacks up against our six Rule Breaker criteria.

1. Top dog and first mover in an important, emerging industry. No questions here: Intuitive invented robotic surgery. It had only one competitor, a company called Computer Motion that it acquired in 2003. By the time we found it, Intuitive was essentially a monopoly. Whether robotic surgery would prove to be an important industry may have been a matter of debate, but fast-rising sales of robotic systems, and the more reliable repeat sales of disposable instruments used with each procedure, pointed to fast-growing acceptance and gave us confidence.

2. Sustainable advantage gained through business momentum, patent protection, visionary leadership, or inept competitors. Intuitive had established a monopoly because no other company had the vision to put a stake in the field. As time went on, traditional bulwarks against competition, such as patents, became increasingly irrelevant. Intuitive had a rapidly swelling installed base of repeat customers who continued to buy instruments and accessories. The company's head start effectively closed out newcomers. Today, with more than 700 da Vinci systems installed around the world, a newcomer would be hard pressed to get a foot in the door without a revolutionary improvement in technology or price.

3. Strong past price appreciation. Intuitive went public in June 2000, right when the stock market was melting down from the excesses of the Internet bubble. It wasn't a friendly environment for small technology start-ups, but even so, Intuitive more than doubled from its IPO price over the following five years. That's a compound annual growth rate of about 15% over a period when the S&P 500 lost ground at an annual rate of about 4%, and the Nasdaq composite fared far worse.

It's worth noting that Intuitive's rate of appreciation accelerated as the "secret" of the company's success became more widely known—the stock went up more than 500% in a period of less than three years between 2005 and 2007. It "looked expensive" to a lot of investors at $50 . . . and $100 . . . and $200 . . . and $300 a share. It turns out the acceleration of the stock price was a fantastic signal to get on board.

4. Good management and smart backing. One of Intuitive's co-founders, Dr. Fred Moll, previously founded two separate medical device companies subsequently acquired by larger businesses. That's an encouraging track record of success, although by the time we came on board, Moll had handed over the reins to

Lonnie Smith, whose background was more in managing an established business. Major venture backers included the Mayfield Fund, a firm responsible for launching Genentech, Amgen, Silicon Graphics, Compaq, and many others. Of course, qualified management and blue-chip investors are no guarantee of success. But it certainly helps to know that a company trying to create demand for an entirely new category of product has the support of investors who have made similar things happen many times before.

5. **Strong consumer appeal.** It might not sound like brand recognition or sex appeal would have much relevance to a medical device. But consumers have been one of the drivers behind Intuitive's success. Surgical patients don't want to experience any more pain, scarring, or complications than absolutely necessary. The da Vinci system first made its mark in prostatectomy (surgical removal of the prostate), and informed patients quickly learned that having the procedure done robotically would get them out of the hospital more quickly with fewer complications. Demand from patients helped push hospitals to purchase the machines.

6. **Grossly overvalued, according to at least one significant constituent in the financial media.** In July of 2005, just a few months after we staked a claim in Intuitive, *Wall Street Journal* financial columnist Herb Greenberg appeared on the CNBC television show *Mad Money*. That's the program where veteran trader and TheStreet.com founder Jim Cramer screams out lightning-fast reactions to dozens of tickers. Greenberg highlighted the risks of owning Intuitive, and Cramer urged investors to cash in on their gains. After all, the stock had moved up from the mid-$40s in April to about $69 per share in July. Greenberg and Cramer, who have made plenty of other good calls, were just two examples of the cautionary voices that abound when a stock rises "too far, too fast." Sometimes caution pays. But this caution was just delaying investors who finally couldn't resist the company and piled in over the subsequent two-and-half years, causing the stock to more than quintuple, topping $350 a share in late 2007. We held it that whole time, and still do today. It has returned 518% for us versus just 0.5% for the S&P 500.

Intuitive created an industry that essentially didn't exist before. It engaged in what might be termed *asymmetrical competition*. The company wasn't trying to put an earlier generation of surgical robots out of business—there was no earlier generation. It wasn't trying to bully, advertise, or price its way into the highest market share. In fact, its real competition was the status quo: surgeons with scalpels. Because of what the da Vinci system could offer in throughput, outcomes, and return on investment, these competitors became Intuitive's most ardent supporters.

Now *that's* a brilliant strategy.

Intuitive didn't need massive amounts of capital; about $80 million in venture capital was used to create a company that would be valued at more than $11 billion less than seven years after its IPO. Its advantage was that no one else saw a market while it did. Of course others see it now, but it's probably too late for a would-be competitor to find a foothold. That's sustainable advantage.

Is Intuitive immune to competition? It's possible a canny, committed competitor could enter the field during an upgrade cycle as users replace older da Vinci systems. It's possible that better technology could offer significant improvements over the current robots. But you should think twice before betting against this company.

THE WORLD NEEDS RULE FOLLOWERS, TOO

So are you ready to go out and discover the ultimate growth companies, like Amazon and Intuitive Surgical, that can single-handedly build your $1 million portfolio? Great! But keep in mind that you're going to lose some money somewhere along the way.

Every investor, no matter what style or strategy he or she chooses to pursue, makes mistakes. Everyone. We can make reasonable assumptions and sensible inferences about the future, but we can't predict it with any accuracy. We make bets.

When it comes to growth stocks, your mistakes will cost you. You're buying companies priced with the expectation that tomorrow is going to be a lot better than today. That new technology is going to work, that product is going to reach the market, that demand is going to climb.

If it turns out tomorrow is only a *little bit* better than today, you'll pay. If tomorrow turns out to be *worse* than today, you'll *really* pay. Rule Breakers tend to be volatile because necessarily rough predictions of the future are constantly being reevaluated, amplifying both good news and bad news. You've got to have the stomach for some volatility to invest in Rule Breakers. If the idea that an investment might lose 30% or more of its value in a single day gives you a stomachache, it might be a good idea to skip ahead to the next chapter.

But remember that you should be buying Rule Breakers as part of a portfolio approach. Just consider: If you own equal amounts of ten stocks and one drops 50%, your portfolio goes down 5%. If you own equal amounts of ten stocks and one goes up 500%, your whole portfolio increases in value by 50%. From just one stock. You can apply that logic on whatever scale you like—a concentrated portfolio of just a few stocks or a less-volatile portfolio of 100 stocks. But if you apply the Rule Breakers approach with diligence and patience, you will find stocks that go up 500% and more, as Intuitive Surgical has for us. You will also pick some that go down 90%. We have. Just remember that your Rule Breaker investments are part of a broader approach to wealth creation.

FLYING INTO THE SUN

Rule Breakers, if they succeed, don't remain Rule Breakers forever. It's the rule of Daedalus: You can't keep flying higher and higher without eventually getting burned. Some companies can manage exponential growth when they are just starting out. Even if a newcomer displaces an older industry with a new product or service, that product or service will eventually reach a level of saturation. Some of the greatest Rule Breakers of the past decades are not Rule Breakers any longer. They've been successful enough to mature into a slower, steadier state of growth.

In your hunt for new Rule Breakers, look at the circumstances and strategies that favored the success of past and present Rule Breakers. Similar dynamics surround some of today's fast-growing contenders.

It's Not Too Late to Wake Up and Smell the Coffee

There's a decent chance that you'll be enjoying a cup of Starbucks coffee at some point during your reading of this book.

But when did you *first* hear of the company? Was it when you bought some fresh beans from a tiny storefront in Seattle in the early 1970s? Probably not. Was it in the mid–1980s, when Starbucks first became America's answer to the European coffeehouse, selling espresso drinks from its Pike Place location and giving customers a place to gather and relax? Again, pretty unlikely. Maybe it was in the late 1980s, when Starbucks coffeehouses had spread around the Pacific Northwest. Or when the company went public in 1992, by which time there were 165 stores operating. Perhaps it wasn't until the chain opened its first store in Cincinnati in 1995, by which time there were 676 locations.

Eventually, though, you heard about the chain. No one can blame you for your ignorance of the brand—or for missing the shares at their 1992 debut price of 65 cents (split-adjusted). But by the time Starbucks was starting to expand in Asia in 1996, you could still have gotten shares for between a split-adjusted $2 and $3.

By June of 1998, the brand was so ubiquitous that the humor magazine *The Onion* ran a satirical article headlined "New Starbucks Opens in Rest Room of Existing Starbucks." That same year, Starbucks was both a plot point and a joke in the romantic comedy *You've Got Mail*. It was a secret to no one. Yet you could *still* have grabbed shares for an adjusted $6. That was still a pretty sweet embarkation point for a ride to $40 in late 2006.

Admittedly, few people scored the potential 62-bagger that this company offered between its debut and what is (thus far) its peak price in 2006. But as we sit here today, you could have bought too late and held on too long and still crushed the S&P 500 with a compound annual return of 10.3% from mid–1998 to mid–2008, a period during which the S&P returned a mere 2.7%. This company, really no longer a Rule Breaker, created one of the world's best brands. It used its early Rule Breaker advantages— first-mover and top-dog status—to build itself into an iconic presence. The ubiquity of its stores reinforce the brand. That Starbucks was so *obvious* by 1998 is a good deal of what still made it a great investment.

Online Auctions: Going, Going, Gone!

Monopolies were first outlawed in the U.S. by the Sherman Antitrust Act of 1890. For well over a century, it's been illegal in most circumstances for one company to exercise exclusive or near-exclusive control over an entire market or industry. Monopolies stifle competition and can, among other things, lead to artificially high pricing and low levels of innovation. That's bad for consumers. But monopolies sure can be good for investors.

In fact, there are monopolies in this country. Microsoft, itself a former Rule Breaker, has long held a near-monopoly on computer operating systems. It was tolerated as such until the 1998 case *United States v. Microsoft* declared the company to be an "*abusive* monopoly" [emphasis added]. Following appeal, the company was not forced to break up, and today still holds overwhelming market share in PC operating systems.

Such de facto monopolies form when competitors can't gain an effective foothold against a market leader. And as long as the dominant company doesn't do anything illegal to hinder competition, such monopolies are allowed to exist.

Not all de facto or natural monopolies are Rule Breakers. Utilities, for instance, have such high start-up costs that they generally operate as monopolies in their local regions. And by now you'll probably recognize that most utilities aren't Rule Breakers by a long shot. But outside such capital-intensive situations, successfully creating a de facto monopoly is probably enough to satisfy most of our Rule Breaker criteria. We already discussed how Intuitive Surgical accomplished this feat, but it's not alone. Some businesses are prone to winner-take-all effects.

Consider eBay, the world's largest virtual garage sale. The company operates an online marketplace for almost anything (short of human organs and a few other controversial items). All eBay does is put together buyers with sellers, and facilitate a bidding process that lets transactions take place. That's it. It doesn't carry inventory, it doesn't ship goods, it doesn't take legal responsibility for buyers and sellers living up to their mutual obligations.

In fact, there's nothing innovative about this concept. It's been around for decades in other forms such as newspaper classified ads. What was revolutionary is that eBay took the process online and made it work on a global scale—which has really hurt the newspaper business.

Your local paper probably once had a near monopoly in your community. Even the largest cities only support two major papers at most. That's what made the classified ads work. If you had to list an item for sale in 20 different publications to have a decent chance of success, you'd probably look for an alternative marketing channel. For exactly the same reason, eBay was able to take a visionary idea and a good head start to create an enduring competitive advantage. Sellers sell on eBay because that's where buyers go to shop. They may grumble about the fees eBay charges, but that's where the game is played. Would-be competitors have been singularly unsuccessful at wresting away any sort of meaningful market share from eBay.

Its rule-breaking days are in the rearview mirror for eBay, but its stock offered exceptional returns to investors who got in on the ground floor. Even investors who bought at the very peak of the Internet bubble would still be ahead on their investment if they held shares through today.

Was eBay unique in exploiting the network effect? Not at all. We like to think The Motley Fool, with its critical mass of smart investors engaging in intelligent dialog, offers something of a network effect in the financial world, especially when it comes to the world of CAPS (sorry, you'll have to wait a few chapters to learn more). And there are other companies out there achieving similar leverage. You just need to hunt them down!

Cutting Down the Competition with Lasers

IPG Photonics was founded in 1990 with the mission of becoming a leading manufacturer of lasers. That was a tall order. Lasers have been around since the 1960s, and IPG's aspirations put it up against some venerable competitors, including Coherent, Rofin-Sinar Technologies, Newport, and even defense contractor Lockheed Martin.

But IPG doesn't just make lasers, it makes fiber lasers. Without getting into a lot of technical detail, suffice it to say that older laser technologies rely on special crystals or carbon dioxide gas. Years of technological improvements have created some powerful and precise devices that can do everything from cutting and welding steel to excising small amounts of tissue to correct your vision to determining the sequence and structure of proteins in biomedical research.

Fiber lasers, in contrast to older technologies, consume low amounts of power, don't require special cooling or other special environments, and need far less maintenance. Unfortunately, for many years, they were so low in power that they weren't useful for many applications.

This is where things started to get interesting. Because fiber lasers were of little interest to its competitors, IPG had free reign to innovate, develop, and improve the technology. As it found niche applications for low-powered fiber lasers, the big companies were happy to concede a few unimportant markets. As it found more customers for its not-quite-so low-powered fiber lasers, the larger players still didn't see a significant threat.

By the time IPG went public in late 2006, it had nearly three-quarters of the worldwide market for fiber lasers. More importantly, fiber lasers were beginning to dominate the field of materials processing—that is, the use of high-powered lasers for cutting, drilling, welding, and etching that had been the mainstay of the older companies.

IPG is still a young company, and we don't know how the story will end. Its competitors have all belatedly embraced fiber lasers and are fighting back. But IPG has a serious head start in patents, expertise, reputation, recognition, and infrastructure, all of which will prove tough obstacles for its rivals.

Bursting Blockbuster's Bubble

Many of you probably receive little red envelopes from Netflix. If you're a fan of movies or just about anything else recorded onto DVD, there's a good chance you appreciate the convenience of having your latest selections mailed to your home for a modest monthly fee, with almost unlimited choices and no worries about late fees.

Netflix started with a rule-breaking vision and executed on it almost flawlessly. Despite its imitators, it has benefited from its first-mover and top-dog status, not to mention its excellent management and its keen focus on customer satisfaction.

But Netflix has also benefited from something else: Its most significant competitors proved unable to mount any kind of coherent defense against its steady pull of market share. In many ways, Blockbuster embodies the idea of the inept competitor spelled out in our Rule Breaker criteria. But let's take a little pity on the company—it was put in a tough place.

The advent of the DVD changed Blockbuster's business. Blockbuster dealt in VHS tapes—a bulky, fragile, and relatively expensive medium not readily suited to a mail-order business. DVDs, on the other hand, are light, durable, inexpensive to replace, and easily mailed in flat envelopes for a low bulk rate. These differences, perhaps subtle at first blush, made Netflix possible. They also spelled Blockbuster's (near) doom. Block-buster management was slow to adapt to DVDs, and once they did, they treated them as just another medium to stock on the shelves. This slow reaction doesn't reflect well on Blockbuster's management, but there were also powerful forces at work that made it difficult for the company to counter its new competitor effectively.

If management had been incredibly nimble and armed with bold and accurate foresight, Blockbuster would have begun shut-tering many of its more than 5,000 retail locations back in 2002 when Netflix was heating up and Blockbuster stock was at an all-time high . . . and Blockbuster shareholders would have stormed the headquarters in protest. Perhaps if Blockbuster had tran-sitioned its business model and executed on the plan well, it might have been able to use its high-profile brand to prevent Netflix from dominating mail-order movie delivery.

But realistically this wasn't going to happen.

For one thing, Blockbuster still does a lot of business through its retail outlets and brings in more than four times the annual revenue of Netflix. Getting rid of the stores wouldn't have made sense (and that about a fifth of them are operated by franchisees would have further complicated the matter). On the other hand, keeping them meant continuing to support expenses that Netflix, operating out of centralized warehouses with relatively few em-ployees, simply doesn't have. Between 1996 and 2007, Blockbuster reported only two profitable years. Netflix has been profitable every year since 2003.

Blockbuster was stuck with an inferior business model. Chang-ing it to compete head-to-head with Netflix would have been tantamount to liquidating and starting all over, an option that management would not have seriously considered, and that shareholders would not have accepted. Netflix has a structural advantage in its business, which led us to recommend the stock in *Stock Advisor* back in 2004. Since then, Netflix has risen 96% while Blockbuster has fallen 68%.

A RULE BREAKER GONE WRONG

As we noted, checking off companies against our Rule Breaker criteria, and the deeper diligence that should follow that first step, doesn't always guarantee success. We were handed a big loss in our Rule Breakers portfolio by a company that seemed to be a sure thing.

Force Protection essentially invented mine-resistant, ambush-protected vehicles, known more commonly as MRAPs (pronounced EM-raps). The realities of modern urban warfare with roadside bombs, improvised explosive devices, suicide attacks, ambushes, and rocket-propelled grenade attacks created a whole new battlefield paradigm. Early in the Iraq War, soldiers in traditional Humvees suffered a terrible death and injury toll from such attacks. Even when heavily armored, these older vehicles often couldn't survive.

Force Protection created an innovative V-shaped vehicle hull that deflected blasts from mines and other explosives outward, protecting the vehicle and its occupants. In early use, these vehicles amassed an almost perfect safety record. All of a sudden, the military was awarding billions of dollars in contracts for MRAPs, and talking about replacing its entire fleet of Humvees. Force Protection was the top dog and first mover, and there was no question that this was an important market. In early contracts, the military appeared to favor Force Protection's vehicles over those of its relatively few rivals. Sales exploded—almost 20-fold in two years—and so did the stock.

Moving down our checklist, we also believed the military would gravitate toward only one or two models of MRAP, not wanting to complicate the parts and maintenance issue that would come with multiple manufacturers. Force Protection, the innovator and seemingly favored vendor, looked like it would win the bulk of the contracts. There was our sustainable advantage.

When the military awarded the bulk of a large contract to

Navistar, a company that had actually been delisted from the New York Stock Exchange because of persistent problems with its financial bookkeeping, we were surprised. But we reasoned that the government was still in exploratory mode, testing out different models in real-world applications.

But contracts kept going out to Force Protection's rivals. It turned out that the company's size worked against it. It was able to grow rapidly because it was starting from a much smaller base than the major defense contractors, but the military was worried the company wouldn't be able to keep up with the production demands that went with the large contracts. Force Protection forged manufacturing partnerships with BAE Systems and General Dynamics to keep up with demand—cutting out much of its profit margin in the process—even as the military increasingly seemed to favor other models. Worse yet, the company made a large investment in its own manufacturing capacity just in time to see demand for the vehicles start to slacken, and the bulk of contracts to go elsewhere.

Force Protection is still in business, and is winning some government contracts for certain vehicles. But it did not offer the growth prospects we originally expected. When we sold the stock, it had lost about 90% of its value.

It was painful to our wallets, but that 90% loss bought us some valuable lessons. Force Protection wasn't prepared for the demand it created with its innovative product, pushing its customers to larger, better-capitalized competitors. At the same time, it relied on too few customers, where just one decision-maker could dramatically affect its business. Though it was the innovator, it had no real protection against better-heeled imitators that moved in on an obvious opportunity.

Of course, we knew there were risks when we made the investment. Force Protection's shortcomings look clear in hindsight, but we also considered most of them upfront. The company offered a set of risks in which we thought the odds favored success. It turns out they didn't. That happens sometimes. There's a lot to learn from Force Protection, but one of the most important things to remember is that you will always make some mistakes as an investor. The upside is that even against such losses—such expensive, dramatic losses—a few winners will tilt your portfolio heavily into the black.

THE PIECE OF YOUR PORTFOLIO

Even the most committed, risk-loving, growth-craving Fool would be loath to suggest that you put your entire savings into Rule Breakers. While the right stock could catapult your net worth into the stratosphere, you'd be taking on far too much risk of steep, potentially unrecoverable loss. Even with a successful set of Rule Breaker stocks, the inevitable volatility alone would probably turn you into an insomniac.

But we feel that Rule Breakers should make up a portion of your stock portfolio. We've got no hard and fast rule as to the exact proportion, except for the general rule of thumb that your risk exposure should generally decline as your age advances and retirement draws nearer.

We also think most investors should own a Rule Breaker or three *no matter what their age.* They can be tremendous fun, and the right investment can make a real difference to a portfolio. When a world-changing company comes along, and you're smart enough and lucky enough to recognize it, you should grab it. Believe us, the company doesn't know how old you are or what your risk profile is.

And consider this: Bell curves, that favorite tool of statisticians, don't describe most of reality. They work fine for some things. Take height, for example. Most people are between about 5 foot 4 inches and 6 feet 2 inches. The number of people shorter or taller than this decreases at an accelerating pace as you retreat from the statistical norm. You'll never find somebody two inches tall or 30 feet tall. It's not physically possible.

But bell curves fall short (no pun intended) when measuring, say, wealth. After all, how much wealth can a person have? Not less than zero, certainly (assuming we're not counting debt as negative wealth). But what's the upper limit? When it comes to earning power, you *can* be 30 feet tall.

When you invest in Rule Breakers, you can lose money. But unless you're engaged in short selling or an aggressive derivative strategy, you can't lose any more than 100% of your investment. That's the total downside.

How much can you gain? We've talked about companies that have increased 10, 20, 60 times in value over relatively short periods. There's no upward constraint here, just as there are no limits on creativity and innovation. Rule Breaker investing is an expression of that aspiration.

So here's to being 30 feet tall.

Motley Fool Analyst Karl Thiel contributed to this chapter. A key part of both the Stock Advisor *and* Rule Breakers *newsletter teams, Karl enjoys running with scissors, swimming after eating, and wearing white after Labor Day.*

Visit us at mdpbook.com for the Rule Breaker *team's best growth stock pick.*

CHAPTER 8

WE ARE THE WORLD

In our first book, *The Motley Fool Investment Guide*, we made the point that one can do just fine in this life never looking beyond the shores of the United States for investments. After all, the American economy is the largest, most diverse on earth; the American legal and regulatory regimes offer the most protection for minority shareholders; and the U.S. market is less prone to wild swings than most foreign markets.

We still believe this to be true—we think it would be small-*f* foolish to think that one cannot find fortune among American companies. But we also believe that our previous view was incomplete. There are opportunities among the 36,000 public companies based beyond our borders that dwarf those of the 18,000 public companies based in the United States. So while you need not ever invest a dime overseas, we have updated our previous view—a steadfast refusal to consider international companies makes about as much sense today as investing only in companies with two syllables in their names. Aiding us tremendously in our understanding of and enthusiasm for these incredible opportunities is

Bill Mann, one of our top investors at The Motley Fool and the founding advisor of our *Global Gains* international investing service.

Many overseas markets, including the growing monsters of China and India, have improved their regulatory oversight by leaps and bounds. There are markets with all the legal framework of 19th-century Deadwood, to be sure. Those tend to be obvious. No one today would confuse the Zimbabwe Stock Exchange with the London Stock Exchange, for example.

Besides, the increasing globalization of markets, and the explosion in individual company cross-listings and exchange-traded funds (ETFs), have made buying foreign shares easier than ever before. In fact, international investing can be as easy as picking a foreign country and buying an index fund based on the performance of its market. Malaysia? Check. Brazil? Check. Japanese small caps? Check. European bonds? You get the idea.

Of course, the trouble with international investing is that we can generally only be in one place at once. It is challenging to tell, for example, what the feeling is on the streets of Jakarta, unless you happen to be on the streets of Jakarta. To buy foreign equities, you have to understand some additional considerations and challenges. In the six months after October 2007, the Shanghai Composite Index lost nearly 50% of its value, wiping away $2 *trillion* in wealth for investors. This wasn't supposed to happen— the ascendancy of China is considered inevitable. Did this drop portend cracks in the China thesis or a once-in-a-lifetime opportunity? Only investors extremely familiar with the Chinese economy had a hope of knowing the right answer. Point being, an investing thesis constructed on a skin-deep understanding of a country is likely to end with a suboptimal outcome. And we try to avoid suboptimal outcomes.

A FOREIGN STOCK JUNKIE

Bill Mann was in Mongolia in the summer of 2007 visiting a company with enormous mining concessions—"metal veins the size of boxcars." As Bill tells the story, his host took him on a whirlwind visit of Ulan Bator, the Mongolian capital, and stood before him in the center of Sukhbataar Square describing his company's prospects. Bill learned a few things that day. He learned, for instance, that he should stand in the same direction as his companions, even while having a conversation, to keep the damage from windborne sand to a minimum. He also learned that the company had an agreement before the Mongolian congress that it hoped would be ratified before *Naadam*, the Mongolian festival that marked the end of the legislative session (after which most Mongolians would live in the steppe for the next few months). He learned that Mongolia was blessed with mineral wealth, but that Mongolians' connection to the Gobi Desert was so strong that they were willing to leave that wealth in the ground rather than put the Gobi at risk of destruction.

As he stood there, in the middle of the main square of a nation where even legislators are semi-nomadic, talking to a representative of a company that hoped to convince them to let it dredge up a corner of their precious land, it hit him. "Wow," Bill thought, "this right here is pretty foreign to me."

BUYING THE WORLD

Foreign investing is not just a means of diversification—although diversification is the chief allure for many U.S. investors. Spread your bets across industries, countries, and market caps, the reasoning goes, and you're less susceptible to a huge hit if one of those bets goes bust.

We Fools believe in diversification—revisit any previous or future chapter for a refresher—but it's *not* the reason to own foreign stocks. The one and only purpose to invest in companies based outside the United States is far less complicated: the opportunities beyond our borders are too good to pass up. You want your long-term savings tied to the best companies with the best prospects. If those companies all existed in Rhode Island, then so be it. But they don't.

With no offense to the many publicly traded Little Rhody-based businesses (all 32 of them), you'd miss out on many great stocks by imposing an arbitrary geographical limitation on your investments.

In fact, even if you view it as a simple math problem, it's unlikely that the best investments are all going to be American. Only a third of the world's publicly traded companies are in the United States. If you focus exclusively on American companies, it's the equivalent of refusing to consider any company that comes after *J* in the alphabet.

"Ah," you say, "but the United States is the most developed economy in the world. Foreign companies are riskier, right?" Well, not so fast. Where the U.S. market once dwarfed all others in size, today American public companies make up little more than 32% of total world market capitalization, and this percentage is decreasing—rapidly.

A look at the top 20 stock exchanges by market cap is illustrative:

NAME AND RANK	MARKET CAPITALIZATION (IN TRILLIONS OF U.S. DOLLARS)
1. New York SE	$14.2
2. Tokyo SE	$4.0
3. Euronext[1]	$3.9
4. Nasdaq	$3.5
5. London SE	$3.4
6. Shanghai SE	$2.6
7. Hong Kong SE	$2.2
8. Deustche Börse	$1.9

continued

NAME AND RANK	MARKET CAPITALIZATION (IN TRILLIONS OF U.S. DOLLARS)
9. TSX Group (Toronto)	$1.9
10. BME Spanish Exchanges	$1.7
11. Bombay SE	$1.5
12. São Paulo SE	$1.3
13. Swiss Exchange	$1.2
14. National Stock Exchange of India	$1.2
15. OMX Nordic Exchange[2]	$1.2
16. Australian SE	$1.1
17. Korea Exchange	$0.96
18. Borsa Italiana	$0.95
19. Taiwan SE	$0.72
20. Johannesburg SE	$0.71
Total Global Stock Market Value	$55.6

Data as of March 2008. Source: World Federation of Exchanges.
1. The Euronext is the combined exchanges of Paris, Amsterdam, Lisbon, and Brussels.
2. OMX consists of the exchanges of Copenhagen, Helsinki, Reykjavik, Stockholm, Tallinn, Riga, and Vilnius.

Things that have "always been true" just no longer are. We would never talk down the U.S. economy and its stock market—in the long term, an investor who believes she will be more comfortable keeping her money in companies only headquartered in the United States has the potential to do quite well. But both demographic and economic trends point to much greater opportunity beyond our shores. Again, this is a math problem. The United States represents 5% of the population of the world and 21% of its gross product. We have had our day as the greatest growth economy in the world. In 2007, the U.S. economy grew at a rate of 2.2%. Azerbaijan's economy grew 23%. Are you going to invest in Azerbaijan? Pretty unlikely. After all, Azerbaijan today is a fairly unstable, underdeveloped country with high levels of corruption and dependence upon a single commodity—oil. But what about any one of the following, all of which outpaced the U.S. economy?

COUNTRY	REAL GDP GROWTH RATE, 2007
China	11.4%
India	9.2%
Argentina	8.7%
Vietnam	8.5%
Singapore	7.7%
United Arab Emirates	7.4%
Poland	6.5%
Czech Republic	6.5%
Indonesia	6.3%
Hong Kong	6.3%
Taiwan	5.7%
Brazil	5.4%
Israel	5.3%
Chile	5.0%
South Korea	5.0%
Spain	3.8%
Norway	3.5%
Canada	2.7%
Sweden	2.6%
United States	**2.2%**

Source: CIA World Factbook.

These GDP figures are not, by the way, adjusted for currency fluctuations. In 2007 the U.S. dollar declined against nearly every global currency that wasn't somehow pegged to it. Those outperforming the sawbuck included the murderer's row of the Honduran lempira, the Mauritanian ouguiya, the Nepalese rupee, and the Mozambique metical. In other words, when measured in dollars, most of these economies grew even faster when compared to that of the United States.

THERE IS ALMOST NO DIFFERENCE BETWEEN INTERNATIONAL AND DOMESTIC STOCKS

So if you're thinking about sticking to domestic stocks, you're eliminating the majority of companies in the world, and moreover you're turning your back on thousands of companies benefiting from economic tailwinds no longer blowing in the United States. If you could go back to 1980 and invest in the United States when the Dow stood at 1,000, would you? Today, that kind of economic growth is standing directly before you in countries like China, India, Vietnam, and even Colombia.

This chapter is a little bit different from any of the others in this book. International investing isn't a single strategy, much as some asset-allocation specialists like to claim that it is. What is the right level of allocation to foreign stocks? 10%? 20%? 70%? To us it's a crazy question. After all, giant European pharmaceutical companies have nothing in common with Chinese startups or South African mining companies. And just the same, what's the difference between owning a California-based networking company like Cisco Systems and one from Finland, like Nokia? And what of Aflac, which is based in Columbus, Georgia, but does 70% of its business in Japan? Is it more or less "international" than India-based Infosys, which does more than 60% of its business in North America?

Our approach at *Global Gains* is the same as the Fool's overall approach to stock-picking: we're bottoms-up, business-focused investors. The key difference is not the *how*, it's the *where*. Our approach encompasses small caps and fast-growers and dividend payers and value stocks. It's just that we disregard borders in our search because there is almost no difference between international and domestic stocks.

This ought to be somewhat obvious. Just like domestic companies, foreign companies—generally speaking—seek to reward their investors by generating profits. Even if these profits are denominated in dong, gourds, or escudos, they're still profits, and they can be converted to dollars. The scorecard for foreign stocks isn't based on kittens, buildings, or ennui. It's based on their ability to turn profits.

WHY GLOBAL GAINS INVESTING WORKS

Economies around the world are growing quickly. As illustrated in the table above, China's economy (measured by GDP) grew 11.4% in 2007. The U.S. economy will *never* again reach those levels—it's just too big and too developed.

Those economies resemble the trajectory America was on decades ago—and *that's* why international investing works. The Chinese economy, for instance, looks a lot like the U.S. economy . . . of the early 1900s. Industrialization is propelling China much like it did on our home soil, bringing plenty of growing pains along with it. One example can be seen through the efforts of China Fire & Security, a company helping China write, develop, and implement national fire codes in industrial buildings. These are the sorts of safety regulations we take for granted in the United States, but in China their absence poses a clear threat—and the company is booming.

It's not an exaggeration to say that foreign investing is a "time machine" for U.S. investors. We have an opportunity to examine mature industries domestically and find those same industries in their high-growth phases elsewhere. Think back to when Bank of America began consolidating the banking industry many years ago, and then look at HDFC Bank, which is doing the same thing in its home country of India. Think back to the online auction industry that eBay created out of thin air, and then consider that MercadoLibre is doing those same things in Latin America . . . a decade later.

THE 0%/100% RULE

Diversification, while important, is not the goal of investing. To the extent it can help you make money—and prevent you from losing it—it's a worthy endeavor. But in the end, you want 100% of your money invested in companies that don't suck, and 0% in companies that do—and that's regardless of whether a company is headquartered in Paris, France, or Paris, Texas. Do not make the common mistake of lumping "international" together with "consumer staples" or "energy" or other diversifiable sectors. That's crazy, especially when you consider that foreign markets in aggregate exceed the size of all U.S. stocks. Is "crazy" a bit harsh? Let's look at two stocks in this would-be "industry."

America Movil provides wireless and fixed communications services. It is a $90 billion company headquartered in Mexico City, and it generates most of its revenues in Latin America. Teva Pharmaceutical, a generic drug maker founded more than a century ago in Israel, has a market value of $35 billion and does most of its sales in Europe and North America.

Now, would you consider America Movil and Teva Pharmaceutical to be part of the same "sector"? They aren't located in the same country—or continent for that matter. They don't compete in the same industry. They denominate earnings in different currencies (pesos and shekels, respectively). They draw on different labor pools, and they do not rely on the same supplies or commodities. The only reason they'd belong to the same sector is that they're (1) for-profit entities that (2) are not based in the United States.

So *Global Gains* investing is not about exposure to a particular sector or style. It's about opening up all the doors available for our portfolio. And that's why it works—it broadens frontiers.

THE ENVELOPE, PLEASE

Let's briefly look at a few markets worldwide—what they did for investors in 2007 as well as how they performed on a five-year annualized basis.

MARKET	2007 RETURN	FIVE-YEAR ANNUALIZED RETURNS*
Australia	28.3%	28.5%
Brazil	74.8%	59.8%
Canada	28.4%	27.2%
China (FTSE/Xinhua 25 index)	54.8%	N/A
France	12.1%	20.3%
Germany	33.7%	26.5%
Japan	(5.5%)	15.6%
Malaysia	44.6%	22.0%
Mexico	11.3%	37.1%
South Africa	15.5%	N/A
South Korea	31.7%	28.5%
Spain	20.9%	27.0%
United Kingdom	6.5%	16.1%
United States (S&P 500)	**5.2%**	**10.5%**

Data from Morningstar. *Through May 2008.

The U.S. market was outdone—by a significant margin—by almost every market in 2007, which was an OK year domestically, based on historical standards. While we did cherry-pick the examples in the above table, we did so only for the sake of brevity. Had we included every market in the world, the results would have looked much the same. The MSCI EAFE index of foreign stocks, for example, returned 8.6% in 2007 and averaged 18.8% gains over the past five years—that's an index tilted toward mega-caps in developed countries, beating the pants off the U.S.

Early in 2008, *The Wall Street Journal* ran a fascinating story of "The Lost Decade" of stock returns. The data showed that from March 1999 to March 2008, U.S. stock market returns were up only slightly on an annualized basis—well behind the returns bonds and Treasury Inflation-Protected Securities (TIPS) offered. D'oh. Over that same period, though, the *best-performing* "sector" was the stocks in emerging markets, which averaged annual returns of more than 18%.

Plenty of U.S. investors rode the coattails of those markets. Pull up five-year charts for PetroChina, China Mobile, Potash, Petrobras, Cemex, Baidu.com—we could go on and on—and you'll likely see stock returns that dominated any competitor from our home soil.

DOLLARS OR DINARS?

When the subprime mortgage mess first began to spread through financial institutions, ultimately resulting in what was poetically called a "credit crunch," the Federal Reserve aggressively lowered interest rates to spur lending. This didn't help the U.S. dollar, which declined in value versus just about every foreign currency in 2007 (except those pegged to our greenbacks). While a weak dollar might make you rethink that vacation to Bavaria, it makes a good case for owning international stocks.

If your paycheck is denominated in dollars, it's a good bet that almost all your currency exposure is to U.S. dollars. That makes a lot of sense—if you live in the States and try to pay for a latte in loonies, you'll be laughed at (even if the loonie is worth more than the dollar). Nevertheless, you're missing a big opportunity. Over the past five years, as the dollar has declined in value, Americans who have invested heavily in overseas companies have seen a powerful diversification (there's that word again) benefit—because earnings denominated in pounds, euros, rupees, dinars, and, yes, loonies, are worth more for folks investing in dollars.

If you're worried about the future of the buck, you don't need to research foreign exchange derivatives or such bets. The easier move is to buy solid companies that produce growing cash flows in stronger currencies. As they churn out more cash, that cash will become more valuable in dollar terms—effectively giving you two ways to grow your savings.

Let's look at Canadian coffee and donut chain Tim Hortons. During a three-month run-up in late 2007, the company's shares on the Toronto exchange jumped from CAD$28 to CAD$34.59, a respectable 24% gain. Meanwhile, over the exact same period, Tim Hortons shares on the New York Stock Exchange went from $25 to $34.14, a 36% jump. The sliding dollar made the difference.

Now let's dig a little deeper into a foreign stock case study.

BUILDING AN INTERNATIONAL FOUNDATION

Cemex is a dynamic Mexico-based multinational cement company we first recommended five years ago. It has tripled since then. Cemex is the real deal. In fact, we are still big fans of this three-bagger, although the investment thesis today is a bit different from when we originally singled it out.

Cemex was founded in 1906 and dominates its home market of Mexico. Though its largest markets are Mexico and the United States, the company operates in more than 50 countries. The sheer size of its footprint means it is less tied to the construction industry of any single country.

Over the course of the 20th century, Cemex transformed itself from a domestic near-monopoly into an international power-house. The company went public in the mid–1980s, but only in the 1990s did it branch out of Mexico. What Cemex actually does is not difficult to understand—although it may be difficult to stay awake for. The company produces, markets, and distributes cement, ready-to-mix concrete, and aggregates. A lot of it. All over the world.

When we first recommended the stock, we saw several very attractive things:

- The management team, led by Lorenzo Zambrano, was transparent, fiscally conservative, adept at managing risk, and respectful to minority shareholders.
- The company was secure within its industry. It dominated its home market and had a substantial foothold in Spain and the United States. It was also branching off into emerging economies around the world. Such an international reach meant that the company could be somewhat protected from slowdowns in one country or region.
- Part of Cemex's strategy at the time was growth-by-acquisition, which meant it carried a heavy debt load. All things being equal, a company that grows by acquisitions is riskier than a company that grows organically, so this would have been a red flag, if not for the superb talents of the management team.
- Also, the company had several weak quarters leading up to our recommendation, which reflected not poor operations but poor economic conditions in its larger markets. Nevertheless, the market didn't think much of Cemex—it carried a price-to-earnings ratio of 8—in spite of its superior free cash flow margins and more than 2% dividend yield.

Cement is *sort of* a commodity business—"sort of" because cement is much more asset-intensive than just about any other commodity. There are steep costs to develop a cement plant, and because cement doesn't travel well, it's not cost-effective to transport or ship cement from a large plant to a job site thousands of miles away. In developing countries—which made up 60% of Cemex's revenues when we recommended it—poor infrastructure poses problems for moving a time-sensitive material like cement. Cemex had production facilities in 16 countries, but because those facilities had access to the sea and the company's own shipping fleet, it sold concrete in more than 30 countries.

Having successfully conquered its home market—a developing market, no less—Cemex began applying those practices to new markets. The company put the then-nascent technology of global positioning systems (GPS) in its mixing trucks, turning cement deliveries from a "when we get there . . . perhaps next week" scenario down to 30-minute windows of time. Cemex also reached out to distributors in Mexico who sat between the manufacturer and the end customer. In an outreach program called Construrama, it gave those distributors cost reductions, IT sharing, and branding benefits in exchange for the exclusive marketing of Cemex products. In barely a year, Construrama created an additional 2,000 points of sale. These initiatives were good for customers and shareholders.alike. They afforded Cemex remarkable brand strength in a not-quite commodity business.

It was easy to like the company back then. Competitive advantages? Check. It had a strong brand, superior leadership, and the ability to acquire competitors (and then digest those acquired companies without a hiccup). Superior leadership? Check. Zambrano had been on the job a decade and a half; Cemex had some of the best corporate governance practices we'd seen in *any* company, regardless of nationality. Growth catalysts? Check. It was positioning itself in the emerging markets while not losing focus in the more developed markets it already dominated. Reasonable valuation? Check. It sold for only eight times earnings. Since then, Cemex has been a three-bagger.

FEAR OF FLYING

Yet how many times have you heard a Mexican cement company being hyped at a cocktail party? Exactly. That may be because of a subconscious—perhaps even a natural—reason many U.S. investors don't care for international investing. It's called home equity bias and, according to Professor Jeremy Siegel's *The Future for Investors*, "Recent data show that U.S. investors, both professional and individual, hold only 14% of their stocks in non-U.S.-based companies, less than one-third of the indexed proportion."

International investing may frighten more than just the xeno-phobes. There are added layers of due diligence that create more work for you—keeping up with not only the minutiae of compa-nies, but entire countries. We do this every day in *Global Gains*. For example, early in 2008, Venezuelan President Hugo Chavez decided to nationalize the domestic cement industry. Cemex gen-erated 2% of its revenues from operations in Venezuela but had no say in the decision. For U.S.-based Cemex shareholders, it was a reminder of the sometimes Wild West nature of operating in emerging (or frontier) economies.

But you should be up for *Global Gains* investing anyway. You are likely familiar with some of the other companies affected by Chavez's nationalization plans: American oil concerns Exxon-Mobil and ConocoPhillips, to take two examples.

"Foreign" events don't just affect "foreign" companies. Exxon and Conoco both do significant business outside the U.S. As I mentioned earlier, Georgia-based Aflac—originally the Ameri-can Family Life Assurance Company of Columbus—does 70% of its business in Japan! Heck, iconic American brands McDonald's and Coca-Cola actually generate more than 65% of their revenue outside the United States. If you hold these "U.S." companies, you already have a lot of exposure to the idiosyncrasies of inter-national investing.

That's not to suggest that owning foreign stocks is no differ-ent from owning American stocks. There is almost no difference, but there is a difference.

LET'S FOCUS ON THAT MAGICAL WORD "ALMOST"

Almost no difference, is, of course, not the same thing as *no dif-ference*. There are, in fact, differences between foreign compa-nies and American ones. Some of these matter, some not so much. But it's good to be aware of them all.

1. An ADR (American Depositary Receipt) is not common stock.
2. Foreign companies use different accounting methods.
3. Foreign companies have different shareholder laws and practices.
4. You may have little recourse if something goes really wrong.
5. Your dividends are taxed immediately, and some foreign countries have been known to jack up their taxes on foreign shareholders.
6. Some of the companies you can invest in sell absolutely no products or services in the United States.
7. Your risk of having the company delist is somewhat elevated.
8. You have currency risks.
9. Many countries have stock markets that are substantially more volatile than that of the United States, and as such your shares might rise and fall much more quickly than a comparable company's would in the U.S.

Most of the concerns on this list are not huge deals. OK, they tax dividends—so does the U.S. Investors might not be well represented in case of a problem. Well, how many gigantic checks have the folks who owned shares of Enron received? We've just listed some of the problems and differences with foreign companies. On the flip side, we offer the following:

1. China currently has 24 cities larger than Chicago, and due to internal migration must build infrastructure to handle a population the size of Houston *every month*.
2. India, one of the world's poorest countries in 1980, has a middle class equal in size to the population of the United States—and its members are rapidly increasing their level of consumption.
3. Argentina has some of the most fertile farmland in the world, valued at a tiny fraction of what the comparable land would cost in Iowa.

4. Some regulations and practices in the United States, compare quite poorly to many foreign markets. The gross overpayment of executives and "heads I win, tails you lose" mentality so pervasive in American executive suites is generally nonexistent overseas. Certain countries, like Mexico, are extremely protective of their biggest private companies, which benefits shareholders.

5. The expansion of the European Union has caused a rapid development in the economies of Eastern European countries, which have a combined population equal to that of the United States.

6. In 2007, only one major emerging market index underperformed the S&P 500: Chile. This massive, wide-ranging outperformance took place in spite of the existence of all of the risk factors enumerated above.

7. Regardless of the problems and challenges of owning foreign securities, most foreign markets are growing faster than the United States—and will generally continue to do so. While stock market performance and economic growth don't perfectly correlate, over the long term there will be more wealth created in markets that grow the fastest.

8. These are huge opportunities, but it's hard to get at them if you only focus on U.S. companies for fear of the foreign. The key is making good decisions.

DIGGING IN AROUND THE GLOBE

If you've never owned a foreign stock before, let's get started on setting up your foreign stock brokerage account. Are you ready?

Step 1: Log onto your existing brokerage account.
Step 2: You're done. Go make a sandwich or something.

Your domestic brokerage is perfectly capable of handling trades in shares of hundreds, if not thousands, of foreign securities. We live in a country with the largest base of investors in the world. So instead of having to set up brokerage accounts in a number of countries, you can buy many foreign companies right here. There are approximately 850 foreign companies listed on the three major U.S. exchanges, plus another 5,000 listed on the over-the-counter and Pink Sheets exchanges. Every company in the first group can be bought exactly the same way you'd buy an American stock. If you type in GE, you buy shares of General Electric. If you type in E, you buy shares of Italian oil exploration giant Eni.

Almost all foreign companies trading in the United States have their primary stock market listing in their home countries. Even though the majority of Finnish wireless communications giant Nokia's trading volume takes place on its secondary listing on the New York Stock Exchange, its primary listing is in Helsinki. This leads to an interesting phenomenon: Whereas there is no company on the S&P 500 that constitutes more than 4% of the total value, Nokia's market capitalization represents more than 60% of the value of the Helsinki Stock Exchange. As goes Nokia, so goes Finland.

It's only been in the past two decades that cross-listings have become popular. For the most part, the primary beneficiary is the company, not you. By listing shares in the United States, they access cheap, copious capital. That we get to trade in these shares is but a by-product, but that's the reason a thousand companies have secondary listings in America, and why no companies have secondary listings in Albania.

Some companies, particularly those from China, Bermuda, and Israel, do not bother listing on their home exchanges. A Chinese citizen could not, for example, buy shares of New Oriental Education & Technology, a Beijing-based company, on the Shanghai or Shenzhen Stock Exchanges. Its sole listing is on the NYSE, so if you buy shares of New Oriental, you're not buying ADRs of a Chinese company, you're buying stock. What's the difference? Ultimately, almost nothing.

Finally, the companies on the Pink Sheets and the OTC exchange are much more of a mixed bag. They tend to have much lower trading volumes, and some brokerages are better at getting shares than others. Furthermore, while you'll receive an annual report and have voting rights with companies that trade on the major exchanges, the OTC and Pink Sheet foreign companies have lower reporting standards for American shareholders.

HOW TO APPROACH INTERNATIONAL STOCKS

You know everything you've learned so far about stock investing? Yeah, those are the same basic principles for foreign stock investing. The game hasn't changed—it just has a few more boxes you need to check off.

What you *don't* need to pay much attention to is the size of the country, the richness of its natural resources, or how awesome a time your nephew Ronny had when he visited over fall break.

Of course, and at the risk of sounding like a broken record, there are foreign elements to foreign investing. "Country risk" is a catch-all way to measure the goings-on of a particular country. What's the political environment? Is corruption a problem? How is the country's debt structured? What are its plans for economic development?

A subset of country risk is political risk. For instance, is there a real threat of nationalization, rebellion, or military action?

The last risk unique to foreign investments is currency risk. Zimbabwe's insane inflation rate—it hit 66,000% in the early months of 2008—may be extreme, but it's a helpful reminder to pay attention to the level of exposure a company has to weak currencies.

These risks shouldn't supersede the other risks you're examining—the existence of competitive advantages, suspicious management, or an outrageously high valuation—but you need to add them to your due diligence process.

And finally, and this might seem obvious, you should make sure that you can actually buy shares of a company before you get down to the business of analysis. When we created the Awesome International Portfolio Featuring 30 Awesome International Companies and Please Pay Special Attention to the Awesome Diversification (AIPFTAICAPPSATTAD), which you'll encounter on the next page, we selected 30 companies listed on the major U.S. exchanges. A fabulous study of Qatar Telecom does you no good unless you have access to one of the exchanges it trades on.

So to boil this down, *Global Gains* looks for countries with:

1. Respect for rule of law, strong rights of appeal, and low levels of corruption
2. Political stability and a government that doesn't dominate the local economy
3. A stable currency
4. Investability

THE PIECE OF YOUR PORTFOLIO

When it comes down to it, international versus domestic is almost a difference without distinction. It would not be hard to construct a balanced portfolio entirely out of international companies. It would be scarcely more of a challenge to do so only with companies domiciled in emerging markets. In other words, a targeted percentage allocation to international stocks in a portfolio is nonsensical. Some investors would be perfectly comfortable having 100% of their portfolio in international companies.

Did You Get a Little Nervous Just Then?

Look, while we stand by the 0%/100% rule, proper allocation is always an important consideration. In *The Future for Investors*, Professor Siegel found that a balanced portfolio that included a hefty dose of foreign stocks increased returns while decreasing risk. Sounds pretty good, doesn't it? Professor Siegel recommends a 40% allocation to foreign stocks, via broad-market foreign index funds. Even this conclusion is "aggressive," according to the standards of many money managers. (How 40% can be aggressive when foreign stocks in aggregate outnumber U.S. stocks is anybody's guess.)

While the 40% rule makes sense for passive investors who have little interest in rolling up their sleeves (or just wearing T-shirts) and digging for stocks, *Global Gains* investing is all about *outperforming* the indexes. It's about a bottoms-up search for the best companies with the brightest prospects. So, for example, we wouldn't recommend an 18.4% stake in companies domiciled in northwestern Europe. Because when building, refining, or rebalancing your overall portfolio, your top priority is to invest in your best ideas—ignoring country, sector, or number of vowels in the ticker. Your secondary concern should be ensuring that you're not overexposed to any specific geographic region or industry sector.

Investing only outside the United States, you could achieve a level of diversification at least as meaningful as one that was 30% domestic, 60% domestic, or 100% domestic. Further, you could do it by only focusing on the international companies trading on the major U.S. exchanges. If you did an analysis of the following companies, bought in equal size, you'd have a list of companies diverse in every way except one: 0% of these companies suck.

THE AWESOME LIST OF 30 AWESOME INTERNATIONAL COMPANIES AND PLEASE PAY SPECIAL ATTENTION TO THE AWESOME DIVERSIFICATION

COMPANY & TICKER	INDUSTRY	MARKET CAP	COUNTRY
New Oriental Education (EDU)	Education	$2.3 billion	China
Veolia (VE)	Infrastructure	$25 billion	France
Lihir Gold (LIHR)	Metals & Mining	$5.5 billion	Papua New Guinea

continued

COMPANY & TICKER	INDUSTRY	MARKET CAP	COUNTRY
Banco Itau (ITU)	Banking	$58 billion	Brazil
HDFC Bank (HDB)	Banking	$10 billion	India
Toyota Motor Company (TM)	Automobiles	$147 billion	Japan
Sanofi Aventis (SNY)	Pharmaceuticals	$95 billion	France
Cresud (CRESY)	Agriculture	$670 million	Argentina
Turkcell (TKC)	Telecommunications	$13.5 billion	Turkey
Sasol (SSL)	Energy	$35 billion	South Africa
Ctrip.com (CTRP)	Travel Services	$2.8 billion	China
Melco PBL (MPEL)	Gaming/Hotels	$3.3 billion	Hong Kong
Infosys (INFY)	Software Services	$24 billion	India
Wimm-Bill-Dann (WBD)	Food	$4.3 billion	Russia
Rio Tinto (RTP)	Metals & Mining	$156 billion	United Kingdom
WPP Group (WPPGY)	Media & Advertising	$10.7 billion	United Kingdom
Nokia (NOK)	Telecommunications	$93 billion	Finland
Potash Corp. of Saskatchewan (POT)	Fertilizer	$66 billion	Canada
Brookfield Asset Mgmt (BAM)	Real Estate	$18 billion	Canada
Autoliv (ALV)	Automotive	$3.2 billion	Sweden
Endurance Specialty (ENH)	Insurance	$1.8 billion	Bermuda
Vina Concha y Toro (VCO)	Wines & Spirits	$1.2 billion	Chile
Cemex (CX)	Basic Materials	$19 billion	Mexico
Sadia (SDA)	Food	$4.4 billion	Brazil
CGG Veritas (CGV)	Oil Services	$5.6 billion	France
Teva Pharmaceuticals (TEVA)	Pharmaceuticals	$35 billion	Israel
Willbros Group (WG)	Engineering	$1.5 billion	Panama
Posco (PKX)	Steel	$37 billion	South Korea
Diageo (DEO)	Beer/Spirits	$45 billion	United Kingdom
Diana Shipping (DSX)	Shipping	$2.1 billion	Greece

That's 30 companies—the number of non-related companies that classic financial texts claim is necessary to achieve diversification. None is based in the U.S. (though plenty of these companies have big exposure to the American market), and each is a leader in its market, even the small caps. Does this look like a risky portfolio to you? We'd be content holding this portfolio if the markets closed for a decade.

A POSTSCRIPT ON ETFs

We would be remiss if we didn't point out that while we have focused on foreign equities in this chapter, over the past decade hundreds of exchange-traded funds (ETFs) have sprung up, covering all sorts of foreign markets. There's even one such fund, the iShares MSCI ACWI ex US Index, that seeks to track the index of all of the world's stock markets *except* the United States.

Using ETFs gives you the ability to make national, regional, sector-based, even combination investments using extremely low-cost index products. In fact, some ETFs give you access to markets and segments that you simply cannot buy on a stock-by-stock basis. For example, there are no Malaysian companies trading on the major U.S. exchanges, but there is an ETF that will give you exposure to the country: iShares MSCI Malaysia. Just the same, though there are plenty of Japanese companies trading on the U.S. exchanges, most of them are large caps. Exposure to the Japanese small-cap market is most easily achieved through the SPDR Russell/Nomura Small Cap Japan Index.

These products are generally wonderful. They give international exposure to anyone who wants it but does not have confidence in his or her own stock-picking abilities (the famed "know-nothing" investor, who tends to do much better than those claiming to know something), and can be used simply to get broader exposure than one could through buying individual stocks alone. You should be careful, though. Generally speaking, we'd recommend that you stick to ETFs that are based on world-recognized indexes, like anything created under the SPDR (run by Standard & Poor's, a division of McGraw Hill) or MSCI (a division of Morgan Stanley) headings. Some ETFs, most notably the Xinhua China 25 Index, were constituted by non-indexing organizations and include companies that do not accurately reflect the composition of the country's market.

FINAL THOUGHTS

An increasingly global economy has erased one of the longstanding reasons for holding foreign stocks: diversification due to low correlation. With the U.S. market moving in lockstep with overseas markets—a trend that certainly doesn't seem to be reversing itself—diversification is no longer the reason to consider foreign equities for your portfolio. In fact, one of the key conclusions of *The Future for Investors* is this: "Where a firm is headquartered will become increasingly irrelevant to investors."

The reason to look overseas is much simpler: opportunity. Pull up the five-year charts for almost any international index and you'll see that it's outperformed the S&P 500. Just as you'd never limit your stock search to companies based in Rhode Island—or those that have names beginning before the letter *J* in the alphabet—you don't want to ignore foreign stocks.

Motley Fool Advisor Bill Mann and editor Brian Richards contributed to this chapter. A founding advisor of Global Gains, Bill has traveled all over the world and can speak several languages. His favorite foreign word is jäätelö (Finnish for "ice cream"). Brian heads up our advocacy team, writing and editing articles on every one of our investing strategies.

Visit us at mdpbook.com for our favorite international stocks.

CHAPTER 9

CAPS: THE POWER OF COMMUNITY INTELLIGENCE

While an investment thesis of any public company necessarily must change with time, the principles we've outlined in this book are timeless. As you'll find in our reference section at the end of this book, we've built our approaches by reading intensively. There are libraries of great business and investing books. These strategies have been tested for years and, when used correctly, will lead to superior results.

But while the principles are timeless, the companies are constantly changing. How might you find the best of these for your portfolio? We've built our entire business around providing you that advice, in the form of membership services at fool.com. But a funny thing has happened on the way to providing all of this advice. We've learned, over time, that some of the greatest original research anywhere in the world is being done by millions of people who visit fool.com each month.

To understand the concept, think for a second about this book. The two of us, working with our team of advisors, analysts, and editors, have laid out our entire approach to stock investing. And while we hope you've thoroughly enjoyed the read, we can't help noticing that you haven't had an opportunity to share *your* insights. Your sticky notes, your underlines, your constructive criticisms, your questions and opinions serve an audience of one—*you*. What a remarkable waste of creative energy—the energy of the thoughtful reader.

This is exactly what David was thinking a few years ago when he began to develop a concept for linking investors together online. He was starting to find more and more investment ideas on the discussion boards of the world's greatest investment community at Fool.com. And as a company, we began hiring more aggressively out of our community. Today, most of our investment analysts proved themselves to us by showcasing great analytical work online at fool.com. Why then, David asked, should we anchor exclusively on the work we're doing in-house? Why limit ourselves, when we have millions of monthly visitors to our site? Why not build a platform to allow investors around the world to share their insights, learn together, and prove their mettle?

In 2005, we began making the largest capital allocations in our company's history into the creation of CAPS, home to more than 100,000 active investors. In less than two years, CAPS has grown into the largest and deepest stock ratings database in the world, exceeding long-standing ratings services such as Value Line, Morningstar, and Schwab by a two-to-one margin. The service features ratings on more than 6,000 public companies. And every day CAPS gets smarter and more powerful, as investors input more analysis into a ratings system that tilts toward the very best contributors. Now we can leverage this powerful network to improve your investment returns by overlaying our proprietary data across stocks you find using any of the strategies outlined in this book.

Before we explain how CAPS works, we want you to know why it matters. The CAPS system rates public companies from one to five stars, with five indicating a "most attractive" buy rating. These ratings emerge from the more than two million stock

picks that have been entered into the system since inception, and
here are the results thus far during a tough market:

5-Star Stocks:	+10.3 points annualized
1-Star Stocks:	–14.3 points annualized
S&P 500:	+1.3 points annualized

Data from 1/3/07 through 5/12/08.

Given the breadth and depth of coverage, those results are
stunning. We're putting them to work in our newest service, *Motley Fool Pro,* where we are using our CAPS data to drive
market-beating results. We'll talk below about how this system
can help to improve your investment returns as well. But first, let
us explain how CAPS works so that you can get the most out of it:

Step 1: Members make stock predictions. It begins with
investors around the world making stock picks. With every
stock pick, we ask a simple question: Will this stock outperform or underperform the S&P 500?

Step 2: We keep score. As soon as investors answer that
question, we score them. If they choose "outperform" for a
stock and a month later that stock is up 8% over the market, the investor is rated in two ways, as (1) "Accurate"
since the pick was correct, and (2) "Positive" with your
score being credited +8 to indicate the outperformance.

Now, Foolish investors like you know that we invest for
the long term, so why are we scoring after a single month?
For the simple reason that we want to provide all viewers
with a moment-by-moment view of all the competitors and
all the company ratings. In this way, CAPS gets smarter
every day.

Step 3: Members receive CAPS ratings. Once an investor has made seven or more stock picks, they get their own
personal rating. We then continue to aggregate their results over time. To tabulate their score, we factor in their
performance based on accuracy (the percentage of right

calls about the direction of a stock) as well as their total performance against the market. We then compare performance across every investor, stacking up competitors against each other across our database. Just like high school seniors with the SAT, CAPS participants are scored by a percentile ranking. An investor who is rated 77.34 is in the 77th percentile of the entire marketplace of investors.

Step 4: Stocks also receive CAPS ratings. In our database, we're able to see which stocks are rated highly by our smartest members—those members with the highest score. This is a very important point. CAPS is not a democracy but a meritocracy. The most successful investors carry the most weight in influencing the ratings of public companies. Through the magic of computing, we're able to crunch numbers across all these stocks and stock-pickers every 15 minutes to give what equates to a "Doppler radar view" of the stocks our community likes most and which they like least. We break all our stocks up into quintiles—assigning five stars to the most attractive stocks and a single star to the dregs of the market. In the two years that CAPS has been running, our star rankings are pretty accurate in predicting which stocks will beat the market. As mentioned above, 5-star stocks, taken in aggregate, have beaten the S&P 500 by a full nine percentage points and 1-star stocks have trailed the benchmark by 13 percentage points. Here are the exact figures again:

5-Star Stocks:	+10.3 points annualized
1-Star Stocks:	−14.3 points annualized
S&P 500:	+1.3 points annualized

Data from 1/3/07 through 5/12/08

Step 5: CAPS gets smarter. Finally, every day we get better at rating our community's intelligence. In the Step 2 example above, our investor had a score of +8 after one month. That doesn't tell us a lot. She might be the next

Warren Buffett or she may just have been lucky. Time will tell. That's exactly what CAPS uses to get smarter. As time passes, our ratings of both people and stocks become more accurate. Our CAPS members are getting smarter every day, too. They learn from their successes and mistakes; they gain a greater understanding of the stock market; they don't have to put their own money on the line to learn; and they begin to pick more winners and fewer losers.

HOW CAPS CAN HELP YOU BEAT THE MARKET

Housing more than two million stock picks, featuring the selections and blogged research of more than 100,000 investors, and showcasing star ratings that look predictive, CAPS can be used in a variety of ways. It's worth mentioning at this point that CAPS is a free service that can be accessed at caps.fool.com, or by typing "CAPS" into Google.

Let's work through its best uses.

1. To find the best stocks. Yes, there are more than two million stock picks out on CAPS, but how might you sort through it for the best of the lot? Simply by using the CAPS Screener at caps.fool.com. You can quickly find the highest-rated stocks in any industry or style of investing.

2. To get a second opinion. Most investors get stock picks from isolated sources such as a broker, a magazine, or their Uncle Bob. It's difficult to know just how good these picks are. CAPS is an ideal sounding board for verifying the quality of stock ideas you come across anywhere. A third of U.S. stocks aren't even covered by Wall Street analysts, meaning that there's little information available on these companies to help you make intelligent decisions. CAPS allows you to drill down into just about any public company in America, by studying the information and analysis from other investors. A plethora of investment analysis, ranked according to the performance of each contributor, is available to you on any stock you own. Still not convinced? CAPS had it right on Bear Stearns, the oil industry, and home-builder stocks.

3. To track some darn good investors. As you go about your research, you'll undoubtedly run into the names of the top players over and over again. If you find fellow members who strike you as smart, take a look at their CAPS pages and their blogs. These pages and blogs serve as a repository for all they think and do as investors, and it's open for you to study.

4. To evaluate your own performance. In CAPS, every action you take is archived and publicly accessible. A public showing of every prognostication you've made on stocks is a fantastic learning tool. Look back over your permanent track record and compare it to those of other investors. Get your investment club, friends, and family members to track their results for free on the platform, as well.

When we launched CAPS two years ago, we could not have imagined the breadth, depth, quality, and investment performance emerging from the network. By combining the investment strategies we've taught throughout this book with our CAPS system, your odds of superior investing results rise dramatically. If you use CAPS for no other reason than to get second opinions on any stock you own or are considering, you will have improved your chances of success.

Visit us at mdpbook.com for more on putting CAPS to work for you.

CHAPTER 10

YOUR NEXT MILLION

So, by now, you've put all of our advice to work and built your one million dollar portfolio, right? No? That's OK. We hope you at least know where to start (and when—now!). But no matter how far along you are in your investment journey, building a portfolio is not enough. You also need to know how to protect and grow it.

That's what this chapter is all about. We're going to explain how you can use all the investment strategies illustrated in this book to create a solid, intelligent portfolio, and arm you with some portfolio-management techniques to help boost your net worth, regardless of what kinds of investments you ultimately choose.

ASSET ALLOCATION

When some people hear the words "asset allocation," they also hear the word "diversification," which is a dirty word in some investment circles. They cleverly call it "di-*worse*-ification," claiming that it waters down returns. That might be true for skilled investors—those with a demonstrated ability to identify the best assets to own over the next ten years or so. Unfortunately, if you ask the average investor, "What will be the best asset to own over the next decade?," he's likely to reply with the asset that had the best returns of the *past* ten years. This is true of do-it-yourselfers as well as professionals. How has investing in the winners of yore worked out? Pull on your bell bottoms as we look back at investment returns over the past thirty-six years.

A Brief History of Chasing Hot Assets

Let's say it's January 1, 1980, and our investor is deciding where to invest $10,000 for the next ten years. He's narrowed down his choices to U.S. large-cap stocks, real estate (in the form of real estate investment trusts, or REITs), international stocks, and commodities. Looking back to 1972 (the first year with complete data on all five assets), he sees these returns:

CAGR*	LARGE CAPS	REITS	INTERNATIONAL	COMMODITIES
1972–1979	5.1%	11.1%	10.5%	22.1%

Source: Large caps from Ibbotson Associates; REITs from NAREIT index; international from the Morgan Stanley Europe, Australasia, and Far East Index (FAFE); commodities from S&P Goldman Sachs Commodity Index.

* CAGR=compound annual growth rate

Our investor says to himself, "The prices of oil and gold are going through the roof!" With the 1973–74 bear market in stocks still fresh in his mind (remember the "Nifty 50"?) and having read the August 13, 1979, issue of *BusinessWeek* (cover story: "The Death of Equities"), he decides that "hard assets" are the place to be. He invests all of his money in commodities throughout the 1980s. The returns over that decade were:

CAGR	LARGE CAPS	REITS	INTERNATIONAL	COMMODITIES
1980–1989	17.5%	15.6%	22.8%	10.7%

Of the four assets, commodities fared the worst. Still, they turned his $10,000 into $27,608. Yet that was well behind what international stocks returned. Our hypothetical investor says to himself, "I better get on the international bandwagon. Heck, the Japanese just bought Rockefeller Center!" So he invests all his money in international stocks for the 1990s. Here are the returns of the four asset classes during the decade.

CAGR	LARGE CAPS	REITS	INTERNATIONAL	COMMODITIES
1990–1999	18.2%	9.1%	7.3%	3.9%

Despite one of the greatest bull markets in U.S. history, our investor's portfolio grew to $56,027 over the course of the decade, barely doubling his money. (That's still better than what happened to the Japanese-led firm that owned Rockefeller Center, which went bankrupt in 1995.) He's nearly brought to tears when he realizes he'd have almost three times as much if he had just invested in an S&P 500 index fund during the 1990s.

So our investor, duly chastened, decides to bring his portfolio back home to the blue chips of the red, white, and blue. Once it was clear the Y2K bug was nothing but sound and fury, he invested his entire portfolio in U.S. large caps in January 2000. You know how this has turned out so far:

CAGR	LARGE CAPS	REITS	INTERNATIONAL	COMMODITIES
2000–2007	1.7%	16.3%	5.5%	13.3%

So far, this has been the century for real estate (at least until 2007). As for large caps . . . not so much. Our investor's original $10,000 stake has grown to $63,915.

Meanwhile, our hypothetical investor had a hypothetical neighbor—a boring guy who didn't seem to care about the hottest thing. Instead of shifting his investments around each decade, he invested equal amounts into each of these assets, and rebalanced his portfolio annually. Losing money in just four years (instead of our first investor's six years of losses), the neighbor ended up with a tidy $302,186—except he wasn't the neighbor anymore because he was able to move to a much nicer community.

Chase What's Hot, Get Burned

Granted, our story was a little contrived—but perhaps not by much. Many studies have shown the extent to which investors chase the hot investments, a recipe for buying high and selling low. According to research firm Dalbar's "Qualitative Analysis of Investor Behavior" study, the typical equity fund investor earned just 4.3% a year from 1987 to 2006, compared to the S&P 500's 11.8% annual return. Why the lousy returns? Investors tend to sell what has already declined and buy whatever has already risen.

And that behavior is not exclusively for the itchy individual investor, according to a study titled "Assessing the Costs and Benefits of Brokers in the Mutual Fund Industry." Written by Daniel Bergstresser and Peter Tufano of Harvard Business School and John Chalmers of the University of Oregon, the study compared the performance of more than 4,000 mutual funds sold by financial advisors with those chosen by do-it-yourself investors from 1996 to 2002. The results aren't pretty, at least if you're a full-service broker (or one of their clients).

The study found that the returns of equity funds—net of all expenses—chosen by individual investors earned an average annual 6.6% versus just 2.9% for broker-sold funds. The study's authors conclude: "There is no consistent evidence that funds sold through the broker channel exhibit substantially greater or less trend-chasing behavior." In other words, the evidence suggests that brokers chase the hot assets just as much as individual investors. Incidentally, the study also found that advisors tend to recommend investments that earn them the most money. Not very heartening.

Putting all your money into recent winners can lead to a significantly smaller portfolio. What was "in" during one period might be "out" the next. We call it the "asset hokey pokey," and it can shake your portfolio all about. If you want to increase your wealth, if you want to protect your wealth, and if you want to parlay that wealth into a long and comfortable retirement, an intelligently created and maintained asset allocation strategy is the way to go for most investors.

THE BEAUTY OF BALANCE

If you started your reading with this chapter, you might now be dialing your broker to invest 25% of your portfolio in each of the aforementioned assets with a plan to rebalance annually—not a horrible idea, considering that strategy outperformed the S&P 500 13.7% versus 11.2% annually from 1972 to 2007. That's considerably less horrible when you look at the dramatic impact such a seemingly small edge could build over time—$10,000 invested in the S&P 500 in 1972 would have grown to $454,614 by the end of 2007; that same ten grand invested equally in U.S. large caps, international stocks, REITs, and commodities, with annual rebalancing thrown in, would have grown to $871,984, almost twice as much, just by squeezing an extra two percentage points of return out of the portfolio each year. (We must add that the same effect can be gained by reducing your investment costs by a couple of percentage points a year.)

But no, that's not our final answer. Our saunter through investment history is intended to show how holding a bunch of assets that don't move in the same directions at the same times has the benefit of enhancing returns *and* lowering risk. Let's look a little closer at the long-term numbers of U.S. large caps, international stocks, REITs, and commodities, as well as a four-asset portfolio holding each asset with annual rebalancing, courtesy of Roger Gibson, CIO of Gibson Capital Management and author of *Asset Allocation: Balancing Financial Risk*, one of the best books you'll ever read about constructing a well-diversified portfolio.

PORTFOLIO FROM 1972–2007	U.S STOCKS	INTER-NATIONAL STOCKS	REAL ESTATE INVESTMENT TRUSTS	COMMODITIES	FOUR-ASSET PORTFOLIO
Return*	11.19%	11.75%	13.01%	11.65%	13.22%
$1 Turned Into ...	$45.50	$54.53	$81.79	$52.81	$87.31
Standard Deviation	17.02	21.66	17.37	24.52	11.00
Sharpe Ratio	0.39	0.35	0.48	0.34	0.68
Worst 1-Year Return	−26.45%	−23.20%	−21.42%	−35.75%	−12.77%
Worst 3-Year Return*	−14.56%	−17.00%	−10.49%	−9.58%	−0.56%
Worst 5-Year Return*	−2.31%	−2.61%	3.29%	−4.53%	3.34%
Worst 10-Year Return*	5.91%	4.30%	9.14%	2.11%	8.74%

Source: Roger C. Gibson, Chief Investment Officer, Gibson Capital Management.

* Compound annual total return; data from 1972–2007.

Let's start with the number we understandably care the most about: compound annual return. We see that the four-asset portfolio is the winner. Down on the next line, we see how earning a percentage point or two more a year can make a humongous difference when compounded over decades. The four-asset portfolio turned $1 into $87.31, almost double the $45.50 created by the lowest-returning portfolio (U.S. stocks), even though their returns—13.22% versus 11.19%—don't seem all that far apart.

Now let's take a look at the other side of the coin: risk. The first measure is standard deviation. The higher the number, the more likely the portfolio was to vary widely above or below its "average" return. Here, the clear winner is the four-asset portfolio, with a standard deviation (11) dramatically lower than its rivals. And look at its Sharpe Ratio! That's a metric developed by Nobel Prize–winning economist William Sharpe, who developed the ratio as a way to measure risk-adjusted returns. The higher the number, the more bang you're getting for the amount of risk your buck is taking. But you don't need that fancy-pants number to figure that out. All you have to look at is the worst one-, three-, five-, and ten-year returns. The four-asset portfolio had a darn good compound annual return over those three-plus decades, yet its bad years weren't quite so bad, relative to the other portfolios.

HOW DID THEY DO THAT?

How can a portfolio have a greater return than the sum of (most of) its parts and have lower volatility than each of its parts? The answer is intelligent and true diversification, which means selecting assets that don't move in the same direction at the same time. Some asset classes thrive in an environment with low interest rates, for example, while others wilt a little bit more with each quarter-point cut from the Fed. Finding the right blend brings the best chances of success.

In the academic world, this dance is measured by "correlation"— how much two investments tend to move in or out of sync. And when you combine assets that don't perform similarly at the same time, the standard deviation of the entire portfolio declines. Throw in regular rebalancing and you not only get less volatility, you also increase your chances for an enhanced return because you're selling the investments that have done well to buy the investments that have lagged. Since assets take turns sprinting ahead and then taking a breather, rebalancing often leads to selling high and buying low.

BACK (AGAIN) TO BUFFETT

As we mentioned earlier, one of our favorite Warren Buffett quotes is "Rule No.1: Never lose money. Rule No.2: Never forget rule No.1." While it's impossible to find investments that won't have their down days (or years), it is possible to minimize the volatility of your overall portfolio. Why does that matter? Let's look at four hypothetical portfolios to see how fewer ups and downs can lead to more dollars. Below are the portfolios' returns over ten years:

YEAR	NO VOLATILITY	LOW VOLATILITY	MODERATE VOLATILITY	HIGH VOLATILITY
1	10%	12%	18%	30%
2	10%	8%	2%	−10%
3	10%	12%	18%	30%
4	10%	8%	2%	−10%
5	10%	12%	18%	30%
6	10%	8%	2%	−10%
7	10%	12%	18%	30%
8	10%	8%	2%	−10%
9	10%	12%	18%	30%
10	10%	8%	2%	−10%

The simple arithmetic average return of those portfolios is the same: 10% a year. Go ahead, whip out a calculator or spreadsheet if you have doubts. Now, let's see how much money someone would have under three different conditions:

- A lump sum investment of $100,000
- An investment of $100,000 with additional $4,000 contributions each period (just like someone saving for retirement)
- A $100,000 initial investment and $4,000 withdrawals each period (as a retiree would do)

The chart below shows the value of each portfolio after the ten years:

	NO VOLATILITY	LOW VOLATILITY	MODERATE VOLATILITY	HIGH VOLATILITY
$100,000 Lump Sum	$259,374	$258,946	$252,587	$219,245
$100,000 Plus Annual $4,000 Contributions	$319,124	$318,039	$309,142	$268,554
$100,000 Minus $4,000 Annual Withdrawals	$199,625	$199,853	$196,032	$169,935

In every case but one, the dollar value drops as volatility increases. The biggest difference can be seen in the lower values of the high-volatility portfolios. The more a portfolio rises and falls, the less money you'll have in the end.

The bottom line is that lowering volatility isn't just about enduring short-term declines. Lower volatility, over the long term, leads to more money in your portfolio. A well-allocated portfolio minimizes the downside while maintaining excellent upside.

"But I must endure the volatility of the stock market to get stock market returns," you're saying—and you're right. However, by combining assets that have similar returns over the long term but dissimilar returns over the short term, you get that nice double-digit long-run return with a fraction of the volatility—which, again, leads to a bigger portfolio. Let's look at just two assets—U.S. large caps as represented by the S&P 500, and international stocks as represented by the Morgan Stanley Europe, Australasia, and Far East (EAFE) Index—to dig a little deeper into this phenomenon. As shown earlier in the table from Roger Gibson, the average annual returns from each asset since 1972 are pretty close—11.2% for U.S. stocks versus 11.8% for international stocks. However, let's once again look at their returns for each of the past four decades (as discussed earlier in this chapter), except this time we'll show *total* returns, rather than annualized returns, over each period.

TOTAL RETURN	S&P 500	EAFE
1970s*	48.6%	122.7%
1980s	403.7%	678.0%
1990s	432.4%	102.9%
2000s**	14.1%	53.7%

*Returns for 1972–1979
**Returns for 2000–2007

This back-and-forth would emotionally devastate our hot-class-chasing hypothetical investor from earlier in the chapter. But for his stick-to-his-guns neighbor, a $10,000 investment in the S&P 500 in 1972 would have been worth $454,614 by the end of 2007. Not bad. However, if their neighbor across the street had invested $10,000 in the EAFE, it would have grown to $540,343. (We'll once again take the opportunity to point out how a couple of percentage points pay off over the long term.)

Now, take a guess how much each neighbor would have if they pooled their thinking and each began 1972 with a portfolio that was split evenly between the S&P 500 and EAFE and rebalanced annually.

We can't read minds, but we suspect you have a figure of around $500,000 in your head—somewhere in between that $454,614 and $540,343. But the correct answer is $548,346. Combining the two assets created a better return than the assets achieved individually. Put another way, even though S&P 500 had a lower return than the EAFE over this period, a portfolio exclusively of international stocks lost out to a portfolio that was half international stocks and half of an asset that had a *lower return*. As that lower-returning asset (U.S. stocks) was up at some times when international stocks were down (or at least not down as much), the addition of the laggard still created more wealth.

While the additional $8,004 earned by the combined portfolio over the EAFE-only portfolio isn't life-changing money, keep in mind that the combined portfolio was a true no-brainer—half in each investment, no questions asked. When you combine investments that have similar *long-term* returns but dissimilar *short-term* returns, diversification can lead to better *portfolio* returns—and that means more money for you!

Assets that offer this type of diversification must differ from one another in a few important respects. We've covered most of them already in this book. We'll now take a look from a higher-level, portfolio-construction perspective.

SIZE

In Chapter 6, we explained how small stocks beat large stocks. But just as the population can't accurately be broken into tall and short, the nearly 10,000 publicly traded companies in the U.S. really shouldn't be divided into just two sizes. It's a spectrum, spanning from tiny companies to gigantic multinationals. To illustrate, let's break the U.S. stock market up into ten groups, or "deciles," with the help of research firm Ibbotson Associates. The table below displays the returns and standard deviations from 1926 to 2006 for stocks in each decile, with the first decile representing shares in the largest 10% of companies and the tenth decile representing the smallest 10%.

SIZE DOES MATTER

MARKET CAPITALIZATION	ANNUALIZED RETURN	STANDARD DEVIATION
1st decile (largest 10%)	9.6%	19.1
2nd decile	11.0%	21.7
3rd decile	11.3%	23.5
4th decile	11.3%	25.8
5th decile	11.7%	26.6

continued

MARKET CAPITALIZATION	ANNUALIZED RETURN	STANDARD DEVIATION
6th decile	11.8%	27.7
7th decile	11.7%	29.8
8th decile	11.9%	33.3
9th decile	12.1%	36.3
10th decile (smallest 10%)	14.0%	45.2

Source: Ibbotson Associates.

There's a gradual progression in returns and standard deviations. The most drastic differences come at the extremes—there's a big jump in return from the first to the second decile, and again from the ninth to the tenth. So it might be more accurate to break up the market into the *really large*, the *bulging middle*, and the *itsy bitsy*.

It's clear that the biggest boost in return comes from the smallest of the small—the tiniest 10% of the market. When Ibbotson Associates published its 2007 yearbook, the largest company in the tenth decile had a market cap of $314 million. That is *very* small. Consider that of the 586 small-cap mutual funds in Morningstar's database, only 14 hold companies with an average market cap less than $314 million—including the intriguingly named Ancora Homeland Security Fund. (With an expense ratio of 3.3%, homeland security better be a booming business for this fund to succeed. Or perhaps it can be considered as a way to hedge your portfolio against a terrorist attack.)

While smaller stocks do outperform larger stocks over the long term, this doesn't happen each and every year—or even each and every decade. Consider that (again according to Ibbotson), large caps beat small caps by an average 5.24% a year from 1984 to 1999. Investors go through periods—sometimes long periods—when they favor some size segments of the market over the others. A well-diversified portfolio should own companies that range in size, from microcap to giant cap.

VALUE VS. GROWTH

As we've said a few times now, exactly how "value" and "growth" are defined depends on whom you ask. The famous Fama-French studies referenced in Chapter 5 simply break up the market by one criterion: the book value of a company divided by its recent stock price, known as the book-to-market ratio. Companies with a high book-to-market ratio are considered "value" companies. Mutual fund research provider Morningstar, on the other hand, uses ten different characteristics to differentiate value from growth stocks, taking into account stock valuation as well as estimated earnings growth.

If you asked each analyst at The Motley Fool for their definitions of "growth" and "value," you'd likely get a broad and entertaining array of responses. But this much we all agree upon: The market goes through cycles of favoring one over the other. Unless you're reading this book when you should be paying attention to your fifth-grade social studies teacher, you're old enough to remember the go-go-growth days of the late 1990s. Traditional value investors were being mocked; Warren Buffett's Berkshire Hathaway was down 20% in 1999, a year the S&P 500 was up 21%.

Then the bubble burst; dot-com was out and dividends were in. From 2000 to 2006, value-oriented companies as a group walloped growth stocks. The tide changed again in 2007, as growth once again assumed the throne. To benefit from this irrational value-growth seesaw, simply include both styles in your portfolio.

DOMESTIC VS. INTERNATIONAL

You read plenty in Chapter 8 about the benefits of international investing. And, earlier in this chapter, we demonstrated the value of sending money overseas. But again, the world can't be divided neatly into United States and Other. There's more than a subtle difference in the opportunities for investing in Japan as compared to Kyrgyzstan, the economic considerations in Argentina versus Cameroon. It's important to diversify your non-U.S. investments by size, region, and level of development.

We have more than once referred to the Morgan Stanley Europe, Australasia, and Far East (EAFE) index, the best-known index of non-U.S. stocks. While it's useful for research purposes, it's not an ideal international investment, even though it can be easily added to your portfolio by buying shares of the iShares MSCI EAFE exchange-traded fund. As an investment, the EAFE treats the 21 component countries as one, and there is no rebalancing.

Asset manager Richard Ferri, author of *All About Asset Allocation* and *The ETF Book*, argues that you can beat the EAFE just by investing in its dominant components separately and rebalancing annually. If you had invested 25% of your money in the United Kingdom, 25% in the MSCI Europe (excluding UK stocks), 25% in MSCI Japan, and 25% in the MSCI Pacific Rim (excluding Japanese stocks) from 1970 to 2007, you'd have earned a return that beat the EAFE by 1.1 percentage points a year.

1970–2007	EAFE NET DIVIDENDS	50% EUROPE, 50% PACIFIC NET DIVIDENDS	25% UK, 25% EUROPE (EXCLUDING UK), 25% JAPAN, 25% PACIFIC (EXCLUDING JAPAN) NET DIVIDENDS
Annual Return	10.9%	11.8%	12.0%
Annual Standard Deviation	21.5%	23.7%	22.2%

Source: Richard Ferri, CEO Portfolio Solutions; data from 1970–2007.

So as you look beyond your own borders for investment ideas, make sure to look east, west, north, and south. Just owning a few large multinationals headquartered in Western Europe or

Japan won't result in all the benefits of international owner-ship.

INDUSTRY

No need to dwell on this one too long. You're smart enough to know that your portfolio shouldn't be filled with just bank stocks, or just tech stocks, or just oil stocks, or. . . . you get the idea. A tidal wave sinks all ships, so if a sector gets walloped, every stock gets dragged down. We saw this with dot-com stocks in 2000 and, more recently, with financial stocks in 2007 and 2008. Make sure your financial future isn't riding on a single industry.

Does this mean you should aim to own a stock in every sector of the economy? No. But if diversification is what you're after, a rough guide is to own stocks in five industries.

And broad diversification means more than a basket of stocks and funds. The illustrations from earlier in this chapter include real estate and commodities, which could be considered sectors. The proxies used in those illustrations—the NAREIT index and the S&P Goldman Sachs Commodity Index—measure the per-formance of investments that have different structures than common stocks. Real estate investment trusts must pay out 90% of their income for the company to receive special tax benefits, which is why they have a significantly higher dividend yield than most other stocks.

The S&P GSCI does not measure the price changes of actual commodities, but of fully collateralized futures contracts. If you happen to know what that means, terrific. If not, no worries. Just know that this investment vehicle is not an index that measures the performance of publicly traded oil, mining, and agriculture stocks. As Goldman Sachs says on its Web site, it's designed to provide investors with a reasonable benchmark in the commod-ity markets.

If you're looking to diversify a portfolio dominated by U.S. stocks, REITs and commodities will do the trick. In 2000, when the S&P 500 was down almost 10%, REITs were up 26.4% and the GSCI was up 52.6%. Of course, low correlation works the other way, too; while the S&P 500 was up 28.6% in 1998, REITs were down 17.5% and commodities declined 35.8%.

If you're forced to pick between the two for some reason, a stronger case can be made for including REITs in your portfolio. They're not nearly as volatile as commodities (or even U.S. stocks) and they represent actual companies making actual money. Plus, that higher dividend is pretty sweet. As for commodities, if you own a globally diversified portfolio of common stocks, you likely have plenty of exposure through U.S. stocks that work in commodities-related businesses, as well as stocks in countries with economies tied to the booms and busts of oil, agriculture, and metal prices. However, if you're looking for an investment more likely to hold up during times of inflationary and international turmoil, consider direct ownership of commodities.

PULLING IT ALL TOGETHER

Looking back at all the investment strategies discussed throughout this book, what kind of returns would a portfolio that dabbled in each strategy have earned over the past 20 years? It's not particularly fair to go back a couple decades and select Microsoft as our portfolio representative for the growth category, but we can get an idea by constructing a portfolio of mutual funds that follow similar strategies. (For more on investing in funds, don't miss Appendix A.) This isn't an exact science. There's no mutual fund that fully embodies the Rule Breaker philosophy, for example. Plus, we're limited to choosing funds that have been around for two decades. But the investments chosen by the strategies outlined in this book can be found in the six funds selected on the next page—large and small stocks, growth and value, domestic and international are all represented, plus some REITs. I also included a science and technology fund to represent our Foolish penchant for picking investments from cutting-edge industries.

In the chart on the next page, you'll find the returns for the Vanguard 500 Index Fund (VFINX) for comparison purposes, the six mutual funds selected to represent the various strategies, and the returns of an annually rebalanced portfolio equally allocated to the six mutual funds. The returns are computed for five-year periods starting in 1988, as well as for the entire 1988–2007 period.

FUND	CATEGORY	1/1/1988–12/31/1992	1/1/1993–12/31/1997	1/1/1998–12/31/2002	1/1/2003–12/31/2007	ENTIRE PERIOD
Vanguard 500 Index Fund (VFINX)	U.S. large-cap blend	15.6	20.1	-0.6	12.7	11.7
T. Rowe Price Equity Income (PRFDX)	U.S. large-cap value	14.1	20.0	2.4	13.2	12.2
Janus Small Cap Value (JSIVX)	U.S. small-cap value	12.0	21.1	8.5	14.6	14.0
Vanguard Explorer (VEXPX)	U.S. small-cap growth	16.6	13.7	2.9	15.6	12.0
Fidelity International Discovery (FIGRX)	International large value	6.1	12.2	1.4	24.4	10.7
Fidelity Real Estate Investment (FRESX)	Real estate investment trusts	13.7	15.9	4.1	16.4	12.4
Waddell & Reed Science & Tech (UNSCX)	Technology	14.5	14.8	10.9	17.7	15.4
Six-fund portfolio (annually rebalanced)	Asset allocation portfolio	13.3	16.6	6.6	17.3	13.5

Source: Morningstar

For the first ten years, owning just the S&P 500 (in the form of the Vanguard 500) was a perfectly fine strategy. For the next ten years, it was the worst possible approach. Notice also that the absolute best five-year return for any asset came from the Fidelity International Discovery Fund, which returned an average annual 24.4% from 2003 to 2007 . . . but seasoned investors might have shied away after the period from 1988 to 1997, in which international stocks were clearly the laggards in the batch.

So why not just pick the Waddell & Reed Science & Tech Fund, which had the best run for the duration of the period? For one, because the 10.9% average annual return from 1998 to 2002 glosses over the fact that those returns were earned with the following annual returns: 59.3%, 102.9%, –14.0%, –13.4%, –26.8%. Even the steeliest investor would be shaken by that volatility.

Of the seven funds (the six we chose plus the Vanguard 500), the well-diversified portfolio beat five of them over the entire period, with just two down years (compared to five down years for the Science & Tech fund). Not a bad showing, especially since the amount it trailed the No. 2 fund (0.5% annually) was much smaller than the amount by which it beat the other five funds (1.1% to 2.8% annually).

Now, here's a little math to show how the whole is greater than the sum of its parts. Add up the returns of the six funds we chose, and then divide by six to get an average return. The result: 12.8%, which is 0.7% less than the 13.5% earned by the annually rebalanced portfolio. Not earth-shattering, but enough to add thousands of dollars to a long-term portfolio. It's just another benefit of a diversified portfolio, augmented by regular rebalancing. This is why we started our *Million Dollar Portfolio* service—to bring together all of the philosophies in this book in a smart, Foolish, market-beating portfolio.

WHO HAS TIME FOR PROPER PLANNING?

During the 2005 Berkshire Hathaway annual meeting, Vice Chairman Charlie Munger turned to Chairman Warren Buffett and asked, "When was the last time you sat down and wrote out an asset-allocation plan?" Buffett replied, "Never."

So if the world's greatest investors don't bother with asset allocation, why should you?

Because you're not as good as Munger or Buffett . . . yet.

Among the pantheon of legendary stock pickers, you probably won't find many masters who had a checklist with required allocation amounts—Peter Lynch almost assuredly never fretted that he was slightly underweighted in small-cap companies in emerging markets. No, that rarefied club is dominated by people who look for attractive businesses at attractive prices, period. And their ability to do so has led to market-crushing returns. It's also their full-time job.

The problem is that this group is small. As we'll discuss further in our appendix on mutual funds, the majority of actively managed funds lose to their respective indexes over the long term. A study by Thomas McGuigan published in the *Journal of Financial Planning* found that just 10.5% of large-cap U.S. stock mutual funds beat the Vanguard 500 Index Fund from 1983 to 2003. These mutual fund managers aren't dummies (well, most of them aren't), and they have tons of resources at their disposal. It's just very hard to beat the market after fees.

Of course, we think that we (and you) have a distinct advantage as small investors. We have the potential to rub elbows with the other great investors in the exclusive club of market-beaters. But if you're nervous about jumping right in, consider keeping the bulk of your money in a portfolio of low-cost index funds, gradually venturing into individual stocks and honing your skills as you focus on finding great companies, regardless of whether they're small caps, large caps, or bottle caps.

How do you know you're a great stock picker? You keep accurate records, learn every day, and you're honest with yourself. Every person who chooses to invest in individual stocks should be comparing his or her performance to a relevant benchmark. Don't worry about a year or two, since the returns from one year to the next are often full of noise, distractions, and craziness. What you want to see is that your investments have been paying off over a five-year period. If so, that's encouraging news. If not, don't give up, but don't pour too big a portion of your portfolio into individual stocks until you improve your track record.

THE GLASS IS ALWAYS HALF SOMETHING

Owning several types of investments guarantees one thing: Some will be winners and some will be losers. So, you'll always be unhappy with some part of your portfolio. You'll also be happy with some part of your portfolio. Every year, your portfolio will be a mixed bag and the heat will jump from one asset class to the next. The well-diversified asset allocation portfolio is a middle-of-the-road strategy—your portfolio won't double overnight, but it also won't lose half its value in any given day.

If you're looking for the excitement that comes from holding a more concentrated portfolio, asset allocation may not be the strategy for you.

ASSET ALLOCATION REQUIRES PATIENCE

Diversification often does not pay off in the short term. The six-fund portfolio had the third-worst return from 1988 to 1992. It also didn't post the best return over any of the five-year periods. But over the long term, the returns from smart asset allocation will gradually rise toward the top of relative rankings.

For that to happen, however, you have to stick with the strategy, which means holding onto assets that are out of favor. This is especially difficult when U.S. stocks are on top, an interesting behavioral risk that Roger Gibson, author of *Asset Allocation*, refers to as "frame of reference risk." U.S. investors subconsciously benchmark their investments against the U.S. market, clouding their view of diversification. They perceive diversification as a positive whenever the U.S. market is a relative underperformer because they had the good sense to dabble in other areas that are beating the results they see in each day's headlines. And they believe diversification is a bad thing when the U.S. market is taking its turn in the sun.

Anyone holding international stocks in the late 1990s probably had moments of doubt. These investors certainly did not have as much to brag about at cocktail parties. Maybe some decided to swear off non-U.S. stocks for good amidst all the Yankee euphoria. But that would have been a mistake if they didn't buy back in, since international stocks have crushed U.S. stocks since 2002. If you don't have the patience to hold onto investments that can underperform the investments owned by your neighbors, family, and co-workers, then stick with U.S. stocks, secure that you'll all suffer and prosper together.

CAN YOU PREDICT THE FUTURE?

Maintaining a well-diversified portfolio is premised on the assumption that it's difficult to predict the next hot asset or to pinpoint performance. Even the "experts" get it wrong. Back in July 2000, after the stock market peaked early that year and had started what would eventually be a three-year slide—the biggest crash since the Great Depression—*USA Today* published an article featuring the opinions of many of the bigwigs at Wall Street's biggest firms. Did they warn investors of the impending crash? Nope. Five of the seven experts interviewed expected the Dow to end the year above 12,000. By New Year's Eve, the Dow was at 10,788. Here are some choice quotes from that July 2000 article:

"[Abby] Cohen of [Goldman Sachs] . . . remains upbeat on stocks despite a slowdown in corporate profits. 'What matters most is that profits are sustainable and durable, which we think they are,' she says."

" 'Stocks will head higher—much higher,' says Thomas Galvin of Donaldson, Lufkin & Jenrette."

" 'We're pretty upbeat,' says Alan Skrainka at Edward Jones. . . . 'We'll still have solid economic growth and strong earnings.' "

" 'There is no end in sight for the best economic and financial market cycle in U.S. history,' says Jeffrey Applegate of Lehman Bros."

To be fair, you could dig through the Fool.com archives and find plenty of examples of when we were wrong, too. These analysts are far from stupid. Even smart, experienced, well-resourced people aren't so good at predicting where the market will be at any given point. If you can't predict which type of investment will outperform the others, you should own a little bit of all of them.

BUILDING THE PERFECT PORTFOLIO

So how do you create the right portfolio for you? It all starts with our four Foolish rules for asset allocation:

Rule 1: If You Need the Money in the Next Year, It Should Be in Cash

You don't want the down payment for your home to evaporate in a stock market—or a bond market—crash. Find a high-yielding money market fund or savings account—such as those offered by ING Direct, HSBC, GMAC Bank, or Emigrant Direct—that allows you to transfer money to your checking account whenever you need it.

Rule 2: If You Need the Money in the Next One to Five Years, Choose Safe, Income-Producing Investments

Whether it's your kid's college money or the retirement income you'll need in the not-so-distant future, stay away from stocks. As with all investments, risk and reward go hand-in-hand when it comes to "safe" assets. So, in order of "safest" to "still safe but technically riskier," we have Treasury notes and bills, CDs, and corporate bonds. That is, not coincidentally, also the order of lowest- to highest-yielding. CDs are still safe (as long as your account is FDIC-insured), and you should be able to find some that pay a percentage point above Treasuries. Shop around for the best rates. Your local bank is probably not the best-yielding option.

As for corporate bonds, the general rule is to choose bond mutual funds if you have less than $25,000 to $50,000 to invest, as buying individual bonds can be tricky. With a stock, you can pull up a quote on your computer and—presto!—you have a good idea of the going price. But since even bonds from the same issuer will have their own characteristics—different coupon rates, maturity dates, and so on—and thus sell at different prices, it's hard to comparison shop for a good deal. Plus, in addition to charging a commission, many brokerages embed a "markup" in the price of the bond, making it difficult to know what fees you paid.

It is gradually becoming easier (and more cost-effective) to buy individual bonds, so it can be done if you're willing to put in the effort. The advantage of individual bonds over bond funds is you know exactly how much you'll get back when the bond matures. Bond funds, on the other hand, don't technically mature, so you don't know what your investment will be worth when you need the money. In fact, they can lose quite a bit of money, which can be inconvenient if it happens right before you need it.

If you're going to choose a bond fund, stick with short- to intermediate-term bonds (that is, bonds that mature in two to five years). And be vigilant about costs—you can find plenty of good funds with expense ratios below 0.50%. Dodge & Cox Income and the Vanguard Short-Term Bond Index Fund are a couple of Fool favorites.

Rule 3: Any Money You Don't Need for More than Five Years Is a Candidate for the Stock Market

At this point in the book, you've been barraged with stats about the superiority of stocks for the long run. Any cash you don't need in the next few years might wisely be used to buy a piece of a promising company using any or many of the strategies we've outlined.

We'd be remiss if we didn't point out that the long run might have to be long indeed for stocks to pay off. Surely you remember the 2000–2002 bear market—and, more recently, the financial crisis of 2008—when the S&P 500 plummeted 40%, and still hasn't fully recovered several years later. As of this writing, the Nasdaq is less than one-half its March 2000 peak. It will take many years for those who bought at those prices to see a profit.

If another such debacle would increase your blood pressure, impair your sleep, or scare you into selling stocks *after* they've already declined (a real wealth killer), perhaps some of your longer-term money should be kept in bonds. If history is any guide (and it's the only guide we have), you won't earn as much. But when the next bear market comes (and there will always be bear markets), you won't lose as much. So owning a low-cost, intermediate bond fund has merit—not excitement or promise of great rewards, but merit nonetheless.

Rule 4: Always Own Stocks

Even if you're in or near retirement, a portion of your money should be invested for the long term. According to the Centers for Disease Control, a 55-year-old can expect to live another 26 years. A 65-year-old has another two decades. The average 75-year-old lives into her late 80s. (A 110-year-old, however, should sell everything and get to Vegas while he still can.) And those are averages, meaning half of the population will live longer. So unless you're a 95-year-old skydiver who smokes, expect your retirement to last two to three decades. To make sure your portfolio lasts that long, you need stocks. Over the long term, equities are the best vehicles to ensure that your portfolio withstands inflation and your retirement withdrawals.

As Wharton professor Jeremy Siegel wrote in his investing classic *Stocks for the Long Run*, for every rolling five-year investing period since 1802 (1802–1807, 1803–1808, etc.), stocks outperformed bonds 80% of the time. Stocks beat bonds in 90% of the rolling 10-year periods, and essentially 100% of the rolling 30-year periods. For holding periods of 17 years or more, stocks have always beaten inflation, a claim bonds can't make.

Put it all together, and you should arrive at a stock/fixed-income mix that works for you. History tells us that young workers with decades until retirement should have an all-stock portfolio. Those within a decade of retirement should begin ratcheting down their stock exposure, starting with 10% to 20% in bonds, reaching 30% to 40% bonds by retirement. Retirees should maintain that same allocation to fixed income throughout their golden years, including an "income cushion" of the next three to five years' worth of living expenses out of the stock market.

BRING REBALANCE BACK TO YOUR LIFE

But moving money throughout your portfolio is not only for folks who regularly visit the early-bird buffets. By rebalancing throughout your investing career, you can benefit from the ups and downs of different types of investments, while also managing the risk that you'll be overexposed to a hot asset about to turn cold.

By bringing your portfolio back to its target allocation, you're regularly selling your leaders and buying your laggards, which just might add some extra money to your portfolio and get you part of the way to your next million.

Let's look at two hypothetical investors with $50,000 portfolios.

Our first investor (Let 'Em Ride Leroy) puts 20%, or $10,000, of his $50,000 portfolio into each of the following assets in 1997 and never rebalances. Our second investor (Rebalancin' Reba) invests that same 20% of her $50,000 nest egg into each asset— but then rebalances at the end of every year. By the end of 2007, here are the allocations and total amounts for our two investors:

	INTERMEDIATE BONDS	LARGE CAPS	SMALL CAPS	REITS	INTERNATIONAL	TOTAL AMOUNT
Leroy	14.5%	18.1%	25.5%	23.9%	18.0%	$129,395
Reba	21.6%	21.2%	18.9%	16.3%	22.0%	$138,071

What can our hypothetical friends teach us? Two important lessons:

- **Rebalancing can enhance returns.** Reba has 6.7% more money than Leroy, and she earned it with less volatility as measured by standard deviation (11.3 versus 11.9—the lower, the better). In other words, Reba got a higher return with less risk.
- **Rebalancing restores your portfolio to its ideal allocation.** Reba's portfolio at the end of 2007 looks much like her

original allocation of 20% in each asset. Presumably, she chose that risk distribution for a reason. Leroy's portfolio, on the other hand, has grown riskier as his stocks have outperformed the bonds. If history repeats itself, and stocks continue to outperform bonds over the long run, Leroy's portfolio will get riskier and riskier, even though he should be taking *less* risk as he gets older.

Over the years, we've reviewed countless studies on the topic, and it turns out that rebalancing every year is too much—every few years is a better strategy. An asset's relative ranking generally persists for two or three years before turning the other direction. So annual rebalancing has you selling the winners and buying the losers too early. A better strategy is to rebalance when an asset class has moved a certain percentage from your ideal allocation.

To illustrate, let's return to Reba. If she rebalanced only when an asset strayed five percentage points from her target allocation—dropped below 15% or jumped above 25% of her portfolio—she would have rebalanced just three times from 1997 to 2007 and she would have saved on commissions, too. This would have resulted in a portfolio worth $141,078—that's $3,007 more than her annually rebalanced portfolio and $11,684 more than Leroy's left-alone portfolio. Plus, the standard deviation dropped a tad as well, to 11. Even more return with even less risk.

Now, this illustration brings us to a sticky question for stock pickers. For investors whose wealth is mostly in mutual funds, rebalancing makes a world of sense. For stock pickers, it's a tougher question. Your decision to sell a stock should be based on your analysis of its future earnings as they relate to its current price. Permitting a few stocks to dominate your portfolio will increase the volatility, but that alone shouldn't be a reason to cut your winners off at the knees.

That said, many risks that investors face—such as executive malfeasance—may not be revealed by even the best analysis. If a single stock makes up more than 10% of your net worth and a big drop in its value would change your life, consider diversifying.

REBALANCING IN REAL LIFE

While rebalancing is an easy concept, it's not so easy to implement—especially if you have several investment accounts. You can't sell the stocks in your 401(k) to buy bonds in your Roth IRA (that would be considered a distribution, which would incur taxes and maybe penalties). Here are some strategies for rebalancing your overall portfolio across many accounts.

The Add and Subtract Strategy: The easiest way to rebalance is to direct where you put new money or make withdrawals. Savers should add money to the investments that have lagged. On the flip side, those who need cash might sell recent winners the next time assets need to be converted into spending money, starting with the categories that have done particularly well.

The Mother Ship Strategy: If you have one account that contains the majority of your assets, do all your rebalancing there, especially if it's a tax-advantaged account that doesn't charge commissions (for example, an IRA with no load). While rebalancing is important, it actually doesn't affect most of your assets. Rather, it takes place mostly on the fringes—selling a little bit here, buying a little bit there. The rest of the portfolio—including smaller "satellite" accounts outside of the "mother ship"—can stay invested as is.

The Every Portfolio Is an Island Strategy: If you have several accounts that are of approximately equal value, treat each account as an individual portfolio, which means each would have roughly the same mix of assets. You still might tweak the allocations based on each account's tax status.

The U.S. Large Caps in Every Pot Strategy: When you rebalance, chances are U.S. large-cap stocks will be involved—they make up the biggest piece of most portfolios and they tend to move faster than, say, bonds, so they have a habit of growing or shrinking beyond their original allocation. Thus, one way to rebalance across many accounts is to hold a position in large-cap U.S. stocks in each account, ready to be increased or decreased as needed. Their relatively high tax efficiency makes them an appropriate common denominator in all of your accounts.

Make Benefits Outweigh Costs

Rebalancing your portfolio involves selling and buying investments, which could incur taxes, fees, and commissions. Follow these tips to ensure that shuffling your investments doesn't consume your assets.

1. **Invest in no-load or no-transaction-fee funds.** Choose funds that let you in for free, but also watch for back-end commissions or redemption fees when you sell. Even no-load fund pioneer Vanguard sometimes charges fees if you sell too soon.

2. **Keep it in the family.** Ask if back-end fees will be waived if you move your money to a fund within the same family. This maneuver is known as an "exchange" and is common with B-share mutual funds. But an exchange is still a taxable event if the money isn't in a retirement account.

3. **Rebalance in a tax-advantaged retirement account.** Uncle Sam doesn't care about transactions *within* a 401(k) or IRA—it's when you start taking money out that the government takes notice.

4. **Sell the shares with the highest cost basis.** If you need to sell shares of a stock or fund in a non-retirement account, designate the shares that cost you the most (contact your brokerage or fund company to find out how). Your gain will be smaller (or your loss bigger), and you'll pay fewer taxes. If you're selling at a profit, make sure you've held the shares for longer than a year so they'll qualify as long-term capital gains (and a lower tax rate). One final note: Once you've designated a method for selling your mutual fund shares, you must stick with that method until all the shares have been liquidated.

Risk Before Return

Now that we've got you all pumped up about the joy of rebalancing, we must provide a bit of perspective. Our hypothetical illustration doesn't include taxes and commissions, which could wipe out the return benefits of rebalancing. And we only used one time period. As the lawyers say, past performance is not indicative of future returns. There have been periods when rebalancing actually hurt returns, especially for portfolios that have more than 20% allocated to bonds.

So, rebalancing must first be thought of as a risk-control strategy. If the future resembles the past, rebalancing every few years will pay off over the long term (ten years or more). But there's no guarantee. However, steering your portfolio back to a mix you're comfortable with is guaranteed to help you sleep at night. *You* should be the one in control of the amount of risk you take—not the market.

THE $1 MILLION PORTFOLIO AND BEYOND

You've now spent a good chunk of time and thought pondering your financial future—which, incidentally, puts you in far better shape than the vast majority of Americans, many of whom are counting on a combination of the lottery, reality show winnings, and valuable things they find in their attics to see them through their retirement years.

The next step is to apply this knowledge, and to get started on building your first million. Below are three model portfolios that provide reasonable asset mixes, depending on your investing timeline and temperament. You're under absolutely no obligation to follow these guidelines—we promise we won't be checking your brokerage statements—but they might help frame your thinking as you dive in.

Notice that "blend" and "growth" are grouped together. A "blend" mutual fund has both growth and value stocks; S&P 500 index funds are considered "blend" funds. Historically, blended funds, including index funds, tilt toward the growth side, so there's less diversification benefit from owning both "growth" and "blend" funds. So we've grouped them into the same allocation category. If you're picking individual growth stocks instead of mutual funds, then look to the "blend/growth" categories for guidance about how much to own.

YOUNG AND CRAZY
(15 years or more from retirement)

ASSET CLASS	% OF PORTFOLIO
Large-cap blend/growth	20
Large-cap value	20
Small-cap blend/growth	15
Small-cap value	15
Real estate	5
International large blend/growth	8
International value	8
International small	5
Emerging markets	4
Intermediate-term bonds	0
Inflation-protected bonds	0

YOUNG AT HEART AND RESPONSIBLE
(10 to 15 years from retirement)

ASSET CLASS	% OF PORTFOLIO
Large-cap blend/growth	15
Large-cap value	15
Small-cap blend/growth	8
Small-cap value	8
Real estate	5
International large blend/growth	7
International value	7
International small	3
Emerging markets	2
Intermediate-term bonds	15
Inflation-protected bonds	15

GETTING GOLDEN
(5 years from retirement and retirees)

ASSET CLASS	% OF PORTFOLIO
Large-cap blend/growth	15
Large-cap value	15
Small-cap blend/growth	6
Small-cap value	5
Real estate	5
International large blend/growth	5
International value	5
International small	2
Emerging markets	2
Intermediate-term bonds	20
Inflation-protected bonds	20

Whichever asset allocation looks right to you, or even if you think asset allocation is a bunch of bunk, the most important thing is to get started. The sooner you set off on your investing journey, the sooner the clock starts, the sooner your assets begin to grow, and the sooner the magic of compounding can kick in. Challenge yourself to get at least some of your investable funds into the market by the end of this month—whichever month it happens to be when you're reading.

There's no question the first million is the toughest. Investing $100 a month and earning a 10% annual return, it would take you just under 45 years to go from nothing to $1 million. If you were able to increase the monthly contribution to $500 a month, it drops to less than 29 years at the same rate of return. But once you hit the $1 million mark, the second million is a relative breeze. To go from $1 million to $2 million, it would take you less than seven years of $100-a-month investing (also figuring 10% returns) to reach the next milestone. Not that you'd need more money after that, but if you are so inclined, that third million would only take 4.1 years at the same rates of investment and return. But to get to that money-printing stage, you need to start as soon as possible.

Granted, this book has provided you a whole lot of strategies and ideas—some of them seemingly contradictory—and you might not know where to jump in. But don't allow yourself to be paralyzed by information overload.

Start by purchasing some of the index funds we've discussed to get some skin in the game and to begin seeing how much compounding can help you. Or check Appendix A to find a couple of high-quality mutual funds that made sense to you and your investing interests. Then start researching individual stocks. If you're like most people, one of these chapters spoke to you more than the rest—dividends make nothing but sense, you might have said as you dog-eared that chapter, or, I'm all about innovation and risk, sign me up for the Rule Breaker strategy. Use CAPS and your own expertise and experience to find a company that intrigues you, then find out as much as you possibly can about that business, its leadership, its competition, its financial situation, and how others view it as a potential investment—it's likely that there's at least an article or two on Fool.com about the company and quite possibly an enlightening thread on our discussion boards. If it looks promising, buy some shares. If your investment increases in value, good for you. If it drops, also good for you.

Because either way, you're an investor. Welcome to the club!

Motley Fool Advisor Robert Brokamp contributed to this chapter. The fearless leader of the Rule Your Retirement *service, and a Fool for 10 years, Robert would have liked to contribute more, but he had to see a horse about a man.*

Visit mdpbook.com to learn more about how we're building a diversified portfolio—using all the strategies outlined in this book—in our Million Dollar Portfolio *investing service.*

CHAPTER 11

WHAT NEXT?

Did you think you were done? Though we've walked through your first stock purchase, detailed our five most profitable investing philosophies, introduced you to our powerful CAPS community, and showed you how to map out the path to your next million, none of this book's lessons will help you become a better investor unless you put them into action *today*. What does that mean?

THREE ACTION STEPS

1. **Buy a stock.** If you already own stock, buy another stock using the strategy that most appeals to you. If you're not quite ready to buy a stock, buy some shares of an index fund. That single action will pay for this book many times over. Remember, the best time to start investing is right now.

2. **Keep learning.** Reread this book. Read the books on the recommended reading list we provide on page 241. Read

the newspaper daily. The more you know about investing, the world economy, and the companies that keep it
going, the more likely you are to succeed as an individual investor.

3. **Get more help if you need it.** Appendix A will give you
some keys on how to invest successfully in mutual funds.
If stock picking seems overwhelming to you, start there.
Also, you can visit Fool.com to read premium research
from analysts who work within each of these strategies,
or in the case of *Million Dollar Portfolio*, all of them! We
also offer free trials to every one of the newsletter services we've mentioned throughout the book.

Finally, don't forget to visit mdpbook.com, where we offer top
stock picks from each of the investment strategies we've discussed here, provide additional research and tools, and invite
your feedback on the book.

Thank you for allowing us to guide you along your investing
journey. We hope to be your partners for life.

Fool on!

APPENDIX A: PICKING
THE RIGHT MUTUAL FUNDS

Throughout this book, we focused on stock investing, which we believe is the single best path to investing riches. But that's not to say it's the *only* way, and it's certainly not the most prevalent. Given their popularity in 401(k) and other retirement plans, mutual funds are actually the most common type of investment for most Americans. In many retirement plans, funds are the only option. So even though we're predominantly stock guys, we wanted to offer some insight into how to find the best funds available.

There's a lot to be said for mutual funds—theoretically, they allow the average investor to put his dollars and faith in the expert stock-pickers who helm the funds, limiting their downside risk while earning solid if unspectacular returns on their money with relatively little effort.

Unfortunately, there is no way to invest in theory.

In reality, there are roughly 8,000 stock and bond funds on the market in the U.S., the majority of them overpriced, over-hyped underperformers that in the long run serve primarily to make you feel better about your own individual investing. "I could have lost that money myself," is the common lament of the frustrated fund investor. "And without the fees."

With so many funds—and so many bad ones—how can investors find the winners that successfully turn theory into practice?

That's the $64,000 question—or however much you happen to have to invest. The majority of mutual funds are proven underperformers. For the 15 years that ended with April 2008, fewer than 450 domestic stock funds delivered an annualized return greater than the S&P 500's mark of 10% over the period.

Following that math to a seemingly logical conclusion, many investors understandably choose to park their money in index funds. After all, if you can't beat the market with actively managed funds—in which managers scour the market for the stocks they think stand the best chance of big returns—you can at least *match* it by investing in a low-cost S&P 500 index fund. Well, not quite. Investing exclusively in index vehicles means you only get a B-grade: Your funds will lag the market each year by about the amount of their expenses.

BUT WAIT, THERE'S MORE

Just when our quest for quality funds is looking its most dire, it gets a bit worse. Performance is perhaps the worst of the mutual fund industry's woes, but it's far from our only concern. Scandals abound in the world of money management, which counts among its numerous lowlights a handful of shops that permitted favored clients to buy and sell fund shares after the market's close—a practice that Eliot Spitzer (in his pre-disgrace days) aptly compared to betting on yesterday's horse races.

Some fund companies also encouraged their teams to funnel "hot money" into and out of funds—also known as market-timing. While this practice isn't illegal, it almost never benefits long-term fund investors. Managers working in such a rapid-fire environment have to make trades based not on sound investing strategy and research, but in order to meet redemptions or to put short-term cash to work. That leads to higher transactions costs, which means lower returns for investors.

While market-timing and blatantly illegal abuses made head-lines and led to financial penalties for many firms, there are nu-merous other "silent scandals" that await investors who choose the wrong funds.

Many funds have unacceptably high expenses, fattened up by costs such as 12b–1 fees, charges investors pay to help market and distribute funds they have already purchased, and loads, fees that the fund company charges *just because*. These fees make it difficult, if not impossible, for investors to understand just how much they're paying for their funds. Fund companies even obfuscate their overall performance by closing lousy funds or merging them into more successful offerings. This practice—which leads to so-called survivorship bias—makes it difficult to gauge the company's true performance.

90 MILLION INVESTORS CAN'T BE WRONG—OR CAN THEY?

Despite all these pitfalls, mutual funds are the centerpiece of most investors' portfolios. According to the Investment Company Institute (ICI)—the fund industry's keeper of facts and figures—roughly 90 million Americans own mutual funds and, at the close of March 2008, the sum total of their investments hovered near the $12 trillion mark.

And if you do your homework and choose intelligently at the outset, a fund portfolio can turn into a set-it-and-forget-it long-term investing machine, like the fund-dominated real-money **Ready-Made Millionaire** portfolio we offer at the Motley Fool. There's no need to dive into a pile of earnings reports every quarter, no vague sense of guilt if you prefer not to scour balance sheets and financial statements, no nagging suspicion that maybe you should have dumped your shares yesterday.

Even better, you're always free to invest more when a fickle market puts your favorite funds on sale. No single corporate event, no matter how dire, is likely to decimate a diversified mutual fund. You also have an all-star fund manager on your payroll to contend with the slings and arrows of outrageous market fortunes.

The upshot? If you want to build wealth intelligently over time without constantly fighting the urge to click over to your minute-by-minute stock value, funds are, as investment luminary and Vanguard founder Jack Bogle put it, the "finest vehicle for long-term investing ever designed."

That is, if you know how to separate the fund industry's wheat from its plentiful chaff.

AYE, THERE'S THE RUB

Did we mention that the vast majority of funds are overpriced duds without proven management teams, long-haul track records, or strategies that allow their stock-pickers-in-chief to take advantage of varying market conditions? What's more, with thousands to choose from, the odds of throwing a dart and hitting a winner come in two flavors: slim and none.

Good thing we don't believe in dart-throwing. At the Fool, we believe that if you bring the same level of scrutiny to bear on funds as we do on stocks, it's possible to find funds with the potential to beat the market. What's more, you can relatively painlessly put these funds together in a diversified portfolio that outperforms the market while keeping volatility in check.

That's precisely what we've been doing at the Fool for roughly five years and counting in our *Champion Funds* newsletter. Our track record (all data through March 2008) demonstrates that it's possible to leave the vast majority of the fund universe in the dust by focusing on the traits that we think make for a potential champion:

- Long manager tenure (eight years for *Champion Funds* versus just over four years for the broad domestic-stock fund average)

- Low expense ratio (0.92% vs. 1.37%)
- Low 12b–1 fees (0.02% vs. 0.32%)
- Low turnover (64% vs. 87%)

By focusing on those characteristics, *Champion Funds* has bested the S&P 500 by 3.03% over the past three years (compared to 0.12% for domestic-stock funds) and 5.87% (vs. 0.72%) over the past five.

THE MAKING OF A CHAMP

In order to determine if a fund is worthwhile—and whether it has what it takes to beat the market over time—investors should drill down on these key criteria.

Managerial Tenure

With funds, you're investing in the *manager*. Lots of otherwise intelligent folks get stars in their eyes when perusing past-performance figures in the glossy brochures fund companies distribute in order to lure in prospective shareholders. But if that impressive track record doesn't belong to the manager who's currently calling the shots, that showing—in the immortal words of Elvis Costello—means less than zero.

There's nothing inherently magical about a mutual fund, after all. Fidelity's world-famous Magellan fund was an incredible wealth-creator for its shareholders when investment great Peter Lynch was at its helm, but not so much under Bob Stansky, a Lynch successor who turned Magellan into a so-so mutual fund. Moreover, while there are a handful of exceptions, five years is just about the minimum tenure a manager needs to weather at least one market cycle—and to learn how a particular strategy will play out against various economic backdrops.

Perhaps most importantly, as you go about the business of vetting and conducting due diligence on your prospective money managers, approach the decision as if you're hiring someone for a mission-critical job. After all, that's exactly what you're doing.

Style-Neutral Outperformance

If you come across a foreign large-cap growth fund that delivered an annualized gain of 18% over the past five years, it might well grab your attention. But before you buy, remember that context is critical. In this case, it turns out that the typical foreign large-cap growth fund delivered an annualized gain of roughly 20% over that same period. In relative terms, then, the former fund's seemingly impressive 18% gains are actually rather underwhelming.

Similarly, though small-cap stocks as a group began returning to earth during 2007, they have outperformed the market's bigger boys for most of this decade. If five years ago you invested $10,000 in a so-so small-cap fund, you would have nearly doubled your money. A similar investment in a large-cap fund, on the other hand, would have risen to $16,700 and change.

The moral of the story? When you're trying to pick the cream of a category's crop in order to put together a diversified portfolio, it's all relative. While stock picking is a fund manager's focus, part of any fund's success is owed to where it falls on the market-cap and growth/value spectrums—its "style." Given the way investors favored smaller stocks over large caps for most of this decade, for instance, it would be unrealistic to expect even the most talented large-cap manager to have outperformed smaller rivals. Similarly, when value holds sway, investors shouldn't expect growth funds to lead the pack.

As you research individual funds, the way to control for the influence of style is to make apples-to-apples comparisons based on, among other things, relative returns. If a manager has outclassed his direct competitors, that's a good sign he has added value through stock picking or timely asset allocation calls. On the other hand, if a fund looks great in absolute terms but comes up short compared with its peers, that may mean the manager just happened to be in the right place at the right time.

Reasonable Expenses

Another great thing about fund investing is that it's possible to do it on the cheap. The brokerage arms of Fidelity, Vanguard, and Charles Schwab (to name but three) offer scads of funds that carry no transaction fees. If the fund you're after isn't one of them, you can typically go directly through the shop that offers the fund and invest without paying a dime.

Whether or not you pay a brokerage commission, you'll still have to pay the fund's expense ratio—the percent of your assets fund companies shave off your cash in exchange for the services they provide.

Don't make the mistake of thinking you'll get better returns if you pay up for a fund. All things being equal, the lower the price tag, the better the fund is likely to be. The fact is that money that goes into the fund's pockets comes out of yours. So if you're paying less, you're investing more, and your money is doing more for you.

Beyond that, a cheap price tag provides a built-in competitive advantage for managers: They have a lower hurdle to clear relative to pricier rivals when it comes to competing against fee-free benchmarks such as the S&P.

Before you assume that means you should invest in a low-cost index tracker such as Vanguard 500 Index—whose expense ratio is a dirt-cheap 0.15%—remember that with index funds, the best you can do is to underperform the market each year by about the amount of your annual expenses.

We think you can do far better than that. Through a combination of well-chosen funds and individual stocks, you should easily best the benchmark.

The bottom line? While index funds certainly have their place when it comes to providing strategic diversification—indexing is a strategy, just like growth or value investing—we think you should shoot higher without paying to do so. With that in mind, consider that while the typical domestic-stock fund will ding you roughly 1.4% each year, those that have made the grade with *Champion Funds* cost less than 1% on average and, as a group, have handily beaten the market.

A Winning Risk-Reward Profile

Risk and reward go hand in hand, so it's critical to select funds that carry a level of risk commensurate with the returns the fund has delivered over time. This risk-reward profile is critical to consider when it comes to judging whether a fund strikes the right profile in light of your temperament and timeline as an investor.

We also know that losing money is no fun at all. We think the best way to avoid that is through smart asset allocation, divvying up your assets in a way that spreads your bets among asset classes. When one portion of your holdings drops precipitously, another can be there to prop up your assets.

This is where mathematical means of assessing risk come in handy: These quantitative tools can help all of us design smarter portfolios—investment lineups that can weather the market's inevitable ups and downs while allowing us to sleep at night. Picking the particular funds to slot into our personalized pie charts is, for many a fund geek, the fun part of fund investing. But without an asset-allocation game plan—a portfolio construction strategy that suits your timeline and tolerance for risk—that fun can fizzle and fade.

Just ask those poor folks who haphazardly backed their way into a portfolio heavy with tech exposure around the turn of the millennium. In the late 1990s, the sky seemed to be the limit for tech stocks and the funds that invested in them. As we all learned, what goes up must come down, particularly when it comes to high-flying equities with a century's worth of future earnings already priced in.

Judging from conversations on The Motley Fool discussion boards, a good many smart investors lived through and learned from the tech sector's meltdown, the "tech wreck" of financial folklore. The most important of their discoveries may be that even aggressive investors need to practice portfolio risk management.

On one level, the decision to invest in high-caliber mutual funds mitigates risk. Still, every investment carries risk. With that in mind, here's a guide to help you develop and execute your asset-allocation strategy in light of your own risk/reward profile.

Standard Deviation: When it comes to gauging the volatility of mutual funds, standard deviation is a convenient blunt instrument. Standard deviation measures how far from its mean return a fund's performance has swung. The bigger the number, the more volatile the fund.

That's straightforward enough, but standard deviation needs context to be useful. Otherwise, you could end up comparing bond-fund apples with equity-fund oranges. For a quick and useful take on a fund's relative volatility, compare it with the appropriate broader-market benchmark tracker. Over the past three years, for instance, SPDRs—an S&P 500-tracking ETF that comes with a rock-bottom price tag—returned an annualized 8.1% and posted a standard deviation of roughly 9%, while Vanguard's Total Bond Market Index fund gained 4.9% with a standard deviation of approximately 3%.

Translation: As you may recall from your college statistics class, those numbers mean we can be 66.7% certain that, over the three-year measurement period, the performance of SPDRs ranged between roughly –0.9% and 17.1%, while Total Bond Market gave investors a far smoother ride, staying within the comparatively narrow range of 1.9% to 7.9%.

Alpha and Beta: There are certainly techniques more nuanced than standard deviation to help determine a fund's volatility, and in that regard, alpha and beta are useful tools as well. In a user-friendly nutshell, a fund's beta compares its showing with that of a given benchmark, while its alpha figure provides insight into just what, if anything, the fund's manager has brought to the table in terms of stock-picking acumen.

Here's an illustration: A fund with a beta of 0.97 relative to the S&P 500 should lag that benchmark when the market rises while outperforming it when things go south. Notice, however, the word "should." Actively managed funds aren't statistical models, and mathematically elegant though its formulation may be, beta needs what investing scholar Aswath Damodaran calls a "companion variable" to be useful.

That's where alpha comes in, and here's just about everything non-finance geeks need to know about alpha: If the figure is positive, the fund's manager has likely added value. If it's negative, he probably hasn't.

R-Squared: This metric is another of our favorite analytical tools because it helps gauge whether a fund that purports to be actively managed might really be an overpriced index-hugger in disguise. An R-squared score of 100 indicates that a fund has a perfect correlation with a given benchmark. Lower scores indicate the degree to which a manager goes his or her own way.

Admittedly, some managers perform wonders on relatively short benchmark leashes. Nonetheless, when you're trying to zero in on actively managed picks that give you the most for your money, there's simply no reason to pay up for a fund that merely shadows its bogey. R-Squared is a no-muss, no-fuss way of determining if that has been the case.

Each of the above quantitative gauges has limitations. Standard deviation doesn't tell you much in isolation, and alpha and beta are only useful in tandem and if you're measuring your fund's relative risk against an appropriate benchmark. One surefire way to gauge risk, however, is to ask a simple question: How well has the manager played defense? Successful fund investors should seek out reliable capital preservationists whose track records include few calendar-year losing campaigns and who, when they have hit rough patches, have navigated them better than most peers.

Evidence of a Shareholder-Friendly Culture

Last but far from least, the shop behind the fund should stand behind the fund in a way that puts shareholders first. If making that kind of qualitative determination sounds like a head-scratcher to you, not to worry: While many fund companies are far-flung behemoths with dozens, and sometimes hundreds, of offerings to sort though and choose from, getting a sense of their corporate culture in a way that can help you make smarter investment choices is easier than you might imagine.

Here are three core items you should be on the lookout for at the level of the fund shop.

1. **Expense ratios that decline as assets under management rise:** Some of the most successful mutual funds are also some of the cheapest—and that's no coincidence. A low price tag, as we've suggested, provides a built-in competitive advantage because managers of cheaper funds have less of a "cost drag" to contend with relative to those who captain pricier offerings.

    Beyond that, as a fund's assets grow, the fund company has more shares to spread its costs across, and a key way of determining whether a fund has its investors' interests at heart—perhaps *the* key way—is to note whether they pass "economy of scale" savings onto their investors. If a fund's expense ratio doesn't decline as its assets under management increase, that's ample reason to believe that the fund company is putting its own interests above those of its shareholders.

2. **Funds that close well before they suffer dreaded "asset bloat":** There is an inherent conflict of interest built into the money management business: Fund companies have an economic incentive to grow their assets. The more money they manage, the higher their fees in absolute dollar terms. Trouble is, what's good for the fund company's bottom line can be bad news for

shareholders—particularly when it comes to smaller-cap funds.

As a fund with a massive asset base trades in and out of smaller-cap companies, it risks moving stock prices in the wrong direction—up while building a position and down while trying to exit one. These are the so-called "frictional costs" of mutual-fund trading, and while they don't show up in shareholder reports, they affect an investor's returns in the same way as a fund's expense ratio does: These costs are exacerbated by asset bloat, which occurs when fund companies allow inflows to swell beyond the point where even the most talented stock pickers can execute their strategies effectively.

Good thing, then, that there's a simple solution to the problem of mutual fund obesity: The best and most responsible shops close funds to new investors (this is called a "soft" close) and sometimes to all investors (a "hard" close) in order to stave off the ill effects of asset bloat.

If you suspect a fund you hold may have put on a few pounds, here's a tip sheet to help determine if that development is weighing on returns.

The fund's cash position is huge. If your holding's cash stake remains sizable over a protracted length of time, the manager may be having difficulty putting new money to work. A cash position of 15% or more over two consecutive reporting periods (the annual and semiannual reports, for example) is worth investigating. Anything over 20% may well indicate that better investment opportunities lie elsewhere.

The portfolio is concentrated. Funds that invest in 20 or fewer stocks are especially vulnerable to asset bloat. A big base means the manager must stuff new money into a compact portfolio, dialing up the potential for volatility. Adding new stock holdings is an alternative, but the risk is that doing so will water down the strategy (and the returns) that attracted you to the fund in the first place. If you own a concentrated fund and performance seems to be dragging as assets under management rise, that's cause for concern—and a possible sale.

The fund is a drifter. A fund that starts drifting up the market's cap range may be too flush with cash, sending its managers outside their circle of competence. True, some managers are "go-anywhere" types, scrounging for values wherever they can find them. A successful low-turnover strategy can lead to a bigger-cap orientation, too, as successful small-cap selections morph into mid caps and beyond—remember that Wal-Mart was a small cap then a mid cap before it was a world-eating behemoth. Nonetheless, it pays to look out for "style drift," particularly among smaller-cap funds. In addition to being a symptom of asset bloat, a fund that drifts from small cap to large or from growth to value can wreak havoc on your asset allocation.

3. **Management that puts its money where its mouth is:** Another key ingredient when it comes to cooking up a mutual-fund winner is a candid manager. In a fund's annual and semiannual shareholder reports, clear performance attribution breakdowns are helpful, particularly when it comes to determining whether your manager has added value through stock selection or timely sector calls (avoiding financials during the subprime debacle, for example, or loading up on shares of energy companies as the price of fuel has soared).

But even if your managers favor a more minimalist style of reportage, there is a quick way to determine if their interests are aligned with yours. Do they eat their own cooking? That is, do they invest their own hard-earned money alongside their shareholders? If they don't, why should you?

Thanks to the SEC, fund investors now have an easy way of determining whether their managers put their money where their mouths are: the Statement of Additional Information (SAI). The SAI supplements the prospectus and lays out, within dollar ranges, just how much of their own money a fund's manager has riding alongside yours. It's hard to imagine a better values-aligning litmus test: If your managers are significant investors in the funds you own, their interests are your interests too.

WHY THE CHAMPION-FUNDS APPROACH WORKS

As investors, many of us are our own worst enemies when it comes to making buy and sell decisions, purchasing stocks during phases marked by a condition that former Federal Reserve chairman Alan Greenspan famously characterized as "irrational exuberance" and, alternately, selling during periods we might characterize as "irrational despair."

The main advantage of the *Champion Funds* philosophy is that it's tough to screw up. No investment approach comes with a guarantee, of course, but if you put your funds and their managers through the paces we've outlined above—and if you keep investing through good times and bad—odds are strong that you'll grow your portfolio as well as, if not better than, your average stock jock who has to overcome the disadvantage of his outsized brokerage bill.

You'll also avoid "complexity fatigue": If an investing game plan is comparatively easy to follow, you're more likely to stick with it over time. With funds, once your lineup is in place, you're set. You can put your portfolio on autopilot, making regular contributions, rebalancing annually, and tweaking your equity exposure as retirement draws near.

You'll also avoid hyperactive trading. By design, quality mutual funds are buy-to-hold propositions, a profile that serves long-term investors well and helps keep their inner day-trader at bay, too. When it comes to stocks, after all, the temptation to trade in and out can be nearly irresistible. Great companies can be lousy investments if the price isn't right, and trying to determine if Google, say, is a great investment at $450 but not at $600 is enough to drive even the most patient investor to distraction. Should you harvest gains and deploy the proceeds into picks with greater upside potential or, as the saying goes, should you let your winners run? It's a tough call. Valuation work (gauging a stock's price relative to such measures as earnings, book value, and cash flow) isn't for the idle investor. With well-chosen funds, on the other hand, you've hired top-notch money managers to do the heavy valuation lifting for you while you vet *them* with a relatively straightforward set of criteria.

PARTING IS SUCH SWEET SORROW

We've outlined the qualities to look for when hiring managers, but what about when it comes time, perhaps, to fire them?

Any decision to sell an investment should be considered in light of the potential tax hit you would take on the transaction, but as a rule, these are the main reasons you should consider parting ways with a mutual fund:

The manager has departed. You should own a fund on the strength and reputation of the manager. If the manager has left the building and you don't have confidence in the replacement, you should consider moving on, too.

The strategy has changed. If your fund's strategy seems to change over time—or worse, with the winds—you should consider cutting it loose.

A prolonged period of underperformance. Anything over three years is worth looking at, but only if you determine that the reasons you bought the fund are no longer valid. Market trends—for which no manager is to blame—can be surprisingly durable.

Expenses are high or on the rise. Costs count. You want them low to begin with and you want them to stay that way. Creeping expense ratios demand a watchful eye, and as we've noted, you should expect a fund's price tag to fall as its assets under management rise.

Getting too darn big. If a fund shop lets a fund grow to the point where it's no longer nimble, this can be murder on performance.

Lack of shareholder friendliness. If expansive shareholder letters turn evasive or terse, or if the management team isn't meaningfully invested in the fund they run, take a hard look. Be especially on guard when small shops are absorbed by bigger companies.

Scandal. If the unlikely happens and we experience another pervasive scandal like the one that pockmarked the money-management industry earlier this decade—and if you hold an implicated fund—consider moving on.

A QUINTESSENTIAL CHAMP

Now that we've laid out the core principles that investors need for mutual fund research, let's jump from the magical land of theory into reality. Below, we look at a fund that hails from an exemplary shop that has enriched its shareholders over the course of many years, all while hewing to the highest ethical standards.

Investors in Bridgeway Small Cap Value have been well served for many years, both in terms of performance and candid shareholder communications. At just 0.88%, its expense ratio falls more than 30 basis points (0.30%) below that of its average rival. Senior manager John Montgomery has racked up many years of outsized success at other offerings utilizing the same quantita-

our *Champion Funds* philosophy. Rather than allowing these funds to grow assets to a point where it would become difficult if not impossible for the management team to execute its strategy effectively, Bridgeway ratcheted down the inflow, putting the funds' current shareholders first and forgoing the additional fees it could have raked in with bigger asset bases.

Montgomery pursues a similarly successful strategy at Bridgeway Small-Cap Value, though Bridgeway is careful not to divulge too much information about the inner workings of its team's modeling process. After all, if the shop were to reveal its secrets, the industry's lesser lights could arbitrage away Bridgeway's competitive advantages.

That said, Bridgeway's investment strategy isn't a black box. During a chat with Bridgeway co-manager Elena Khoziaeva, we discussed the particular ways in which the shop's approach plays out with Small-Cap Value—and how the team takes a quantitative approach to portfolio construction as well.

Said Khoziaeva: "We have a library of models, each of which has been historically back-tested. We use as much data as possible, and we pay a lot of attention to risk. Our process is not just about the returns; it is about the balance between risk and return."

Finally, strategic consistency is practically a mantra at Bridgeway. Indeed, we once asked Montgomery if he would, for the sake of strategic diversification, ever consider rolling out a more qualitative offering to complement his shop's quantitative lineup. The answer was swift and assured: "A non-quant fund? No. We said we believe in sticking to the knitting, but the knitting at Bridgeway isn't style box: It's numbers and statistics."

A Small-Cap Foundation

Of course, even the best of the best funds aren't bulletproof. Bridgeway Small-Cap Value didn't escape the small-cap meltdown. The fund is down roughly 9% for the 12 months that ended with April 2008 hit by the small-cap meltdown. Remember what we said earlier about relative performance: To judge a fund during stylistic downturns as well as upticks, you have to measure its showing against its peers and benchmarks. And—surprise, surprise—doing so confirms just what an ace pick this Bridgeway offering is, with the fund outclassing the Russell 2000 Value index by more than 6 percentage points and landing in the top 20% of Morningstar's small-cap value category over the period.

Add to that performance profile a cheap price tag of just 0.88%, rigorous strategic consistency, and a track record of outperformance in one of the market's most volatile areas, and you have a winner. Chip in an unwavering commitment to shareholders and an unemotional investing philosophy and you've got a top-notch fund that exemplifies the *Champion Funds* approach, one that could easily serve as a building block for the small-cap portion of any portfolio.

CHEAT SHEET

Now that you know what makes for a true champ, you're ready to venture out on your own. To guide you, here's a handy checklist of our fund screening criteria:

- Managerial Tenure: At least five years
- Five-Year Returns: Higher by 1% or more (on an annualized basis) relative to a relevant benchmark
- Expense Ratio: Preferably 1% or less, though you may find rare exceptions among younger funds still in base-building mode
- Load: None
- Alpha: Positive; the higher the number the better

You'll want to use the other information we've outlined in the previous pages to gauge more qualitative factors such as strategic consistency and shareholder friendliness. Still, vetting funds based on the this five-point set of criteria will go a long way toward helping you focus on the very best funds the money management business has to offer.

Motley Fool Advisor Shannon Zimmerman contributed to this section. We're pretty sure Shannon—founding advisor of our Champion Funds *service and current leader of* Ready-Made Millionaire—*is the only PhD/music critic/fund geek in the world.*

APPENDIX B: FURTHER READING

All About Asset Allocation, by Richard Ferri
Asset Allocation: Balancing Financial Risk, by Roger Gibson
Beating the Street, by Peter Lynch*
The Black Swan, by Nicholas Taleb
The Book of Investing Wisdom, by Peter Krass
Buffett: The Making of an American Capitalist, by Roger Lowenstein*
Common Stocks and Uncommon Profits, by Philip Fisher
The Davis Dynasty, by John Rothchild
Expectations Investing, by Michael Mauboussin and Alfred Rappaport
The 5 Keys to Value Investing, by J. Dennis Jean-Jacques
The Four Pillars of Investing, by William Bernstein
Forbes' Greatest Investing Stories, by Richard Phalon
The Future for Investors, by Jeremy Siegel*
Global Investing: The Templeton Way, by Norman Berryessa and Eric Kizner
Good to Great: Why Some Companies Make the Leap . . . and Others Don't, by Jim Collins*
The Innovators Dilemma, by Clay Christiansen
The Intelligent Investor, by Benjamin Graham
Investing in Small-Cap Stocks, by Christopher Graja and Elizabeth Ungar
Investment Fables, by Aswath Damodaran

*Must-reads!

John Neff on Investing, by John Neff

The Little Book of Value Investing, by Christopher H. Browne

The Little Book that Builds Wealth, by Pat Dorsey

The Money Masters, by John Train

One Up on Wall Street, by Peter Lynch*

The Only Guide to a Winning Investment Strategy You'll Ever Need, by
Larry Swedroe

Passport to Profits, by Mark Mobius

Poor Charlie's Almanac, by Charlie Munger, edited by Peter Kaufman

A Random Walk Down Wall Street, by Burton G. Malkiel

The Single Best Investment: Creating Wealth with Dividend Growth,
by Lowell Miller

Stocks for the Long Run, by Jeremy Siegel*

Valuegrowth Investing, by Glen Arnold

Value Investing with the Masters, by Kirk Kazanjian

The Vest Pocket Guide to Value Investing, by C. Thomas Howard

You Can Be a Stock Market Genius, by Joel Greenblatt*

*Must-reads!

ACKNOWLEDGMENTS

How many acknowledgments pages have you encountered that begin with a complaint?

Well, here's your first, then.

The two of us have always felt that the Academy Awards ceremony could be so much more engaging. How? By requiring the winners to shed light on the magic of their film. Pull the curtain back. Tell a story. Reward us. Say *anything* other than simply reciting the names of character actors we'll never know or meet, along with every makeup artist, set designer, visual effects coordinator, stunt double, dolly grip, second assistant accountant, line producer, and shop foreman on the film. (And then we're supposed to hold our breath past midnight just to see if they remember to mention their spouse.)

Please!

Every great show is for the audience, not the performer. (Shouldn't Hollywood know this?) Likewise, we believe that every great book should be for the reader. Of course, then, the most important person to recognize and thank in the acknowledgements is *you*, the reader. In order to thank you for taking a chance on the counsel of Fools, we're going to offer some rewards to those of you who actually made it to—and through—this page.

But first, yes, we are going to mention the names below of the many all-stars who helped us deliver this book on time, edited, fact-checked, bound, and stitched for you. They are:

- Our William Morris agent, Suzanne Gluck, for negotiating our two-book deal. What's the second book? You'll just have to wait and see!

- Collins President and Publisher Steve Ross, for signing up, with enthusiasm.
- Collins Senior Editor Ben Loehnen, for truly being the best—and nicest—book editor we've ever encountered.
- Collins publishing gurus Margot Schupf, Hollis Heimbouch, Angie Lee, Larry Hughes, and Matt Inman, for believing in a couple of Fools.
- Fool Communications Czar Jonathan Mudd, for rallying us to this project.
- Fool product guru Robyn Gearey, for living and breathing every single page.
- Fool Advisors Bill Mann, Andy Cross, Robert Brokamp, Tim Hanson, and Shannon Zimmerman for their investing genius.
- Fool Analysts Bill Barker, Rich Greifner, Karl Thiel, and Matthew Argersinger for their thorough work on every chapter.
- Fool Managing Editor Roger Friedman, for giving it all the once-over—thrice.
- Fool business leaders Kate Ward and Randy Coon, for keeping us on the rails.
- Fool Publicity Swami Chris Hill, for making sure you've heard of this book.

Now, these Fools put in a lot of hard work on your behalf, so if you would like to thank them with a gratuity, we will divide anything you send evenly among everyone above. Send your gifts to:

> The Motley Fool
> c/o MDP Book Tributes
> 2000 Duke Street, 4th floor
> Alexandria, Virginia 22314

And now, what are *your* rewards?

Here are two.

First—who could have expected this?—we're going to offer a single stock recommendation. It's a company that we expect will quadruple in value by 2019, returning investors a neat 15% per year. Of course there are no guarantees, but Dolby Laboratories (NYSE : DLB) meets the criteria of greatness that run throughout this book: great leadership, sterling financials, strong market positioning, and a tremendous opportunity—

delivering next-generation audio and video technologies to the world of entertainment.

And for our second reward, we are offering Motley Fool baseball caps to the first five readers who find a typographic error in this book (horrors!) and report them to us at MDPBook.com.

Who knew that acknowledgement pages could be so profitable?

Fool on!

David and Tom Gardner

INDEX

The Contributors to *The Motley Fool Million Dollar Portfolio*

Top row: Shannon Zimmerman, Rich Greifner, David Gardner, Bill Barker, Brian Richards, Robert Brokamp

Bottom row: Karl Thiel, Tom Gardner, Tim Hanson, Andy Cross, Bill Mann

Photo credit: Matt Mendelsohn Photography

Ready to Build Your Own Million Dollar Portfolio?

Invest alongside Motley Fool co-founder Tom Gardner as he applies the wealth-building principles outlined in this book to invest $1 million of The Motley Fool's REAL MONEY.

Here's just a sample of what individual investors like you are saying about this groundbreaking project Tom calls *Motley Fool Million Dollar Portfolio*:

> "This new approach makes me feel as if we are partners…"
> *- Arie L., San Antonio, TX*
> "I have been waiting so long for this service. This is perfect!!!"
> *- K. Miller, St. Charles, IL*
> "This is a great opportunity to learn how to recognize the best of the best, the fat pitch!"
> *- L.H., Sequim, WA*

Million Dollar Portfolio gives you complete access in real time to every move Tom makes as he manages The Motley Fool's $1 million real-money portfolio. You'll never have to decide when to buy a stock, how much to buy, or even when to lock in your profits!

Membership in *Motley Fool Million Dollar Portfolio* isn't always open. For a limited time, we are enrolling new members who were kind enough to read this book. We've even arranged a special new member discount.

Please accept this special invitation to get in the ground floor as Tom Gardner attempts to grow his $1 million into $1 BILLION over the next 50 years.

Visit <u>www.yourmilliondollarportfolio.fool.com</u> right now!

HarperCollins does not sponsor or endorse this offer.